Nerds in New Zealand

the nitty gritty of living in NZ

PG W Nerding

*Our mission is to efficiently provide the world's finest, most comprehensive
book publishing service, enabling every author to experience success.
To find out how to publish your book, your way, and have it available
worldwide, visit us online at www.trafford.com*

Trafford rev. 11/5/2009

 www.trafford.com

North America & international
toll-free: 1 888 232 4444 (USA & Canada)
phone: 250 383 6864 ♦ fax: 812 355 4082

Dedicated to Kiwis, wherever you live in the world,
in recognition of your friendliness, values and not least
the beauty of your country.

Just why you would let someone like me in
to enjoy these qualities defeats me?

Contents

Preface

Warning: Irreverent and sometimes silly material follows

Do not attempt to read this book if you are the sort of person that can be easily offended. It is all right if you have borrowed, or stolen it, you deserve to be offended.

If you are expecting a beautifully constructed work of satire rippled with irony or parody, you had better put it back on the shelf. It is a clumsy, tautologizing work bolted together with six inch screws banged in with a club hammer, in fact, glued rather badly to double entendre, shored up with quick setting sarcasm and as coarse as 60 grit sandpaper. A sort of Benny Hill of travel literature.

I will tell you how it is here in New Zealand, warts and all, with cheap jokes at everybody's expense. You will not be able to sue me for deformation, slander or libel because? .... because?.......because I have warned you about it and because no one is immune from my humour, not even me.

While I understand that one man's humour is another man's insult, I make no apologies to anyone, I live my life the way I want and I don't give a damn about anyone else.

Sorry, I'm not in the way here am I?

Slightly more serious disclaimer

While this book is a mixture of fact and anecdote and I hope it is clear in the text which is which. I have made every effort to check each fact but I cannot be held responsible for inaccuracies that arise, that would be too responsible of me.

I am afraid I cannot cover everything in all the detail each topic deserves. The book is not intended as an encyclopaedia of facts but an instrument to give you an overall idea and feel about living in NZ by someone who lives here, but like you maybe, has also lived in Britain.

How the book works

I hope that all the practical and nerdy advice enclosed will encourage you to bring the book with you on holiday or at migration, to use as a reference for how life works out here. I have tried to keep it to less than 950 pages to respect your baggage allowance. I had no idea at the start of this project, just how much greenhouse gas is generated in transporting 1 kg from Britain to New Zealand. Check it out for yourselves on one of the links later on.

In places throughout the book some important facts and figures are in bold for easy reference if you need to refer back to them. The garrulous rubbish that accompanies each point is my subjective opinion on the statement or my first hand experience on the topic for what it's worth.

I have included as many website links as possible so you can form an opinion or gather further information from the comfort of your home or work computer before you come out here. This method of information gathering feels better when it is downloaded at work and in work time. Hell, they know you want to go to New Zealand and they realize you are doing your research at work. Consider it a perk of the job you are leaving and try not to think of it as theft, which it is.

The choice to include any particular site does not mean I endorse them or any of their products or services. While I will give credit where credit is due, it is where I have personal experience of a good service. This is very subjective, I know, and your experiences may not reflect mine.

The websites listed, serve to give you a feeling of what the country is like and the more common names, websites or companies you are likely to encounter. In preparation for our move and as a Prisoner of Mother England* chained to my desk in the galley of a large corporation, I had no idea of the websites I was browsing and if they were the "big players" in New Zealand or contained any useful or trustworthy information at all. I would have happily given up my back for another thirty lashes to possess a book pointing out the more useful sites to visit.

The book is a cross between a travel guide, an account of our trials and tribulations, and an irreverent look at life down under and life in general. While it is an outlook on life, I draw no parallels with other great works to live your life by, like "How to organize your life starting with that drawer in the kitchen where everyone dumps anything".

Hopefully I will try to get across as many aspects as possible of living in New Zealand and Christchurch in particular. If I am missing things you want to read about, let me know. You won't get a refund on the book you've bought but I will put it into the next edition if there is one.

There are also some checklists at the back giving a summary of some of the important things to bear in mind if you are renting or buying a house out here.

If you read the book to the end you may even learn some new words, (there is a glossary of pretentious words in one of the appendices). I hate pretentiously written books with words you may only come across once in a lifetime let alone use in typical conversation, except with intelligent people. Let's face it most of us don't move in those sorts of circles. So if you will excuse the sesquipedalian in me, here we have our first didactic expostulation.

However, life is about expanding your horizons and we are privileged to be speaking a language that the rest of the world wants to 'speaky without hurty of the head'. We owe it to ourselves to keep complicated words alive to make it more difficult for the remaining 6.2 billion souls on this planet to master and give us English something to be good at for once.

I have tried to remain mysterious, slightly sinister, and shadowy throughout the book. This is to make me seem far more interesting than I really am. Bits of my life can be pieced together from the text. By the end you may have jumped to the conclusion I am a thirteen year old boy with acne who lives in Kent and has done all this from his bedroom covered in Baywatch posters having never actually left England. Well you'd be wrong (except the bit about the spots and Jasmine Bleeth).

I have organized the book into sections to allow you to pick it up and just read a section, rather than create it as a travel book where juicy bits of information are hidden in the text which you then cannot find when you want them most. While the prose may not flow like a travel book, it does mean that you can read a small but complete section between Victoria and Green Park while giving me maximum publicity for the book. Make sure you keep your thumbs off the title so it can be clearly read by people who are trying not to be nosey but finding it too hard to resist.

It is fully intended to be read in conjunction with other texts on the subject of NZ migration but I feel it has the "nitty gritty" that can get overlooked by some books, for instance the impact of bank charges or a subjective opinion on the cost of living in general.

I have some big chapters which are the bread and butter of moving to New Zealand, like how to get a ticket when The Lions are in town or how to use an NZ post box. Smaller chapters cover incidentals like children's education and somewhere to live.

My experiences of this country are obviously centred on Christchurch as this is where I have lived. Many of my points are equally sound for most places in New Zealand. I just use Christchurch as a living example.

I love writing in books, my books are my friends and while I enjoy writing on my friends as well, they sometimes object. I have left a bit of space at the end of each section for scribbling so that any research can be kept together. I admit in places there isn't much space, so use a sharp, fine pencil and not a wax crayon otherwise make some more friends to write on.

In summary, knowledge is power and forewarned is forearmed and I know I would want to do with four arms .... juggle of course.

nerdsinnewzealand@hotmail.com
March 2009

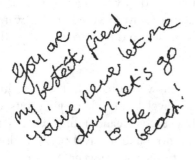

*Footnote
The acronym pom is believed to refer to pomegranate and the red skin immigrants enjoy after a few weeks in Antipodean sun, though "prisoner of old mother England" works and sounds better.

A ship in a harbour is safe, but that is not what ships are built for.

William Shedd
Theologian (1820-1894)

I have no idea what it means, I chose it because New Zealand men love their "shedds" and workshops. So much so there is a dedicated magazine called:

"The Shed. Where dreams are made real"
www.theshedmag.co.nz

Chapter 1

Introductions and the story of our move

I write this first paragraph on Tuesday the 15th of May in Christchurch New Zealand. In terms of seasons it would be the equivalent of November the 15th in the northern hemisphere. Whether it would be a Tuesday I cannot be sure. The reason I am sharing this inane fact with you is because I have just hung the washing out to dry in the garden and the blue sky is the kind of sky only New Zealand can deliver. A warm, gusty Nor'wester is blowing. It is twenty degrees on the thermometer and I'm quids in on the weather front and life feels good today.

Climate has to be one of the big factors for moving to New Zealand and I hope to convey to you in the following chapters the dozens of other reasons to give living in New Zealand a go. Nothing is ever what it seems and often few things ever pan out how you imagine them. Our dream to live in New Zealand is a case in point and I won't pull any punches, I'll tell it how it is and at the end of the day, how it was for us and I will try and do it without as many clichés as there were in the last few sentences.

Setting the story straight?

People have some startling preconceptions about what goes on in New Zealand and what life and living here is really like. Close to home my mother asked us if they have Christmas trees here, while my brother in law thought we lived in a shack on the beach. Perfectly understandable misconceptions but I am duty bound to set the record straight having lived here. Firstly, let's put that old chestnut to bed: New Zealand babies don't become deaf, if they learn to walk without crawling first.

You only get out of life what you put into it and a move, or even a visit to New Zealand is a big project to research. I would have liked a book like this when I was aimlessly surfing NZ internet sites during work time, trying to make head or tail of what I needed to do or what was awaiting me here. Hopefully this publication will go some way to answering your questions, possibly generate more, but ultimately give you some power over how best to deal with those challenges.

The story of our move

Probably the best way to illustrate the mistakes that can be made is to show you ours and that leaves you free to make a whole load of your own unique ones. I will attempt to punctuate what we should have done had we had a second bite at the cherry. Oh no another cliché, "d'oh"!

We had thought about the idea of migrating, back in 1998 but as with so many ideas they stay just that. It all seemed too complicated and difficult to do so we moved house instead. We revisited the thought in 2003 but being the sort of people never to act on impulse we decided to visit New Zealand on holiday to see what all the fuss was about. There had recently been a number of TV relocation programmes about New Zealand and the country looked beautiful. So bags packed we went on a reconnaissance mission for three weeks.

I would advise everyone to visit first, as New Zealand may not be what you want out of life and we know of three English families who have sold everything in the UK moved out here, didn't like it as much as they thought they would and moved back. Their children's education was disrupted and they found house prices had left them worse off when they sold up here to move back to England. Now this might just be the English. The Welsh and Irish are more sensible while I know the Scottish wouldn't do something like that if it left them out of pocket.

Come for a holiday and the worse that the experience will do is convince you that your dream to live in New Zealand was not that realistic and you can focus on something else. At the very least you will have hopefully seen a truly stunning country. It is not going to be for everybody, so test the water with a toe first.

We tested the water, liked it, and liked it enough to roll our British Home Store jeans up to our knees and consider a paddle too. We landed in Auckland and spent two weeks exploring the North Island, and all the usual tourist places. The one place we did like the look of was a small town called Orewa to the north of Auckland. Not far from Waiwera a thermal resort a few miles out it is a pleasant seaside town with a nice feel to it. Like many Brits we could see ourselves moving to the Auckland area. It is highly

2

populated by New Zealand standards but I think it felt familiar and exotic at the same time. Many British come to NZ for the climate and the North Island is sub tropical and the thought of those nice winter temperatures appeals to us all when February in Britain is four degrees and dishwater grey.

The whole North Island stage of the trip went well but for two hours of uncertainty which morphed into blind panic. We left Taupo for Napier on just over half a tank of petrol, a journey of only a few of inches on the map. The Evey suggested we get petrol before we leave Taupo, while I replied that that wouldn't be necessary. The hire car we had rented was equipped with an on board computer that reminded me of what a fool I'd been as we watched the "km" of fuel left in the tank run down and The Evey got increasingly quieter.

Believe me when I tell you there is not a lot between Taupo and Napier. The places on the map aren't towns as you'd expect. They are probably smaller than hamlets and funny enough none of them had a service station or even a Little Chef. My bottom lip quivered more than a bit as we still had an inch to go on the map and the computer calculated we had 20 km left in the tank. I had visions of spending the rest of my life in the dog's bed while the dog wore my bathrobe and read the FT in the morning. We hit the outskirts of Napier shortly after The Evey hit me, with 6 km in the tank and the on board computer reading "you're in big trouble you shmuck, just be nice and we can run this as a damage limitation exercise, try buying flowers but don't for God's sake say "I told you we'd be OK"".

We left ourselves only one week to explore the South Island, which with hindsight was not enough. We took the car ferry as foot passengers and crossed the Cook Strait. A most beautiful sight though the small ferry listed and the wind was amazing, and if you suffer from travel sickness it may be interesting to see how far you can get your breakfast to travel on that wind. We landed in Picton and collected a new hire car for the tour of the South Island, having left the last one in Wellington. This is what most people do.

We came to New Zealand in April which is obviously their Autumn. While the days were warm, the evenings were drawing in and we saw most of the scenery at dusk or in complete darkness. Outside of cities on moonless nights, darkness is absolute, believe me. We travelled from Picton to Greymouth on the West Coast at night, saw nothing at all except the twenty metres of road ahead of us and was amazed how windy the roads were after the windy ferry crossing (sorry but I couldn't resist using a homonym).

3

We realized that our pre-booked itinerary would never get us down to Queenstown or the Fjords in time and we would be facing the remaining week of our holiday in the car before a stressful flight home. We decided to cut short the bottom half of the island and transfer our accommodation to give us more days in Christchurch.

This was easily achieved by telephone and, admiring the beauty of Arthur's Pass, at night once again, we trundled into Christchurch for our last few days and a more relaxing end to a holiday. We still need to see Arthur's Pass in daylight but as we live here now there is no hurry. Christchurch had always been, for us, a bit of an exit point from New Zealand having always thought that if we liked the country and decided to move here we would be in the action up Auckland way.

I have to say Christchurch was, and still is, delightful. It is more than that, it is beautiful and bijou and yet the biggest city in the South Island. Its feel, layout and look are very British, I dare to say English but that isn't fair on Scots, Welsh or Irish. It is "British feeling" but then I'm British. To the Irish it may have an Irish feel. Whatever it was it had a good feel to it. Please include Christchurch in your tour of New Zealand it is the gateway to the south, a bit like Balham only sunnier if that is indeed possible.

In many ways it felt like a parallel or alternative Universe, (because as a nerd I ponder that sort of thing a lot), strangely familiar yet light switches and plug sockets distinctly different. More on that later.

The lessons in hindsight to take from our reconnaissance mission are:

- You need three weeks minimum, two in each island preferably. Hang on that's four weeks?

- **You need four weeks minimum, two in each island preferably.**

- Be aware when planning the distances may not seem long but **the roads are very windy,** framed by beautiful sights I agree but these don't go down well with younger folk stuck in the back of a car for 8 hours. There is nothing much between your leaving point and your destination except nature and it is not like you can stop off at the equivalent of Swindon for a cup of tea, so plan carefully and **always run a full tank of petrol between places.**

- **Travel light.** With the value you get for a British Pound things seem cheap and virtually everything can be bought here. It will also help your fuel economy.

- Come out here after Christmas, in deep winter for the northern hemisphere but the best weather and longest days in the southern hemisphere. **January and February are the most settled months.**

- Be opened minded about other places outside Auckland, to live in. Almost everyone settles in Auckland. Be different. **You also get more points towards your total migration score if you settle outside of the Auckland region.**

- Use the internet as much as possible to fact find for your mission. As I keep saying, better still, do this at work and let your boss fund some of the trip.

Looking for a job: My story of being interviewed

Back in England, and over a period of many months we made the decision as a family to move to New Zealand. By Easter 2005 all parties were on board. We would have a family conference each Sunday morning at the dining table to ensure that we were all "still on board" and to thrash out what was needed to be done in the week ahead to work towards this goal. Charlotte, our youngest, has since confided she never thought we would go through with it. She learnt a valuable lesson.

I spent some time sending off CVs to prospective employers and to be fair they were very polite to me. **I understand now that they would have been more interested in me if I had approached them with a working visa already in place. It makes the employer's job so much easier if you have this already.**

I did not receive my visa until the eleventh hour, after I had been given a provisional job offer. I was delighted in getting a job offer particularly since in my opinion the job interview was the worst one I think I have given.

No that's not true. In 1999 I went for an internal job interview where I was known to all the interviewers, all of them important respected people within the organization. The interview had gone well up until they asked for

5

any questions from me. I had none and they all looked down to finish scribbling their thoughts before dismissing me when I announced that I had to say just one thing. Fully aware of being an internal candidate I attempted to ease their discomfort if they felt the other candidate, a somewhat unknown entity would prove to be stronger on the day. I meant to say "I understand and respect your choice for the post and if it is not to be me I hold no ill feeling and will respect your decision as we continue to work together" Unfortunately under the stress of interview conditions it came out as "look if I don't get the job I won't be crying buckets." I watched four pairs of eyebrows raise and at least two mouths fall open across the table as one of them managed to thank me for my time.

Determined never to make that mistake again I spent all weekend preparing for my telephone interview with Christchurch New Zealand. It was late Sunday evening British time when the phone rang. I was impressed that there was little or no time delay on the line as each of the three senior officials from the organization quizzed me. I sat in my study on my lucky office chair from Ikea that moved in three dimensions, round and round and tilting backwards and forwards on a pivot. In my nervousness I was fidgeting so much on the chair it made a belching sound every time I rocked backwards on it and a farting sound every time it straightened up. I rocked on oblivious for 15 minutes until the interview concluded with that dangerous line "do you have any questions?"

Experience being the best teacher, I fought to keep that earlier nemesis suppressed. I had a better question. I stated that I would very much like to cycle to and from work and were there any showers I could use? After a long pause the lead interviewer pointed out that many people cycled to work as Christchurch is very flat and bicycle friendly but he was sure there must be showers somewhere in the institution that I might be able to use. I knew Christchurch was flat I had been there not a year before so I slapped my forehead with my hand, groaned inwardly and the interview terminated.

The Evey and the small people came in as they were waiting outside offering moral support behind the closed door and the first question in unison was "what was that awful sound we kept hearing?" I slapped my head again as I realized the farty chair would have been heard in New Zealand and coupled with my question about showers it dawned on me that my personal hygiene may be called into question and the weal on my forehead stung again. I attempted damage limitation by emailing the lead interviewer and apologizing for the farty chair. He never replied.

6

A few days later I received a job offer and some paperwork to screen me for MRSA the superbug rampant in some hospitals. Did my potential employer think I was some sort of walking infectious sewer? I slapped my now bandaged forehead. I couldn't shake the thought that after my follow up email my potential boss had raced down to the mail room only to discover the job offer had left the building two minutes earlier and if he hadn't stopped to hold a door for someone on crutches he would have made it and been able to pull the envelope from the post.

I found out a few weeks after I started the job here they were so desperate for my profession they would have taken me if I had been the faecally incontinent grand master, body odour king and farting world champion, unifying all three belts in the process.

Packing up to leave for New Zealand

Winding up and closing down our affairs was a long, slow process and I thought I had left enough time to do it, finishing work eight weeks before our departure. Unfortunately there was the little obstacle of The Ashes (2005) in the way. My productivity fell as I watched every ball from the second test onwards. We expats residing in the Antipodes paid heavily for that triumph as England capitulated 18 months later in Australia. The Poms out here were considered fair game for every imaginable jibe following the five nil whitewash. Why we couldn't have just posted them the urn from England and saved all that trouble I will never know?

Anyway I am getting ahead of myself. We had decided to rent our house out in case we didn't like New Zealand and keeping a foot on the property ladder, while hopefully experiencing some capital growth. While this was a sensible move it came with a lot of extra work as the house needed to be made ready and all those little jobs like a toilet door that shut, had to be done. An agent had to be found and insurance cover had to be arranged. An inventory had to be drawn up and electrical and gas safety certificates printed from that website that supplies fake IDs, MSc's and doctorates from the Irish International University.

We had never intended to bring all our material possessions to NZ, just the things we couldn't live without. We researched removal companies and decided on moving just twenty tea chests of gear with us. Each member of our family had four chests (which turned out to be cardboard flat pack boxes) to pack their precious things in, leaving four boxes for communal house-ware. These all took twelve weeks to arrive by sea. With hindsight I should have bought just the clothes in my suitcase. You can buy everything here that you need. I didn't need eight ties, I never wear them and haven't for over two years now. Funnily enough you can buy ties in NZ. I worked with a lady who sold everything she owned before coming out here, furniture, crockery and kitchenware and that was a good move and I would recommend it.

We stored all our furniture in a self storage unit. I was amazed how we fitted 111 years of combined possessions in such a small lock up. Maybe the door the other end was opened and it was just spilling out unseen. I don't think so, I think it was efficient use of space and I would like to thank my Mum, Dad and our friend Mark for helping us, though we haven't heard from Mark for over two years now. Come to think of it the last time I saw him he was backing a very large wardrobe into that storage unit.

If you go down this same route you need to do the "maths" to see if it is viable. We pay £28 per week plus VAT for the storage but there comes a time in the not too distant future where our stuff is worth less than what we have shelled out for in storage so my advice would be sell everything, give it away, fly tip it, set light to it, whatever. It's only stuff. Sentimental toot, precious memories, old photos, the children's first clay pots and numerous toilet roll "animals" covered in crepe paper, and by now, mouldy glue. Bin it or as the Kiwis would say "biff it".

Transporting Pets

We had a cat and a dog who were very much part of the family and it was always intended that they would be coming out with us even when I found out how much it would cost to send them. I pointed out to the transport company that they weren't celebrity pets and didn't need to travel club class and that they would be quite happy to fly in the hold. I was told that the price was for the hold. They cost us over £3000, but to be fair most of that was bubble wrap and postage stamps.

We flew them with Air Pets who were very good. They could have travelled on the same day as us but we needed to establish a base camp first so they flew out a week later. Besides we stopped off at Dubai and Sydney for a few days so they would have been kicking their heels waiting for us.

You have to have a delivery address for all the paperwork and we had nowhere to live in NZ. It would have been quite interesting if our plane had crashed because a cat and a dog would have arrived at my work place a week later. I imagined the conversation, "Where do you want this cat and dog? Says here you shipped them out from the UK…not my problem mate…"

If you intend to fly pets to NZ check out carefully what needs to be done to export them from the UK and import them into New Zealand. Quite apart from the cost, contributing to the balance of trade between the two countries there is a lot to process. For instance they need micro-chipping, vaccinating, screening and boarding. Your vet will be able to help add a bit extra to these costs. The dog was touch and go as the airport vet couldn't locate her microchip. All the paperwork was there but their scanner couldn't find the electronics under her skin. She was allowed to board her plane, but the delay meant she missed out on the duty free shopping.

Actually come to think of it, it was touch and go for the cat too. She needed to do a stool sample to check for the absence of parasites. This would take two weeks to analyse and for the "all clear" to be given. We had cut it very fine with our own departure date, but we did still have time and so we shut her in the spare bedroom with a litter tray. She consumed a lot of food but supplied nothing in return. For three days we kept her in. Still nothing. We massaged her belly. Nothing. Running out of time before her flight day, and needing a negative result from the sample before she would be allowed into New Zealand, we rang the vet for advice. "Just how do you get a cat to deliver the packet?" we asked. My thoughts were to put a small pot plant in the bedroom, cats seem to like that sort of a challenge.

No, apparently the best way to make a cat pooh is to wipe its anus with cotton wool soaked in warm water. Immediately I could see this was a job for The Evey because I was very busy with my 2020-21 tax return which had suddenly propelled itself up my to do list. I later found out that in my absence The Evey had pulled rank and delegated the job to Charlotte. Still nothing happened, but now her anus was nice and clean.

The whole experience reminded me of something my friend Mark had said twenty years previously. He was adamant that if you tied a piece of wool around a cat's middle it can't walk in a straight line and it falls over. When he told me this I was completely sceptical and immediately had to try it out on the cat we had at the time. We tied some wool around the cat's belly but nothing happened. We, and the cat got bored and she wandered off into the other room. About five minutes later we were hit by the smell which means just one thing.

Most cats don't like being ridiculed as they are proud creatures and have no sense of humour and this one was no exception. The biggest cat do-do I had ever seen stared up at me and next to it was the piece of wool we had used. Maybe Mark had been confused about what tying a piece of wool to a cat actually did? Twenty years on, with that line from Shaun of the Dead about dogs not being able to look up ringing in my ears, I found myself desperate to try anything. Armed with two feet of finest angora I wrestled to tie it around the cat. It didn't produce the desired effect in 1985 and it didn't produce the alternative effect in 2005. Disappointed we had to place our trust in God.

The Almighty moves in mysterious ways indeed as the eagle finally landed that afternoon. We rushed the sample to the vet before closing time and the day was saved. However I couldn't help wondering that maybe the wool thing does work but it is a sort of *delayed* reaction, like in Kill Bill Volume 2 when Bill gets killed.

Space For Your Research

www.airpets.com

Air Pets. This was the company we used to transport some of our team and they seemed very efficient.

www.pss.uk.com

Personal Shipping Services, the international removal company we favoured and they didn't let us down.

Chapter 2

Reasons to come to New Zealand

Why would you want to go through all that bother to pack up your life in one country and start a new one on the other side of the world? Here I attempt to put together some thoughts on why anyone would leave the safety of their birthplace and travel twelve thousand miles to a country tucked away from the rest of the world on the edge of the Pacific Ocean.

New Zealand is a relatively large country, the language barrier is small and the beaches are beautiful to behold and often deserted. The pace of life and society makes you feel you are in the Britain you remember from the nineteen seventies. If you are younger than me this would be the Britain of the eighties but without the Poll Tax. However there are many more reasons to come to NZ other than language, beaches and nostalgia.

The topics that follow are in no particular order of merit but I include quality of life first because all the things that follow can easily make up that concept. You choose which order fits your priorities.

Quality of life

The quality of life is high here. Now I know this is a very subjective thing, and it is down to the way you, yourself measure it, but there are some useful markers.

We are worse off financially, but I almost always finish work on time. Don't misunderstand me, New Zealanders work long hard hours but there is time to go down the pub after work on Friday and with the climate, relaxing is invariably outside.

New Zealand is a country built on migration. True that Maori were here before the Europeans but the bulk of the population has come from migrants. All humanity has been migrant in its way. My point is migrants are welcomed here. 1830 wasn't that long ago and many Pakeha (foreigners or non Maori) are only a few generations at most from their mother countries. Many New Zealanders still have family in the old country be it Scotland, England, Korea or Holland.

Kiwis are an honest, positive, tolerant, secular, egalitarian and humorous bunch with decent moral values. They are stoic beyond belief in many situations and you can't help warming to them if you have any of those characteristics yourself. (I am definitely none of these).

To support my case and if you can measure quality of life, a 2007 poll found 91% Christchurch residents rated their quality of life as good or extremely good.

Friendliness

Being from the south of England I don't do friendliness. However Kiwis have a way of drawing you into this somewhat alien sentiment. People say hello and good morning wherever you go and I actually know my neighbours here and they have become friends. I was at work only two days when a nice old boy struck up a gardening conversation with me and the following morning he gave me a packet of bean seeds having endorsed the variety. I have grown them for three seasons now and he was right. "Tendergreen" dwarf beans are disease resistant, stringless, crisp and ready to eat in six weeks.

Religious tolerance

New Zealand is a tolerant place full stop. Its religious tolerance comes from the early settlers who escaped Britain to NZ to practice their Christianity in peace and quiet. As a result all sorts of denominations are here in Christchurch. Evangelists, Baptists, Presbyterians, Seventh Day Adventists, Church of the Latter Day Saints, you name it, it's here. All the world's big religions are also well represented in Christchurch; Judaism, Islam, Buddhism and Hinduism all reflecting the welcoming and multicultural makeup of the city. Yes even the Hari Krishners are here. They have a large and fantastic float in the Christmas Parade which they pull along by ropes. It's like watching the pyramids being made. Sadly found a School for Jedi have I not.

August 2007 saw the Ministry of Ethnic Affairs launch Islam Awareness Week in New Zealand where mosques around the country open their doors to everyone to help improve understanding and to dispel the mistrust felt of Islam. Most of the country's 40,000 Moslems are from Fiji. There aren't

12

many places in the world where an openly gay government minister is welcomed into a mosque. I did wonder afterwards though on his choice of salmon coloured socks and asking the Imam to hold his clutch bag for him.

Crime

If you have ever read the comic 2000 AD you would know that poor old Judge Dredd had his hands full dispensing law and order in Mega City One. One storyline explored the relationship between crime and life and concluded that dead people don't commit that much crime and so in a parallel universe it became illegal to live. It seemed to work for their universe and they reported criminal activity down year on year. Everyone was happy. The problem came when the Judges from this parallel universe crossed over into Mega City One. The result : Judge Dredd and Judge Death do battle, and lots of innocent people get caught up in it. A great read when you are 13, and still a great read when you are 43 but don't tell anyone.

The point I wish to make is quite obvious and I did not need that previous paragraph to make it. Wherever there are humans there is crime. I am afraid that New Zealand is no different than elsewhere in the world. However the perception here is that crime is not as endemic as the UK and that is refreshing. The reason may be as simple as there are fewer people here. The whole of NZ has only half the population of London. I discuss crime and its causes, socio-economic impact and some possible solutions in detail in the chapter on some of the downsides to New Zealand. Return this book now for a refund if you think that my solutions involve hugging criminals.

Terrorism? What's that?

At the moment there is little or no risk or threat of terrorism, except of course that act of French sponsored state terrorism, and I am talking about the Rainbow Warrior incident of 1985. There was a bomb blast in 1984 at Trades Hall Wellington (a Trade Union HQ) which killed the caretaker. No one was ever caught or punished for it. It has been speculated that it was some anti union thug. In August 2007 three bottle bombs were found in Christchurch at various places. The one at the bus exchange exploded slightly injuring a cleaner's hand and affecting his hearing. The other two were deactivated. It was believed they used solid carbon dioxide as the explosive, the devices were poorly made and the CCTV pictures published of the suspects looked more like student pranksters rather than Al-Quaida sleepers.

Of course living your life here is not without its stresses but suffice is to say that we never think of terrorism as one of them. You only remember it is a world issue when it features in the news here when they are reporting other countries who are suffering it.

Nuclear-free living

If you are a nuclear power it is always good to do the testing of it in someone else's back yard. The Kiwis put paid to that in 1987 with legislation banning nuclear powered craft within 12 miles of the country. This upset the Americans which is always a good thing. The upshot of this stance is that it helped reinforce the country's sovereignty and identity as a free thinking nation, while greatly reducing the risk of nuclear accidents or leaks from visiting nuclear reactors. I guess the ulterior motive may have been "we've got enough radiation coming through that bloody hole in the ozone the world has given us and we don't need any more thank you very much".

There is a certain irony in the country's nuclear-free stance as the land mass sits on a very thin part of the Earth's crust. Consequently there is more than the odd volcano, geothermal field and subducting tectonic plate, all of whose volatility, heat and driving force come from the thermonuclear energy generated below ground in the magma.

The Sky

The sky is bluer here than what we are used to in Britain, partly because of the latitude in which New Zealand sits but also because they don't have the same amount of air pollution.

The Milky Way is beautiful if seen from the southern hemisphere in winter and is visible at night (obviously) just outside the City. If we are travelling home on a clear night we will stop the car and I will point out the Via Lacta to the children and show them the constellations of Xbox, Britney, Posh and Becks and tell them the often sad and tragic mythology behind these legendary creatures.

14

Evergreen natives and trees

Eighty percent of the plants in New Zealand are only found here in New Zealand. (You may have to re-read that sentence to make sense of it.). Many are evergreen making the winters seem pleasantly coloured. The European-introduced species all shut up shop for winter but Cordylines, Hebe, Griselinia, Olearia, Pittosporum, Eleagnus, Flax, ferns, tree ferns and so on all keep trading throughout the colder darker months and it definitely gives the feel of a greener place. This colour, albeit mainly green, together with the "higher" latitude and later winter sunsets help make winter days feel less depressing than northern ones.

Population density

It was Jean-Paul Sartre who said "Hell is other people". If like me you lean to that side of the line then you may find New Zealand a pleasant sort of purgatory. NZ boasts an average population density of only 15.15 people per square kilometre. I have still to meet the 0.15 person in my square kilometre but obviously the cities especially Auckland buzz more than the wop wops but compared to Britain with 243 people per square kilometre there is plenty of breathing space here.

Since the 6 billionth human being was born in June 2006 there are at least another 620 million newbies on the planet. New Zealand has just the right sort of comfortable feel about it. Not too many people, not too few, just about enough. The population of New Zealand is projected to reach 4,418,600 by 2015. That is still 13 times less people than live in Britain today. Think of all those elbows in the January sales hacking and flaying to get to the bargains. You rarely have to queue and wait for things here, from parking spaces to toilet cubicles to traffic light changes, though I suspect some Aucklanders and the odd Wellingtonian would beg to differ.

In his book "A land of two halves" Joe Bennett has commented that New Zealand has the same population in the reign of Queen Elizabeth the Second as Britain had in the reign of Queen Elizabeth the First. And before you ask there is no Black Death here to the best of my knowledge.

If you are that way inclined, living in a small country is a good way to get on telly. I never appeared on British TV once in forty years. Out here I have been on TV twice, once on live TV and once in a recorded format. The latter was a fleeting 2 second appearance when the All Blacks scored a try against South Africa. I was working as an extra in the crowd on both occasions. I will admit I looked a little seedy and could have given the child catcher from Chitty Chitty Bang Bang a run for his money had my wife and children not looked worse.

Traffic

There are 3.15 million vehicles of varying descriptions registered in NZ and I dare say a few that aren't. Compare this to the similar land mass of Britain where we have around 33 million vehicles.

Street names are mounted on posts at every road junction so you know exactly where you are. This may be an Americanism they have adopted but it is so handy as to be a hindrance. I say this because the roads here are long and often based on the grid system so there are many ways to get to your destination. It means that at every intersection you get the street name reinforced on your frontal cortex which offers familiarity and you form a bond with the name. Unless you have a street map and a mental image of where the road goes a familiar name is just that: a familiar name. To this day I am very fond of Idris Road, Innes Road and Greers Road but I couldn't tell you where they go to.

Road works

You rarely see them. I remember reading somewhere that there are as many traffic cones in Britain as there are people. This is probably the case in New Zealand too but apart from the occasional one or two the rest are very shy, most likely existing in symbiotic relationships with students in student accommodation. Road works are handled quickly and efficiently in my opinion. This may be because they don't have the ancient infrastructure under the road to deal with and they don't have any gas pipes to speak of because of the risk of earthquakes. Wellington has a gas system and has had road work problems though nothing on the scale of what we put up with at times in Britain. Often it is not worth setting up traffic lights. A man or woman, I have seen both in this equal society, just controls traffic with a lollipop sign. Roads outside the cities or between such centres of population just aren't that busy with huge volumes of traffic. I know there are problem spots in the cities but the traffic updates on the radio are short and "sweet as".

16

Scenery

The scenery can be best described as where the Highlands meet Gondor meets The Shire meets Austria but where everyone speaks English. In the South Island where we live it's like having your own Lake District bolted onto The European Alps with a bit of exotic native bush to boot. Isolation if you want it, population if you want it and in many places just a sense of being transported to the Jurassic period. The Kiwis do scenery very well. Sometimes your eyes just can't take it all in. However, wherever you drive throughout the country there is no need to worry about missing the best views as signposts warn you of approaching "lookouts" with ample parking to pull into.

Indeed there are numerous National Parks, beauty spots, picnic areas and panoramic vistas. I am not particularly religious but you can see the hand of God everywhere, with absolutely no sign of Maradona which is always a bonus if you are English.

I won't bore you with details or photos, you have to collect your own, but we have stood on beaches, within coves or up hills with no visible sign or sound of any human being save ourselves and when we turn our iPods off all you can hear are the sounds of nature or pure stillness. I have said to the children there may only be a handful of times in your lives where you can feel as close to nature, your spiritual self, at one with the planet, God, call it what you will and these are the times. Commit them to memory so you can call on them in times when you need them. The tax man can steal your money, scoundrels and scallywags can steal your possessions but no one or nothing, save perhaps dementia, can rob you of your memories and even then strong memories of your youth are often resistant to such loss. Everyone nods in agreement and then we all go back to our MP3 players and the latest gangster rap.

Nothing wanting to kill you

There are no poisonous creatures native to New Zealand except the very rare, reclusive Katipo spider which lives under drift wood and can give you a nasty bite, which isn't fatal. I have been on many beaches and have never seen one, but I would squash it if I did.

The Kiwi attitude in general

New Zealanders don't care what you look like or how you dress. They know better than to throw stones in glass houses. I find it all very refreshing. Look how you like, be how you like, be the real you, though you may need a good lawyer if you take that advice too literally.

New Zealanders are pretty unpretentious. On the whole they dress casually, though you do see them in power suits the majority feel at home in simple clothes and even fewer of them in summer. The uniform is t-shirt or "muscle-back", shorts and jandals but saying that many walk bare-footed.

Kiwis don't take themselves too seriously. When Otago Correction Facility opened in 2006 (a prison to you and me) the authorities opened the doors to the public and people were able to spend the night there. One guy's family bought him an overnight stay for his birthday and he couldn't rave about it enough when the news station filmed him there.

On the subject of the penal system, there are about 270 judges in New Zealand. None appear to be like Judge John Deed or indeed Judge Dredd, more's the pity, judging by the TV that is allowed in the courts. I smile whenever I see the relaxed environment of the court room. I thought even the hardest of "crims" owns a suit in an effort to look like butter wouldn't melt. Well out here most defendants opt for the casual look of a t-shirt and stubbies. The accused is visible to the camera unless they have been granted name suppression by the judge and then they have their faces blurred out. However the sports top can give away who they really are. Indeed you do not want to know how many times number ten Dan Carter has appeared in the dock.

The Kiwis are a stoic breed. A guy here recently lost his hand to a working accident. When interviewed for the paper, after it was stitched back on he is quoted as saying "I remember picking up my hand and thinking, "Oh, that's not so good". The accident, he said, was "just one of those things"

Everyone loves the Kiwis, except maybe the French. The Kiwis don't go around the world upsetting everyone like other nationalities. I have noticed however, that whenever anything happens in the world there is always a New Zealander somewhere around at the time of the incident. Be it a nasty earthquake, a kidnapping in the Niger Delta, a failed clinical trial, an

18

assassination attempt or a lost dog there is always a kiwi involved, or witness to it, or within seconds, or feet from the trouble.

I guess this is because they are a diaspora and because everyone knows a Kiwi. We are all aware of the six degrees of separation where no one person is more than six steps from a link with any other person in the world but did you know that you are never more than three people removed from a New Zealander? A friend of a friend's girlfriend or boyfriend is always a Kiwi, a phenomenon known as the Third Law of Affability that every Kiwi practices.

One thing about the Kiwi attitude that really struck me was the case recently of a Christchurch solicitor coming home from holiday to find his home being burgled and someone in his drive pinching his television. He jumped on the bloke while his wife phoned the police who carted the burglar away. Not much to note there but the police inspector interviewed for the paper said "He (the homeowner) did a really good job, we encourage people to take on burglars if they find them in their home: you just need to make sure you use caution and common sense." This sums up the Kiwi mentality if you ask me. Women here are just as tough. Only the other day a 40 year old mother of two, rugby tackled a burglar to the ground and held him until police arrived. Respect.

Back home you wouldn't tackle a burglar unless you had your mates with you and you were all wearing body armour had a dog to hand, a baseball bat and were up to date with your hepatitis jabs… and then he'd sue you for breaching his human rights to roam freely through your possessions.

New Zealanders could give us Brits a run for our money when it comes to drinking beer. You may remember in the news that a genuine Speights Bar appeared on the Thames for the Rugby World Cup 2007. They loaded a 10 tonne pub onto a barge and sailed it 24779 km via the Bahamas for it to sit on the Thames for nine months. I am pretty sure that "via the Bahamas" isn't the quickest route. Anyway each place they stopped at they set it up on deck, a process that took them a whole working day, just so they could pull a pint of draught for Kiwis around the world who may be missing their native beer. And the world thinks the British are eccentric. A bummer that it arrived after the All Blacks got knocked out, though I'm sure the beer didn't go to waste.

Humour

New Zealanders until recently were brought up on British television humour. Programmes like "Are You Being Served?" "Dad's Army" and "The Dick Emery Show" have helped to shape their sense of humour. They are indeed a humorous breed and are very good at laughing at themselves as well as at others. I believe that if you can't laugh at yourself you have no right to ridicule or lampoon anyone else and so I find Kiwi humour is less brutal than the Australian version. Don't misunderstand me, Australians have a great sense of humour but I find they aren't as good at taking it back as giving it out.

Having said that, while many a New Zealander was brought up laughing at Mrs Slocombe's pussy they do have their own national 'humour' identity. A series of simple billboard posters for Tui beer have over the months delighted me with phrases like:

NZ is going to be the 7th state of Australia	Yeah Right!
Those tissues are for my cold	Yeah Right!
It's a six year undergraduate course	Yeah Right!
We only spooned	Yeah Right!

I think you can tell a lot about a people from the adverts their society puts out. I particularly like the one for a brand of quality crisps where two male office workers are chatting around the water cooler and one asks the other what flavour are the crisps he's eating? Sceptical as to the flavour being genuine he bets "his left one" that they don't taste like the description on the packet and takes one to try. Cut to the scene of a cathedral choir in their finest vestments and as the camera pulls gently out, the air is full of the beautiful sound of the same bloke singing castrato. This also serves to illustrate that Kiwis aren't easily offended.

Yesterday was the first airing of the New Zealand version of the franchise "Deal or No Deal". This morning on the breakfast show of "The Edge" radio station they ran their homage to the concept by calling blindly on a number of houses asking the occupants if they were drug dealers or not and did they have a "Deal or No Deal". The worrying thing was the second house they called on sold them something in silver foil.

20

It is a real shame you probably won't be able to witness the "Undie 500" road car race from Christchurch to Dunedin. It is organised by Canterbury University's Engineering Society and participants have to buy a car for under $500 dress it up in a theme and road trip it the 5 hours to Dunedin. The effort and humour that go into these creations are impressive. I have seen both Thunderbird Two and Thunderbird Four cruising the streets. Another vehicle completely covered in hair, one paying homage to Jamie Oliver the naked chef, driven by naked people and one painted in camouflage colours with the Lara Croft film title, font and design reading "Womb Raider" on the doors. Bit naughty that one.

Most competitors are students, mostly male and it all ends in a big piss up with a few sofas set light to in the streets in a tradition as old as anyone can remember.

It was banned from 2007 because rioting broke out in Dunedin's student quarter and a number of residents' cars were added to the pyrotechnics. The crowd had to be subdued by the police in full riot gear who were taunted throughout by the mob performing the haka en masse which looked very impressive when it was shown on the news.

Then it all ended in an open air dance party, with police giving a light show from their torches while the crowd experienced psychedelic stars as police equipment was employed in the way for which it was intended (see section on police further on). There were 69 arrests and 70 fires to put out. As I mention later you can never have enough students.

What made me laugh was one New Zealand newspaper writing up the incident. They summed up the whole thing with the line "This was no good-humoured student japery."

The last time I heard the word japery was in 1923.

New Zealand has no class

This is not exactly true but class is far less obvious here. True there are people who think they are better than the next person but this has been the case since society was invented at 9am Saturday 17th September 4004 BCE. The ruling class have to rule, that is their duty and don't they do it so very well? Snobbery also exists wherever there are humans and here is no

21

exception. Meanwhile most Kiwis leave these sorts of people alone and get on with their own lives grateful they aren't like them. I find I can't obviously tell the class system in New Zealand save for the obvious trappings of wealth and body language. I certainly can't tell from the accent.

New Zealanders don't call their bosses Sir, Mr or Mrs. They'll call them a lot of other names. Most worker/boss relationships are conducted on first name terms. If a boss says or does something stupid, then the workforce will let them know in no uncertain terms.

New Zealand was formed on equality and the one experiment to bring British society to NZ in the early days failed dismally. This was in Nelson in the 19th century but what the businessmen who set up the company back in Britain failed to realize was the very people who wanted to come to New Zealand were those who wanted to escape the British class system. Those pioneers probably said "bugger this we'll go to Auckland instead".

Interestingly it was only the arrival of efficient Germans migrants who kept the Nelson colony alive. I can just imagine it, lots of upper and middle classes all bossing each other around and nothing getting done because there weren't any working class to do it, so they all starved. Egality rules the day: as it should.

New Zealand may have no class but they have some neat ideas

New Zealand has always been a forward thinking country and has many good ideas and practices, and some bad. Giving women the vote in 1893 was one of those. A good idea I mean, along with The Social Security Act 1938 which was the first scheme of its kind in the world.

Do not underestimate the creativity and focus of New Zealanders, a real David in a Goliath world, albeit in shorts and jandals. Though come to think of it this image is not too far from the original David I suspect. Kiwis number only a few but they have brought us the water jet boat, a nano filament spinning device, a micro-particle to fight Influenza and HIV, conquered Everest, found several new stars and planets and invented the calf length gumboot. Did you also know the plastic disposable syringe was invented by a Kiwi. He didn't profit from it either but considered it a gift to mankind along with the child resistant bottle top and a tranquillizer dart.

Some of the other neat ideas this nation comes up with must be profitable because I have noticed that in the Christchurch Yellow Pages alone there are eight patent attorney firms practising in the city.

While on the subject of litigation there is a "no blame" culture here, underpinned by a system known as ACC. You will hear a lot about ACC so I have a separate section on this but it stands for Accident Compensation Corporation. As a result of this scheme there's not much, if any accident litigation, and none of those awful ambulance chasing adverts.

Among New Zealand's other great ideas is "Pay your fine but there is an alternative" In Safety Awareness Week hundreds of drivers were pulled up and fined for not having their children securely fastened in the car. Each incurred a $300 fine but if they could prove they had bought a certified car seat within 7 days and presented the police with the receipt all fines would be waived. Now isn't this a better idea than wasting energy and money chasing unpaid fines? All that effort involving the courts when at the end of the day the whole idea of the exercise is to keep kids safe and preventing accidents rather than spanking the parents, even though some need a good beating. I would insist on barbed wired wrapped around the cane with a run-up and flick of the wrist on impact. Such punishments never hurt anyone.

Charity

New Zealanders are like the British and have a sense of justice and fair play. They are a generous society, funding overseas projects in developing countries while doing good things closer to home. Recently there was a sad story of a small South African family who came to New Zealand for a better life. On attempting to traverse an unmarked railway crossing the driver was blinded by sun strike at the same time as a train passed. Mum and dad were killed instantly but their 5 year old daughter escaped with just scratches. They had no life insurance. A trust fund was set up and the nation chipped in. This illustrates two things. Kiwis' generosity and the way they welcome migrants into their country.

All the major charities are here: including Amnesty International, Red Cross and Greenpeace plus some Christian based ones like World Vision which I hadn't heard of before. Individual Kiwis do their bit for the world. For instance every grans' favourite, Hayley Westernra is an ambassador for UNICEF.

Even charity reflects the Antipodean humour. Each November is "Movember" and men (and possibly some women) are encouraged to grow full moustaches by not shaving. Money is collected, competitions are run for the best ones and all is done to raise awareness of men's health issues. I tried it in "Movember" 2006 but no one noticed mine except in certain lights and then it was ginger. I suffered big time for my effort that month. For example I found the following advert in the staff room.

"BUY / SELL / EXCHANGE
For sale, one moustache, slightly
used but friendly. Good personality,
pedigree papers available. Owner
unable to maintain. Willing to swap
for a moderate amount of chest hair.
Apply to : Nerdy"

When Christmas came and the department opened their Secret Santa presents mine was a stick on chest-piece and medallion. I wore that "moderate amount of chest hair" for the rest of the day but it couldn't be maintained as it was very itchy and brought me out in a rash. A bit like my moustache.

It is understood that with the success of Movember there is a desire to do something for the ladies and it has been mooted that this may be called Fanuary. I kid you not. We'll wait and see how that one opens up. I am sure there will be no shortage of judges for the competition.

DonateNZ is a website that aims to match people who need to get rid of things (but which stand little chance of being able to be sold), with charities, schools and not for profit organizations that need stuff. This may not be a new idea but the neat slant on it is that donors and recipients can communicate. While charity can be faceless and works well that way, it is nice to know who got your kidney and how well they are treating it.

I include it here because it illustrates the resourcefulness of the New Zealander. The national psyche is such that where you are tucked under the world you make do with what you've got, recycling whenever you can. Most Kiwis of my generation and older know all about cars. They know how to fix a Ford Cortina or an Austen Morris because they had to. Parts were expensive, took forever to arrive and if you wanted a car you had to look after it.

24

The cosy nature of New Zealand

Given the small population it is not uncommon for your work colleagues to know or have been to school, or drink with, an All Black, a Black Cap or a Silver Fern. NZ sport's stars are expected to, and willingly engage with the supporting public, for instance at charity events and public appearances. There is a also a good chance you can bump into a sporting hero in the shopping mall, though just why would a prop be buying size 28 lingerie? Actually Dan Carter owns a shop in Wellington and now Christchurch and has been known to serve customers in it. For fans of the number 10, it is called "Gas" or maybe that's what size 28 underwear that's two sizes too small gives you?

Now it has to be said that in 40 years of living in England I have never met any of my heroes from Highbury except by proxy where my brother in law bumped into Thierry Henry in a posh London hotel, before he went off the rails and joined that Spanish club.

With the small population and the abundant space out here I often wonder what Kiwis coming to Britain and a big city like London, think when they step out on a crowded street for the first time. Do they think "wow, the centre of The Universe" or do they think "What have I done? I want my Mum.'

I think Kiwis, especially those who have travelled the northern hemisphere, know what it is like to be a long way from home. In the Rugby World Cup a Tauranga family paid $11,000 up front for a camper van to follow the All Blacks around the country. However on arriving in France the vehicle never materialized. They had been hoodwinked and then as if things couldn't get any worse they had their credit cards, cash and match tickets all stolen. The New Zealand High Commission were able to lend them a tent and a single sleeping bag. News got out of their predicament and they were interviewed for the telly. The same old Kiwi stoicism shone through and they accepted their plight and were very smiley for the cameras. The New Zealand sponsors this end stepped in and funded a camper van and the All Black team got to hear of it and invited them along to watch a training session.

Not long ago a female newscaster and anchorwoman left to have a baby and they presented her with flowers on air at the end of the news and she said her goodbyes and how nice it had been to work with everyone, and had not the next programme started I am certain we would all have been invited down the pub for drinks. All 4.2 million of us. Most would have gone as well.

It was a sad day for the country when its greatest son Sir Edmund Hillary, or Sir Ed to everyone, died in early 2008. Such was his status he was the first living kiwi to appear on a bank note. On more than one occasion he described himself merely as a New Zealander with ordinary abilities and determination. Like many New Zealanders he was just a good bloke. As an outsider the nation's response sums up the Kiwi mentality. They have no time for pomp. The people they admire and revere, are down to earth, approachable, modest people who have genuinely earned their respect.

Political correctness

Doesn't seem to exist here, which is nice in some ways as we have gone too far in the UK. I do however squirm every time I hear the term handicapped as opposed to disabled which is a more dignified word. Help me I've gone all PC and I never meant to, but there is something unsettling about the image "cap in hand" or "handicapped". People with mental disability or learning difficulties are often referred to as mental retards or imbeciles. I flinch when I hear this. I am not a PC person but there are gentler ways of describing people with disability. Obviously not over here.

Having come from a country that takes political correctness to the cleaners or should I say stain removal technicians, I had to watch in shock at a TV advert featuring a blind man in a telly shop feeling all the televisions on display with his white cane. He hits the biggest flat screen TV in the shop and beams with delight while the voice over hits us with the tag line "You want it we've got it". Maybe the sound is great on that model or maybe I'm being too subtle.

The country's daily soap opera set in an Auckland hospital made me laugh recently when a clergyman character was diagnosed with gonorrhoea. Nothing unusual in that I hear you say. No, it was one of the "doctors" who commented angrily "well he didn't catch it from washing his willy in the font". Living rooms echoed with "what's the matter with his ear Mum?"

Other examples here include the notice I saw in the local newspaper recently for a public meeting with our member of parliament entitled "The Crime Epidemic: How to Keep Prisoners in Prison". Just as amusing was the announcement for a fund raiser for Save the Children that stated "no children under 5".

There was also a photograph in the Christchurch paper of Cup and Show Week (horse racing and county show) and it pictured a city type in a suit pinching the bottom of a pretty girl. The caption read "Cup Week cheek: a keen student of form checks out a filly's credentials on Cup Day". Suffice as to say strawberry blonds suffer for their phenotype in New Zealand.

Sport: "What did you say? You don't like what.......!"

It is probably the Australians who are the most sport mad nation in the world but I'll wager the Kiwis aren't far behind. If they don't regularly play a sport they know what is going on in the world of sport and not just their own nation's sport. I was often told the Arsenal score before I knew it, with analysis of the goals we scored and the quality of our win.

To help with the national team names you may encounter here I have summarized the main ones below:

All Blacks	I won't insult your intelligence.
All Whites	The national "Soccer" team.
Baby Blacks	The national Under 19s Rugby Union team.
Black Caps	The national Cricket team.
Black Ferns	The national Ladies' Rugby team.
Black Jacks	The sport of the older person : bowls.
Black Sticks	The national Hockey team.
Football Ferns	The national Ladies' "Soccer" team
Ice Blacks	The national Ice Hockey team.
Silver Ferns	The national Netball team.
Small Blacks	Little people's Rugby team.
Tall Blacks	The national Basketball team.
Tall Ferns	The national Ladies' Basketball team.
The Kiwis	The national Rugby League team.
Wheel Blacks	The national Paraplegic Basketball team.
White Ferns	The national Ladies' Cricket team.
White Socks	The national Baseball Team.

There can't be any permutations left? The only one I can think of is "The Black Heads" but no one wants those.

Don't come here if you don't like or can't understand rugby. Be warned, the game, in either code, gets ten minutes a night on the sport section of the main news but there may be twenty seconds for premiership soccer, especially in the rugby closed season. However expect the rugby coverage to increase exponentially with the build up to the Rugby World Cup in 2011 (to be held in New Zealand). The main rugby arenas which will be mentioned a great deal are listed below:

Carrisbrook	Dunedin.
AMI Stadium	Christchurch (until recently known as Jade Stadium).
Eden Park	Auckland.
The Cake Tin	The Westpac Stadium Wellington: so called because its round silver exterior resembles a baking tin.

I cannot leave the subject of rugby without the mention of the early shock exit from the 2007 Rugby World Cup. The country was in mourning, far worse than any English exit from the FIFA Soccer World Cup which let's face it, is generally rather expected. The reaction demonstrated their love of a sport in which they excel and I have to say I felt for them. I also stayed indoors with the blinds down the day after, as the referee was English and he copped some of the blame. You can never be too careful and an angry crowd out for a lynching will pick the first nerd they see to test that knot on.

When the match coverage ended and the shock had still to set in, the TV station aired one of the nicest things I have seen in such circumstances. Before the next programme started they ran the Eric Idle song "Always look on the bright side of life (whistle, whistle, whistle etc..)" to clips of the Pythons bashing heads, slapping faces with fish, blowing characters up and so on. A real blast from the past to see the skits and sketches I grew up with. I thought out loud how much I liked the Kiwis and their stoic nature which comes out all the time when you least expect it. Whether this intermission cheered the country up I don't know, but as a Johnny foreigner, I understood its intention and it made me laugh and it made me respect the Kiwi more. Well done who ever thought of that.

Within six hours the first jokes were out in the public domain. My favourite was "a man has been found washed up on a beach wearing pink panties, fishnets, heels and an All Blacks' jersey. Police have decided to remove the jersey to save the family's embarrassment." They'll get over it by 2011 I'm sure.

In the meantime there's always golf. Everyone seems to play golf and there appears to be more golf courses in the country than people. If you are like me and find looking for a small white ball in long green grass a bit pointless, fret not, there will be something else sporty for you to do. Everyone young or old is encouraged to do something and there are regular sporting events if you are truly competitive. Biathalons, triathalons, half marathons, the famous Coast to Coast race and so on. There is a children's "marathon" called the Kids' Mara'Fun and there was a lovely picture in the paper of a young lad of about eight or nine heaving his isotonic drink up all over the pavement. I think the photographer must have used a 1/1000 or less shutter speed given the detail captured. The caption reads "Exertion: the Kids Mara'Fun takes its toll on one entrant". I bet his mum and gran are so proud that he is in the paper, though this is one of those photos you probably wouldn't have sitting on the sideboard.

Sport in Christchurch and the South Island

There are dozens of sports groups and clubs in Canterbury covering almost every conceivable thing you can do with your body (except that). For instance there are 42 tramping clubs, 6 water polo clubs, 45 Tai Chi clubs, 4 Australian football clubs, 57 rugby union clubs, even a wild pig hunting club but sorry, because of global warming no polar bear clubs.

Christchurch is home to The Crusaders, one of the top New Zealand Super 14 rugby teams. Some bloke called Dan Carter plays for them when he's not advertising Jockey underwear, serving in his shop or selling himself to the French. The home games are very atmospheric and real knights in armour on real horses come out at the start, to stirring music and churn up the pitch. Everyone waves their foams swords and blows their plastic trumpets. The whole experience couldn't be closer to the twelve century if it tried.

Cycling is big in Christchurch. The Canterbury Plains, I now realize after my job interview, are pretty flat and lend themselves to cycling. Road bikes are everywhere, their riders training hard for just the pleasure of it. Smooth, shapely, toned, hairless legs do justice to figure hugging Lycra, and that's just the men.

My in-laws were travelling in the Queenstown area by car and on a steep narrow road they passed a unicycle club out training on the mountain. Incredible, they must have buns of steel. It's not like you have a lower gear on a unicycle to drop into. The only gear you can drop into is clown gear. I take my hat off to them.......and out comes a bunch of flowers and a rabbit.

No to Iraq

The NZ government wanted nothing to do with the war in Iraq and they have consistently followed this stance. Despite this they were unfortunately embarrassed by state carrier Air New Zealand, of which they own 80% of the shares. Air NZ was chartered to fly the Australian Army to Kuwait to engage in Iraq, and the government knew nothing about it. Why Quantas couldn't take them I don't know? The relationship between the two neighbours can be strained at times in a big brother little brother sort of way but mostly they are buds and we all know "neighbours are there for one another, that's when good neighbours become good friends". (©Tony Hatch)

Kiwis love beating the Aussies

The Kiwis love beating the Australians at sport more than we do, and sporting controversies tick on between the two countries. Whenever they meet in cricket, and that is quite often as you can imagine, there is always lively discussion on the last ball of the match in February 1981 when Australia bowled underarm to win. What you don't often hear the Kiwis say is that the ball was being delivered to the tenth wicket and that they needed to score a six to **draw** the game. Unfortunately Roy of the Rovers wasn't the tail ender and all that the poor batsman could do, was storm off in disgust.

There has been a long running saga about the nationality of Australasia's greatest race horse who won 37 of his 51 starts. Sired and born in Timaru NZ he was bought and raced in Australia. The Australians say he is theirs, the Kiwis theirs. I am referring to the great gelding "Phar Lap" who actually lived in the 1920s. Eighty years on they are still arguing over him/her/it.

Everything you need is here

I have always been a "towny": born and bred. I always thought you wouldn't catch me living in a city, ever. Here I am living in the biggest city in the South Island. D'oh. In my defence, Christchurch feels like a town. A large town I agree, but its earthquake risk means there aren't too many sky scrapers so mostly everything is on the level and looks and feels low rise.

Everything we need is here. We had a little think about what we have here within a 2 km walk or cycle ride. We couldn't find anything that wasn't on our doorstep. School, dentist, doctors, garage, mechanic, shopping mall, supermarket, swimming pool, parks, video shop, bank, hairdressers, computer shop, gadget shop, library and so on. The only thing that was more than 2 kilometres away was the vets (because we will travel the extra 3 km to a very good vet: Harewood Veterinary Hospital) and the airport about 5 or 6 km away. Even The Evey's "special" cosmetics are available in three locations just along the road whereas in England it was a 25 mile journey to find a supplier.

Kids can be kids here

Everything seemed so much more difficult to do in England. Having two young girls who are into music and wanted to see the latest "long haired lover from Liverpool" at Wembley we'd groan inwardly as it meant a three hour journey to London and all the other effort and stress such a mission requires.

The band Snow Patrol, who I believe are popular at the moment, have visited NZ twice in 6 months. This most recent time, they came to Christchurch and my kids were delighted to be in the front row of the mosh pit to see and cheer them on. I was delighted as the stadium was just ten minutes down the road and I could go home for a cup of English breakfast and a rich tea biscuit in between. Unfortunately one of my daughters was left "chasing cars" as her ticket was on the dashboard and I had to come out again. I was chilled about this though, because just before we left England the kids went to see Maroon 5 in Brixton and my 14 year old and her 12 year old cousin were offered a spliff in the street. In some ways the two countries are a world apart and of course they are–literally.

Ask any young female Kiwi you might come across in the UK if they want children. After the stinging of your face has died down, rephrase the question and ask them where they would like to bring their children up. I guarantee most of them will say New Zealand.

I sat in the sand dunes on New Brighton's beach last summer and watched two young lads through my binoculars. Before I get slapped, I'll

31

just rephrase that, I was "people watching" and two boys of between 14 and 16 were playing on the beach. They kicked a football about, they played with a dog, paddled in the sea and then they dug in the sand and built castles. I felt privileged to witness this. They didn't fret about how un-cool it may have looked. They just played like kids should. Our children grow up too quickly under the pressures of their peers and fashion and society and so on. It was great to watch older children just play without feeling self conscious. Alternatively they may just have been nerds but I would like to think that they made the most of their childhood before all the hassles of adulthood barge into their lives.

Some young people want to be "gangstas". Even the kids of architects and doctors. Of course they make the best gangsters as they know how hard life is in the middle classes. It has always been like that. My parents' generation wanted to be James Dean and act hard in rock and roll leathers. My generation, including me, wished to be highwaymen like Adam Ant, complete with painted stripes and all the menace New Romantics could conjure (usually a pout through heavy lipstick).

Kids, for heavens sake, just be kids for as long as you can. Play with your toys, those days are the best of your life. Some of my best friends were toys (as well as books, but don't tell Treasure Island that). This got me to thinking how much I really miss the "Play-doh charge of the light brigade' set I used to have.

Suffice to say the outdoor lifestyle and landscape of New Zealand really helps children be children.

Other Reasons you might like to come to NZ

- You can still buy paracetamol in boxes of 100.

- While they are aware of Jordan, and the Beckhams are big here, this is definitely a Jodie Marsh free-zone.

- New Zealand was the first country in the world to get Halo 3 when it was released one minute after midnight on September 25th in the year of Our X-Box 360 (2007 in the Gregorian calendar). And indeed Grand

Theft Auto IV upset NZ before anywhere else on the planet in April 2008. This country certainly gets film releases and TV series before Australia and even the UK. In particular I am thinking of that classic of our time "Meet the Spartans". You also get to be the first to see in the next millennium but if you can't wait for that, the annual Earth Hour happens here. Record labels often release in NZ well before the UK.

- People aren't going to call by unexpectedly. It takes effort to come out here so it tends to be those people you know and like, that want to see you. However those that do plan a visit aren't going to know your plans or how things work out here. Just draw the curtains and stay very quiet. They will soon get bored and go to Queenstown instead.

- I heard the other day that the UK is the most watched population when it comes to CCTV and if you ask me that is the slippery slope to big brother. Doesn't anyone realize that it all starts with the desire to improve security for its citizens? Well, I am glad to say that while there is CCTV in NZ it is not as ubiquitous (yet) as the UK. It certainly (to my knowledge) doesn't shout at you to pick up the litter you have just dropped or to stop scratching in an antisocial way or to tell you that orange and purple clash and what were you thinking mixing two strong colours on your baby? Mark my words it will all end up like the film "V for Vendetta" except Natalie Portman won't be around to help out.

- On the subject of blowing up parliament, Kiwis also celebrate Guy Fawkes night in November as technically we share the same upper legislature as New Zealand (The House of Lords or at least the Law Lords). I don't remember, remember the 5th of November out here as being as intrusive as the British ones I have experienced. I should know as I have lived in New Zealand for three whole years, which makes me an authority on the subject. Yes, you do get fireworks go off, but not for two solid weeks either side of the 5th and not into the early hours. There is a huge display of fireworks on the weekend around the 5th in New Brighton. Last year, 100,000 people watched a great display launched from the pier. I think maybe it has the potential to be a social problem as Brits come over here bringing this awful tradition with them.

Footnote: Fireworks are only available here from the 2nd November and you have to be over 18 years old to buy them. Footnote to the footnote: Most under 18s have fake ID.

- If you believe Dr James Lovelock (the creator of the Gaia theory and planetary ecology), by the time the world has sorted out global warming there will only be two places comfortable to live in. The UK, which will resemble Hong Kong for skyscrapers and space (or lack of it), and New Zealand. Both countries are kept just right climactically by virtue of the fact they are islands surrounded by natural air conditioning sea. There won't be anything alive in that sea but it is still water. Where would you rather live? Or more realistically where would you rather your grandchildren grow up and live?

- The electrical supply is 230v and 50 hertz which means anything electrical you do bring will work here, except perhaps the TV. Fortunately the frequencies are slightly different. This is just what you need to hear to justify buying the latest 40 inch flat screen when you arrive. Any equipment you bring will need either a NZ adaptor or a new plug as the Kiwis have different shaped power outlet sockets. Anything that goes through a transformer is just fine because all you need to do is to leave the UK lead at home and buy a kiwi one. I am talking about the length from the plug socket to the device or its transformer.

In Summary

I think it is fair to say that most migrants that come here who are open-minded and adventurous stay here. New Zealand has so much to offer. I sometimes have to pinch myself about living in NZ. It feels great and I feel so cool living here. I have never been cool in my life.

I am a very cynical and sceptical person, so when I was researching our move and came across numerous endorsements of how good NZ was, how people who had migrated loved it here, and how they intend to stay indefinitely, I though yeah, yeah, yeah. I thought I was different. I thought no place could give me what I wanted at this time in my life. I am really sorry to say it and it breaks my heart to admit it but New Zealand is all it is cracked up to be, at least in my opinion. I realize I am no different from those people who have gone before me. I should have trusted their judgement and expertise. I wouldn't want to deprive you of the chance to test this place for yourself which is why I hope you will continue reading.

Yes of course there are people who won't like NZ and move on, or move back to the motherland. Fair enough, you have just one life, live it in a way that makes you happy. I think you would be hard pressed in today's world to find a country as welcoming, laid back and as beautiful as New Zealand.......................except maybe Canada or New Caledonia.

For Your Research

A land of two halves (book)
> Joe Bennett ISBN 074326357 X. Published by Scribner

www.stats.govt.nz/products-and-services/new-zealand-in-profile-2006/climate.htm
> Statistics I know can prove anything, but they are good to quote.

www.tv3.co.nz/VideoBrowseAll/SportsVideo/tabid/317/articleID/30781/Default.aspx#video
> The author appears on TV with the child catcher and her children. The NZ vs South Africa match 2007 in Christchurch. The crowd scenes 10 seconds from the end rival anything from Ben Hur.

www.activecanterbury.org.nz
> Getting Cantabrians to play sport, but you can find parks and groups and events here too.

www.sparc.org.nz
> Sport And Recreation New Zealand. Helping top sporty types right down to top couchy types exercise and embrace fitness.

www.coasttocoast.co.nz
> The popular madness of running, cycling and kayaking across the breadth of the South Island, before throwing up on the pavement.

Chapter 3

Some downsides of New Zealand?

I have to say I have struggled to scrape together enough for this section to offer a balance to the reasons why you should come. Please forgive me if some sound a little trite or superficial.

Ultraviolet light

There's a hole in the ozone that occasionally requires staying indoors if you don't want another ear on the top of your head. The met office gives you warning of such events but the depleted ozone in summer can be a big risk for skin cancer. **One in four New Zealanders develop this sort of cancer.** "Slip slap slop and wrap" is the message and it refers to sun screen. But then you are British and like me you will probably ignore the advice anyway and just slip, slap and wonder why you have a hand shaped silhouette of a burn on you chest. If you are Scottish, red haired and freckly I am completely wasting my time, as you are probably just delighted to be in the sun and you will burn anyway.

Sun damage

The sun is responsible for nurturing life on Earth. What the sun gives the sun will take away. It will age your skin visibly. It particularly likes to age Scots for the above reasons. It can be quite difficult to guess the age of New Zealanders, particularly women. You can be a bit shocked when you find that a woman who looks in her fifties is actually in her mid thirties. I like to check first by cutting them in half and counting the rings. People are much more sensible nowadays and most cosmetics have SPF 30 in them. Unfortunately the damage has been done in childhood, all those halcyon days of growing up in New Zealand. To save yourself embarrassment don't ask ages or if you have to refer to someone's perceived age, take ten years off what you think they are to avoid insulting them. This quite clearly doesn't work for children under ten.

Salaries

Don't come to New Zealand if you want to be a millionaire. You can be rich in numerous other ways here but chances are this won't be one of them, unless you win the twice weekly lottery here called Lotto or the twice daily one called Keno. I took a 40% pay cut on moving to New Zealand. Many Kiwis leave NZ to work in Britain and Australia where they can earn better money and pay less tax.

You have to be self reliant

The population here is small. Don't expect the same degree of support the UK can give, both in benefits and tangible services. If you drive your car off the road between towns or cities don't expect to be found for a couple of days or when someone raises the alarm back home in the UK, say when your birthday present to them doesn't arrive. People have driven off the roads here and been trapped in their cars for several days.

The summers are long and hot and flies can be a real nuisance

My favourite joke of all time goes as follows: two flies sitting on a lump of pooh, one farts, the other says "do you mind I'm eating". The number of flies they get here in summer does not sit well with me, especially when **I'm** eating. The first year we had to shut the doors because they were becoming a real nuisance. I counted those trapped inside after we shut everything and there were 55 of them all trying to defaecate on my things. Now I am a little anally retentive as you will come to understand and as a dog owner too, and surrounded by neighbours with dogs, it doesn't take much to appreciate where these flies might have been two minutes before they visited us.

The first year we had the house chemically treated which cost about $180 and it did the trick and really cut down the fly numbers. However it was an industrial treatment and we were exposed to it as well. Likely to be an anticholinesterase of some sort The Evey often found me on my back wrestling the air with my legs as I break-danced uncontrollably on the floor. She would revive me and then admonish me for licking the walls.

Last year when the chemical effects had worn off the house, I bought an insect-o-cutor in the form of a tennis racket which runs off two AA batteries and now my forehand is pretty close to perfect. Other methods for removing them include the obvious fly spray but if you catch them drowsy you can suck them up the Hoover.

Whatever method you employ it matters not. You have to come to terms with the fact that in the warm months (about nine of them) you will permanently have five flies resident, no more, no less it seems. Last thing at night you can clear them using the methods listed and by morning you have five flies in your house. It pains my fussy nature but I have had to come to terms with sharing my space with the five flies of the apocalypse Death, War, Famine, Pestilence and Darren.

The Mullet

Mullet hairstyles are far more popular here than they ever deserve to be, but it is a good unisex style and the king of haircuts, easily worn by anyone young or old and it does serve to keep the flies off the back of your head in summer.

There seems to be a lot of bureaucracy

You may notice as you read on that there are many governmental departments and ministries of this, that and the other. Apparently in the 1950s through to the 1980s the red tape for literally everything was suffocating. Things are better I believe but there is still quite a lot. At least it keeps unemployment low.

Haves and have nots

Like many economies the rich are leaving the poor behind. In the last 10 years the divide has increased. Housing is less affordable, obesity has almost doubled in both sexes and income in the poorest quartile has hardly changed whereas the income in the top quartile has increased 30%. Incidentally this all happened under a Labour government. These were the findings of a government report which then put a typical positive spin on it. Other negative markers that came out of the social well-being report included:

38

Suicide.	Up on the previous year.
Road Injuries.	Up on the previous year.
Increased severity in hardship of living standards.	I was shocked at the large number of food parcels issued by the Salvation Army and City Mission in Christchurch. Many kids in the poor areas of the North Island don't have shoes. This is almost as shocking as hearing some kids in Britain don't have TVs in their bedrooms.
Decreased participation in tertiary education.	This is a real shame as you can never have enough students.
Local content on television.	Down on the previous year. Everyone has a purpose in life and for some this is watching television. I only watch infomercials and then only the ones for Pilates and female gym equipment.

You are a long way from the rest of the world

Now this can work in good ways, but it can mean if something happens to family in the old country it is a good 36 hours before you can be with them. Take a look at Google Earth or an atlas and just see where NZ sits on the globe and how much water is around it. It has hit home to me twice just how far we are from Britain. The first was on the journey over, when you monitor the progress of the flight on the tiny screen on the back of the seat in front of you. You take a very long time to cross Australia despite the plane on the screen being huge.

The second was an exhibit in the Canterbury Museum here in Christchurch where you stand under a large revolving globe of the world and New Zealand is all that you see. There is an edge of Australia that comes into view but the rest is blue.

On the subject of Google Earth it is worth checking out New Zealand. The resolution and quality of some of the areas is excellent and you can have a look at where you may be thinking of living. We can see our house in reasonable detail. Fortunately for you, the resolution isn't sharp enough to see me sunbathing nude in the back garden. We spend a lot of our time at 43 degrees 31 minutes and 36.33 seconds South and 172 degrees 35 minutes and 26.96 seconds East. Check it out and I'll give you a wave.

On a more serious note, for a number of months in 2007 there was no paediatric oncologist at Wellington hospital. This meant that children with cancer and their families in this part of the country had to travel to Christchurch public hospital or Auckland's Starship hospital for treatment. It seems incredible in this day and age that a country can't run an essential service in its capital city. With stories like this it hits home how vulnerable the country can be when at times, specialists just aren't available and it demonstrates how much the country relies on skilled migrants.

Crime

New Zealand has all the crime categories that exist, possibly with the exception of terrorism though that may change in time I'm sorry to say.

Drunken brawls are commonplace in the early hours of the morning in city centres. Stabbings and serious assaults have also occurred. Only some weeks ago a poor bloke had his wallet pinched, his arm deliberately broken and was hit over the head with a spade (but I don't think he was called Doug?).

The city centres have been described as "war zones" on Saturday nights often because some girl didn't like what some other girl said to her boyfriend of two weeks. What is it with human beings and fighting? Have they never heard of John Lennon, have they never seen Independence Day? There is bigger stuff than fighting, unless someone knocks my fizzy orange then there'll be trouble.

The best advice is stay out of the city centres in the early hours. Police operated CCTV is in place but I guess it is a sign of the times that they have to keep it switched on overnight when they go to bed at 9pm.

In Christchurch, a 2007 survey of its citizens found that only 38% felt safe in the city centre after dark. Police statistics showed that in 2006 Pacific Islanders accounted for 6.6% of the population but 12% of the violent crime and 8.6% of the total offences. Youth Offending Projects are attempting to reverse this state, indicative of the poverty and social standing of impoverished and poorly educated Pacific youngsters.

There are probably more guns per capita in NZ than there are in the UK but most are held legally by farmers and hunters (although there are some illegal ones that pop up). Kiwis don't seem to have the same desire to kill each other with firearms out here when you can hunt wild pigs or deer instead. However there have been some horrible mass murders over the years involving unstable types with access to guns.

There are armed robberies usually involving knives, rarely guns, and there have been some tragic drive by shootings where innocents get killed. Mercifully these are few and far between and often in South Auckland where the gangs are; gangs like Black Power, Tribesmen and the Mongrel Mob. Violence is predominantly gang on gang, but not necessarily so.

There are gangs in Christchurch and we are well represented by the Mongrel Mob, one of the toughest street gangs in the world, and some smaller equally tough sounding gangs like the Epitaph Riders and the neo Nazi Harris gang. Go south to Invercargill and the honourable sounding Road Knights face off with the Mongrel Mob (Invercargill Chapter). None are as tough as Ross Kemp though.

I have only ever, to my knowledge so far, come across a NZ gang, once. I was on my way to the library to return some Asterix and Tintin books and the Jane Asher Big Book of Fairy Cakes that I had borrowed, when I saw this dude on an Easy Rider chopper bike. He wore black leathers, shades and bandana as he revved up and pulled out from the Chapel of Rest's entrance, next to the library. Given that they are very hot on cycle helmets and most people comply for risk of an on the spot fine, a bloke on a motorcycle without a skid lid filled me with anger. I was in two minds to shout out "Oi you there, dog breath where's your crash helmet?" when he was followed by three cars full of Mongrel mob and half a dozen other bikers. The penny dropped and suddenly the pavement with all its cracks was the most interesting thing I'd ever seen.

Kiwis in their twenties and thirties remember a time when any murder in their country was really big news. "Now they happen all the time" is what you hear them say. I believe it is all relative. Not every murder in the UK is reported on the Six O'clock News like it is here and it all boils down to human numbers. Only humans murder humans. I personally feel safe in NZ, and, having spent most of my life in England I do not feel that murder happens in New Zealand anywhere near what I remember it happening while living in the UK.

Having made the above comments, there have recently been some really sad and horrific killings of Maori children by family members. It is not confined just to this demographic, New Zealand apparently has one of the highest rates of child death due to physical abuse in the world.

I have taken a very cursory and unscientific look at the statistics for murder in the UK and NZ (2005) and summarized it below. It is probably open to all sorts of interpretation errors but I think it proves the point that rates are roughly the same per number of people but because there aren't the people here, overall it is less common in New Zealand.

	Number of murders per year	Murders per million of the population	Number per time frame.
New Zealand	60	14	5 per month
UK	765	13	2 per day

Crime in Christchurch

We get all the crimes here that anyone else gets, but August for some reason is the month for the highest number of house burglaries in Christchurch, while Dunedin records its high in September. Maybe in the deep winter months even criminals like to get out for a bit of vitamin D?

Christchurch Aug 2006	363
Christchurch Aug 2005	380
Christchurch Aug 2004	390

In Dec 2007 Christchurch officially became New Zealand's most violent city. An analysis of crime statistics as a proportion of population showed Christchurch has the country's highest rates for violent crimes, assaults and sexual attacks. Much of it is alcohol fueled but this is not to trivialize some nasty behaviour. Our new mayor wants a crackdown on the sale of alcohol. We'll wait and see if that helps, in the meantime mine's a double.

Policing is by consent and the police are visible in many ways. A city wide Neighbourhood Watch bulletin updates all residents on car thefts, burglaries and other things but there is always some space for lost property found. The one report I liked the most so far is:

> "A resident in Clouston Street, St Martins has located two double bed size under-sheets, which appear to have been blown into the street last weekend during the high winds. One sheet is yellow in colour, the other is white with a green floral design. Inquiries in the street have failed to locate an owner, so they may have traveled a considerable distance. If these sheets or yours or you have any information please phone..."

Now isn't that quaint as we all wait to see if the owner and their sheets get reunited. This is just one of many examples of why I love NZ society.

Petty crime

Mail boxes are located on the front gates of properties as in America and this makes delivering letters and papers so easy. It does however leave the thing exposed. Our poor neighbours have had their letter box removed twice now and the post has been given a good kicking on each occasion. The first time it was found up our tree where it probably hid in fear but the second time someone has "re-homed" it. They are a bit annoyed about it but they are Kiwis so it is tempered with stoicism. They reported it to the police not to be pedantic but if anyone ever owns up to it or is caught the perpetrator has to pay for the repairs. Our neighbours wait in hope as their post box is now an old plastic paint container with a slot cut in the side.

I have delivered free papers here, helping my daughter with the paper round and with the footslogging I have noticed more than the odd kerb-planted sapling tree snapped in half.

Footnote: Our neighbour has replaced his empty paint container with a beautiful and anatomically correct scale model of Sponge Bob Square Pants. It is truly a work of art to behold. I'll give it until Friday before the bucket goes back.

Footnote to the footnote: I was wrong it survived Thursday night but was kicked to death on the Saturday night. Poor Sponge Bob.

More than once the concrete litter bins have been kicked out of the ground in the local shopping area late at night and the local paper ran a piece complete with photo of a shopping trolley upside down on a give way sign. Such japery (© 1923) seems to happen on a Thursday night because that is the now the new Friday so that it doesn't interfere with weekend drinking.

I have also noticed that since we have lived here there is more graffiti. Though to be fair property owners on the receiving end do paint over the tags quickly, which discourages further attacks. Utility companies and the council are also quite prompt but who ever tidies up, the result is, there is always a poorly matched colour. It's suggestive that they didn't have any of the original colour left but they had one quite close. So these blocks of light green appear over dark green or magnolia over white spring up where the tags were. Graffiti costs ratepayers in Christchurch $1 million a year to clean up. I'd employ someone who wasn't colour blind if I were king and then the colours may match up better.

The size of the country

Just as the small population can seem cosy and civilized, it can feel a little scary too. Imagine just over four million people on the British Isles and the space that kind of population density offers. Now imagine the downsides that may come with that. For instance modern medical therapies and treatments may be a little too expensive to offer routinely because the tax base is too small to fund them.

This doesn't scare me as much as the story of a lumberjack who worked the giant Kauri trees many years back. These trees are truly old and huge with a circumference of up to 20 metres and can reach heights of up to 50 metres. This lumberjack was working alone deep in the bush and having climbed the trunk to where the branches started, which can be anything over 20 metres, he dropped his rope. I suspect he said a bit more than "d'oh".

44

With no one around he was very much on his own. The tree was felled five years after he went missing and they found his skeleton in the branches.

This may just be another urban myth however I can well believe something like this occurring. Now when this incident happened the population was far fewer than 4 million but it serves to illustrate that NZ still has many isolated places and many people each year go missing in the country, often poorly prepared or inexperienced visitors. Some turn up safe and sound, some turn up dead and some are never found. I prefer to stay indoors watching daytime infomercials as it is safer than climbing kauri trees. Actually I can well believe the story of the skeleton in the tree since recently a body and crumpled car were found deep in thick bush, off one of the windy roads outside Rotorua. Two pig hunters stumbled across the wreckage while tracking their quarry. The man had been missing twenty years! Finally closure for the poor man's family.

Staple foods for Brits aren't here

You can't get Marmite, Bisto, Pickled Onion Monster Munch or Quality Street in New Zealand except from specialist import shops. There are two in Christchurch. Watch for short dated stock. This is not to infer the shops sell short dated stock but that it takes a long time to ship it here. So you can't let it stand in the larder. Best eat it before you leave the shop. This doesn't work too well for Bisto gravy granules or Paxo. These shops, while offering a lifeline to the mother country, are expensive so only go there on pay day. A small bag of three Quality Street costs a dollar. That's ten pence each sweet and it's not like you can put the hard ones back in the jar with just teeth marks in them for someone else to find.

La la la la la America

New Zealand can feel a little Americanized at times. Roadside advertising is big and bold and American-like. American words and phrases have snuck into the vocabulary like dollar, real estate, malls, blocks, state highways and MacDonald's to name but a few. Yankee pronunciations have entered the Queen's English and Kiwis say "data", "yoghurt" and "route" in the American way. Call me an ass and I don't want to labor the point but such Americanisms just suck. Period.

Bird Influenza A H5N1

When you look at the migratory patterns for birds on this side of the world they seem to head south from Vietnam, Thailand and other South East Asian parts. These are the very areas where the human acquired "bird flu" is expected to originate that will see your house equity drop to post-Black Death levels if the credit crunch hasn't already achieved this.

On the positive side, New Zealand is expected to close all borders to the world very quickly and easily and it bought a lot of "Tamiflu" for last winter's panic which didn't seem to happen. Chances are it will be out of date when it is needed though.

During the 1918 pandemic it was believed the returning prime minister was responsible for bringing the virus into the country so I suspect that if the current incumbent, John Key is out visiting when it kicks off this time all the locks will be changed and he won't get back in until it's over.

Food out of season

We seem to find that certain foods are unavailable outside their growing season. Organic carrots and leeks disappear from the shops in summer. This may sound a good thing as it suggests there aren't so many food miles attached to these ingredients but I don't think this is the reason. Whatever it is it can be highly irritating though when you can't get a chocolate Easter egg in November or a mince pie in June like you can in Britain.

We have never been able to find tarragon here. Once in a while you can get the fresh packaged stuff that sits in the fridge until it wilts beyond desirability but you can't buy the herb in a pot as a "growing" concern. I have found *seeds* but I'm at a loss to get them to germinate. Do not come to New Zealand if your staple diet is tarragon.

The Nanny State

While New Zealand appears laid back and chilled, it can also appear the mother of all nanny states outside of North Korea, with rules and regulations and public information broadcasting all over the place. Most Kiwis don't seem to take too much notice of this and do their own thing anyway, but I think foreigners notice it.

Most of the nannying is pretty low level but some comes with high rewards. The local Health Boards who run the healthcare provision in NZ often put adverts in the local papers. "Reduce your risk of stroke by: exercising, eating, stopping this and that, doing this, that and the other". All good stuff I'm sure but I find it all a bit contrary when you see a tiny sign saying stay away from the edge at a cliff side, with no barriers to stop those who can't read.

It is a funny mixture of the attitudes of " if you fall to your death you only have yourself to blame, the very small sign was there to inform you of the dangers" and "thou shalt not smoke and we will do everything we can to stop you". Everyone has to die but I guess from a cynical point of view the latter way costs a small country more than if you plop off a cliff. I suppose the Brits are from a nanny state as well, but then I always liked to be nannied. She'd wrap me in a blanket, stroke my brow and sing to me. However The Evey said that that wasn't right, what with me being a grown man and everything.

Space For Your Research

Chapter 4

Getting to and arriving in New Zealand

The Journey to NZ

Assuming now that you still want to give New Zealand a go, even if it is just for a holiday, I am really pleased for you. As you already realize New Zealand is a long way from the United Kingdom which is a good thing. It remains a virtually unspoilt land (if you ignore the slash and burn of the 19th century) that people want to visit. Had New Zealand lay off the British coast, say where the Isle of White is I guarantee it wouldn't be as untouched, though we may have a better rugby team. And yes, I know, New Zealand wouldn't fit in that space either without bumping into France.

Tucked away under the Earth surrounded by sea it takes some effort to get here, but you are going to be glad you put the effort in, once the jet lag has worn off.

We have travelled here on Singapore Airlines, Emirates and Air New Zealand (the latter via Hong Kong). All were very good. Not so good, I understand is the route through Los Angeles. If you use an 'exotic' airline or an asian route to NZ, be prepared for funny sorts of food or food combinations and feeding times. Singapore Airlines like fishy things with black bean noodles at the equivalent of 2 am body clock time. Emirates like Arabic style foods though nothing along the lines of lambs' brains thank goodness. It is all part of the experience I know.

The second time to NZ we booked our flight through "Dial a flight", a UK telephone based agent who were very good and I would thoroughly recommend giving them a ring to organize a quote.

Consider stopovers unless you really want to do it all in one hit. We flew Singapore the first time, straight through with just a four hour wait at Singapore while we changed planes. Expect to feel a little jaded doing this and stay near a bin in case you need to throw up. For the migration journey we used Emirate Airlines. Emirate stops at their hub, Dubai, to encourage you to spend money there, but there are worse places in the world than the UAE. I loved it. Sea, sand and heat, gorgeous, it could have been Margate but it wasn't. It was however the world's biggest building site. A couple of nights in the warmth of the middle east then a night in Sydney made landing in Christchurch a much more relaxed experience as the body clock, at the very least, is starting to come round to Antipodean time. Many people just like to bite the bullet and do the journey all in one hit. Having done both I aim to do the journey with stopovers if I have to do it again.

Some airlines that fly to New Zealand are listed below

Singapore Airlines via Singapore   www.singaporeair.com
Emirates via Dubai UAE   www.emirates.com/uk/
Air New Zealand via L.A. or Hong Kong www.airnewzealand.co.uk
Quantas via Sydney or Melbourne   www.qantas.com

Almost every large town, city or indeed small town in New Zealand has an airport or airstrip as flying is by far the quickest way to travel here, but there are only three international airports Auckland, Wellington and Christchurch. Be warned Wellington can be at the mercy of fog as can the other two come to think of it, but Wellington is often the worst hit.

It is worth noting that if you stop off in Australia, British citizens are required to have a full passport valid for 6 months after your intended departure from Australia. You also need a visa. This can be done electronically when you book your flight with the travel agent.

If you intend to stop off at Dubai, and why not, the Persian Gulf is very blue, you need cholera, hepatitis A and B, polio and typhoid immunization if you don't want to risk contracting cholera, hepatitis, polio and typhoid all in the same day. If you are travelling through Los Angeles you will need body armour and a lot of patience, as I have heard it is a bit rough and there is little to do between lengthy waits for connecting flights.

Duty-free and Customs in New Zealand

If you take advantage of the duty free allowances to come into the country please be aware they are a little like the UK had some years ago but also that it can change without notice. Essentially you can have:

Up to 2 x 1125ml spirits
200 cigarettes or 250g of "backie"
4.5 litres of wine, champagne, port, sherry or beer

I like going through Customs in New Zealand. This is not because I like intimate body searches, I have never had one. It is because they are very pleasant and when they look at your passport they say "Hello Nerdy welcome home" and smile. Last time we went through Heathrow customs we felt like we were illegal immigrants. We were met with total apathy and almost a sneer and a scorn. Someone needs to send these people on a customer training programme or something. When we shuffled through the "nothing to declare" lane there was only one officer, chewing gum and texting on her phone. Crazy, at least New Zealand immigration will look interested in your imminent cavity search and you are probably safe in the knowledge that they will do you the courtesy of warming their hands first.

Christchurch International Airport

A nice little international airport, if that isn't an oxymoron? Over one and a half million international passengers were handled in 2007. I don't know how many objected.

Leaving New Zealand from Christchurch, the trip to the airport is all very civilized. You are able to reach the terminal in 15 minutes from the city, on roads that have little in the way of congestion. Back home it was always a stress to get to Gatwick or Heathrow via the dreaded M25 and you would leave between four to six hours before your flight to allow for traffic, accidents and check-ins. You still have to leave a two hour window for international check-ins but transit times are not a factor to consider.

The domestic and international terminals have recently (July 2007) introduced a high-speed wireless internet service for laptops and PDAs so it is up there with the rest of the big players now. The airport is receiving a $190m face lift due to be finished in 2010 so use of the facility is expected to grow and Branson's Pacific Blue started flying out of here when the airline launched.

If you are getting a taxi from the airport into town be aware there have been some problems with an insufficient number of cabs in the taxi rank at the time people want them. The airport has raised its charge to taxis entering the taxi rank, they say to improve the customer service. New rules state that the taxis must be less than 10 years old and the drivers must be pleasant, helpful and be able to communicate effectively in English because Christchurch airport often provides the incoming tourist with their first impression of New Zealand. All fair enough, but I think waiting in the cold in a line with 30 other people for a taxi is more likely to form a first impression and cheese more than a few people off.

Apparently the phones in the terminal are all card phones and there may not be a free phone for taxis. I will check this out next time I go to the airport, and then I'll wave to all those poor people in the taxi queue as I drive past them in my empty car which is an old London cab and ten and a half years old.

Jet lag

I find jet lag is a good excuse to top up on carbohydrates. I do recommend downloading the BA podcasts by Dr Sleep via i-Tunes or the British Airways website if you have an MP3 player. His soporific voice alone is enough to send you off to the land of nod. But he offers lots of practical advice about the cursed jet lag and people get it to differing degrees. Be aware that you may witness a number of sunrises in the first few days but then they can be beautiful depending on where you are staying. Three days of waking at 4 am was a little unwelcome. You will also miss some equally beautiful sunsets as sleep will want to smuggle you away in the early evening.

Incidentally, new research seems to suggest a 12-16 hour fast, broken with the correct timing of the next meal in the country of your destination, may override the internal body clock normally controlled by light. Moslems will be much better at this than most of us because of their religious observance of Ramadan and the long period without food needed to make this approach work.

Space For Your Research

www.britishairways.com

>Dr Sleep podcasts from British Airways (free to download).Just enter Dr sleep into the search box. Also available from i-Tunes

www.carbonneutral.com

>How to offset the huge carbon emission your flight here has generated, so you had better not be going back too soon. Warning: all of the solutions cost money.

www.ccc.govt.nz/migrants

>For information on how to open a bank account, choose a school, improve your Inglish without hurty of the head and more.

www.chooseclimate.org

>A useful calculator to illustrate just how much of a contribution you are making in destroying our planet

www.christchurch-airport.co.nz/airport/

>Check out Arrivals and Departures and other services

www.customs.govt.nz

>We can't guarantee John Key will be at the airport to greet you but one of his representatives will if you exceed the allowances.

www.dialaflight.com

>Dial a flight. Good quotes and helpful staff.

www.immigration.govt.nz

>A welcome pack is available from the NZ Immigration Service along with up to date information on migrating and visas.

www.move2nz.com

>A free settlement support service and network, sharing experiences and knowledge to help you settle quickly and successfully. Their tagline is "helping migrants become Kiwis."

www.visitortv.co.nz

>Television for visitors to Christchurch and NZ, useful to all newcomers, giving a flavour of what's out there.

After Customs: Biosecurity and the Department of Conservation

New Zealand has some of the toughest biosecurity standards in the world and rightly so considering its largest English speaking neighbour has given it some right old nasties. At times things have got a bit bitter between the two cousins and at one point Australia banned NZ apples. I suspect because you can't bowl underarm very well with an apple.

Your suitcases will be x-rayed by biosecurity after you have collected them from the luggage carousel. Together with the card you fill in on the plane you present this to the nice person sitting at the biosecurity desk where you may be asked questions about the declaration you have made. Please be honest it is a lovely country and deserves to stay that way. Lie if you want. You will be found out and you deserve the body cavity search, 'tazering', roughing up, probes and beating the Department of Conservation officers *will* give you. DoC officers are tough street wise enforcers of the law and are rightly more feared than the East German Stasi, though the Stasi weren't funded as well or have such nice pullovers as part of their uniform.

On the subject of apples and other foods, dump anything you are not sure about in the amnesty bin before you get to biosecurity. If in doubt dump it. We know of a Kiwi coming back from Oz who missed a single uneaten apple in his luggage and he got clobbered with a $200 fine when it showed up under x-ray.

> **"It is an offence to knowingly spread an unwanted organism with penalties of up to 5 years imprisonment, and/or a fine of up to $100,000."**

As I have already mentioned when we came here to live we stopped off in Dubai, we swam in the warm Persian Gulf and we collected beautiful shells, fantastic. I then had real trouble convincing our youngest, to dump her pretty shells before customs. She wasn't having it. I had to virtually peel her hands open, frisk her and her hand luggage and check her mouth, so adamant was she to bring them in. I can understand it they were very pretty. However I was not going to go down in history as the quickest deport out of New Zealand.

Back home I had seen a fly on the wall documentary programme about an Aussie bloke who collected together a bunch of strippers to tour around New Zealand. Channel 4 or 5 I think, late night, after wives have gone to bed, you know the sort of thing these channels programme for sad old gits. I was channel hopping because my programme on the rights of women was taking a commercial break. I don't remember much about the series, truly I don't, except when they landed in New Zealand one of the girls gets deported immediately and banned from NZ forever because the customs dog detected the smallest trace of cocaine in her luggage. There was no drug there but the bag had once had cocaine in it in the past. I think she may even have borrowed the bag off someone if I remember rightly. Tough stuff but fair I think. Shame though, she was fit and I'd like to have seen her get her kit off.

As a result I bought new luggage to bring out here just in case my grandmother, who borrowed it last, was a crack-headed coke smuggling mule. Maybe the reason she always used lily of the valley talc was to discombobulate the cocker spaniel on drug duty?

When we first came to NZ it was in the aftermath of our first devastating foot and mouth epidemic. Now you can understand the Kiwis being a bit twitchy about this disease as sheep outnumber people six to one or more. We were stopped at bio-security and questioned because we were English. We weren't forced through sterilizing sheep dip but the interrogation felt a bit like that. We did have walking boots in our luggage but in our defence they were brand new and had never been out the box so we didn't have to unpack everything. However they never checked my fingernails or my freakish cloven hooves for caked mud, so it wasn't that thorough.

If you ship any belongings over and you have things like tents, garden tools, walking boots and other similar equipment I would advise you to expand your description of the contents of your boxes or container on the customs forms to say you have sterilized these items with bleach. Obviously clean and bleach them but also state you have done so too as it may save customs opening up your stuff to check and delaying your goods arriving.

Removal companies don't ship your belongings in tea chests anymore as I have mentioned. This is because the wood used in packing crates can contain tropical wood boring insects and diseases which could then hitch a lift around the world. The boxes are the same size but are now made of cardboard, flat packed and self assembled and cost you five quid each plus VAT. Outrageous.

The war against pests

The reason I have included this section is because DoC are responsible for controlling these and spend any time here and you will hear about these problems, so bear with me. (Note: bears are not one of these problems).

Viticulture, agricultural diseases and other pests

While still a young industry, wine making is big bucks. Phylloxera is the infestation to be feared if you grow grapes commercially and is almost impossible to eradicate. Rather like an aphid, these sap suckers feed on the roots of the vine. You will see Phylloxera control areas if you visit a winery because many vines in New Zealand are grown on the susceptible rootstock and humans spread it very efficiently.

You may also see rose bushes planted at the ends of the neat rows of grapevines throughout New Zealand. They are planted not to look nice (I find the rose a particularly ugly plant in every respect), but to give the viticulturists early warning of an attack. I can't find any reference to support this so it may be an old wives' tale and not be common practice. It may be that the rose gets a fungal disease first spread by the aphid, but equally I may have dreamt the whole thing. I remember now, there was my old math teacher and Joseph Stalin's personal trainer in evilness who were actually the same person. Dreams can be so real.

Varroa bee mite

This parasitic mite hitches a ride on the back of the honey bee skateboarding or surfing the air and sucking the blood out of its host, spreading viruses and of no bloody use to society. Close up these parasites remind me of a "hoody", shapeless body, a pulled up cowl, miserable expression. As you can imagine an infestation of these if you are a honey farmer is big trouble as they hang around the hives in large numbers being a nuisance and spitting diseases. So please, leave any teenage hoodies at home.

Please also do not bring out any of the following as they have enough here already. Feral goats, crazy ants, yellow crazy ants, indeed anything crazy, rooks and eastern banjo frogs with or without their banjos.

Even more pesky pests

Australians are a generous bunch and like to share their biohazards and vermin with anyone. To date they have given New Zealand the following delights:

Possums

There are 20 possums to every human in New Zealand. Introduced to NZ in 1837 from Australia where everything is poisonous or spiky they are actually a protected species over there. Over here they eat trees to death because they have no natural defences against these marsupials.

They destroy all the native trees and deprive the native fauna of food, eat bird eggs, carry bovine TB and have even been known to push Kiwis out of their beds for somewhere dry to sleep. A bit of a shock in the morning when you bring in the tea and find your child on the floor.

They are not cute even though they look it. In fact most of the road kill is possum. Clever marketing has turned culled possum fur into socks, jumpers, gloves and nipple warmers, though there probably aren't enough nipples in the world to go round, because you only need a few square centimetres of fur. Possum fur duvets or carpets would be better as 70 million little possums now call New Zealand home.

The fur is one of the warmest so hunters and trappers can get good prices for possum skins in today's market. Having no natural predators they have multiplied out of control. Attempts have been made to poison them so you have to watch your dog so that they don't eat the bait. DoC (Department of Conservation) use Sodium monofluoroacetate, or **1080,** to give it its more sinister name, as the main control method. 1080 is not particularly fussy about what it kills taking other vermin too, like stoats and rats. It is a compound found in tea, funnily enough, but dogs are very susceptible to its toxic effects as they like to eat possum carcasses, after they've rolled in them first of course. **Signs indicate where poison has been laid and when it will be safe again for that area.** You can check what areas have been treated in your region at the site listed later. There is a minority backlash against the use of 1080 but the truth is, it does give indigenous species a chance against over-aggressive, introduced predators.

Didymo

This nasty first presented in 2001 or maybe 2004 possibly on the soles of contaminated footwear by some visiting Australians from south east Melbourne. It's found mainly in the South Island and is an algae that forms thick blooms and blankets of cells, choking out native river dwellers. Colloquially known as Rock Snot it is a fair description of the plant. One drop of contaminated water can spread it to an uncontaminated river. Thorough cleaning and responsible recreational fishing and boating are the only controls. **A $100,000 fine or five years in the slammer helps encourage you to clean those hard to reach places around propellers.** Actually I can find nothing to suggest it was the Australians giving this to their cousins, it was probably Brits as it is found in Northern Europe and the UK. So sorry about that Australia (not really I had my fingers crossed).

White tail spiders

I have only ever seen one of these and the name is pretty accurate, they are definitely spiders. It was in the hammock which got left out overnight. One of the smaller people who I share my house with, Charlotte I think she is called, and a committed arachnophobe beckoned me over as she had tried to settle in the hammock when she felt a tickly sensation. I was all for tickling it back with the heel of my shoe as my grandmother always did with spiders. But Charlotte, a committed animal lover as much as she is a committed arachnophobe, though probably more the former, convinced me to place it in the front garden where it lives to this day. However no one goes to the compost heap without tucking their trousers into their socks first.

I have heard bad things about white tails. They are Australian in origin sneaking over here to settle. If you don't have spiders in your house it is possibly a sign you have a white tail nest because they consider every other species of spider bush tucker. I don't like spiders but I do lay awake at night hoping none call our house home as I have only seen three other small spiders in our house in three years.

There are adverts in the paper for getting white tail infestations treated. I think these companies come in and paint them all one colour. The most horrible tale I have heard about these pests is they like warm areas, being from Australia, and they like to hide in freshly tumbled clothes. There, apparently, has been more than one incident of a mother dressing her young baby in its baby grow with one of these creatures inside. The spider bites, baby cries, mum doesn't know why, carries on, baby wriggles, spider bites again and again and baby dies. Horrible. Whether this is another urban myth I really don't know. It may be baby is just badly bitten and whitetails aren't really as poisonous as some other Australian spiders. If there are any gentlemen reading this, always check your underwear before you put it on or go commando.

Wasps, parrots and wallabies can all be blamed on the Australians but to be absolutely fair the Europeans gave New Zealand heather, rabbits and worst of all stoats, These were introduced to control rabbit numbers but they actually set about beating up and eating Kiwi. It sounds like Wind in the Willows all over again. Do not bring out any of these specimens leave them in Britain they aren't welcome here and to reiterate clean all outdoor equipment before packing it up to bring here.

Our friend Fiona always sends us nice homey presents at Christmas and our first year here was no exception. Christmas came and went but we hadn't received anything from her which seemed unusual. We eventually got a letter in the post saying New Zealand biosecurity had intercepted it because it had "au naturelle" wood in it. It was a front door wreath. When we went to bio-security central at the airport to investigate they would only release it after a fine of $80 and a steam clean. Costing more than the article we declined but they did let us take the wrapping paper and packaging home with us. A word of warning then: they are strict and watch what you send people and how you declare it on the customs sticker. Promise you won't tell Fiona because she doesn't know what happened and it is the thought that counts.

Space For Your Research

www.doc.govt.nz

Department of Conservation. These people are big and powerful in the legal sense. I like their livery. Everything to do with DoC is green and yellow. They have nice pullovers too.

www.biosecurity.govt.nz

A division of the Ministry of Agriculture. This is a good source for what can and can't be imported into New Zealand along with information on bringing pets into the country. Be a pest and disease detective by reporting anything suspicious. You only have to take a look at their list to see that many irritations from around the world want to make NZ home. Michael Barrymore for one.

www.issg.org/database/welcome/

Global Invasive species database. It has a nice snake on the home page. There are no snakes in NZ since St Jonah of Lomu drove them all out in 1995.

Visas and residency

I won't be detailing this complicated and confusing part of migration as there are better books on the subject and the websites available cover most aspects and it is always changing. We arrived in New Zealand on "**skilled migrant visas**", having decided on using a specialist migration company.

We know many people though who have done it themselves with no problems. We used a very good company called The Immigration Group, based in Cheshire. They cost us about £1500 which was expensive I know but it took a lot of the worry out of the process. In fact we couldn't have done it without the efficiency of one of their case workers. Diane Vale was most helpful and efficient even after we had arrived in New Zealand and needed bits and bobs from her.

We finally received our visas on the 16 September just seventeen days before we left England, had we processed our application ourselves I'm not sure we would have done it in time.

Returning Residency Visas

Depending on what sort of visa you came to New Zealand on you may have to **apply for a Returning Residency Visa which is valid for two years and can be converted after this time to Permanent Residency.** It allows you back in the country if you leave. Handy if you have a house and pets and you left NZ to go to Australia for a week. The process and requirements are subject to change so you need to check out the latest from the Government's immigration website. Make this one of your first jobs as it takes time and we had to submit medicals and x rays. Because we applied for this quickly we were able to use the medicals and x-rays we had done in England. We don't call The Evey "Mrs Thrifty Bun Arms" for nothing.

Permanent Residency Visas

When you have been here two years and worked so many months of those, you can apply for permanent residency. You used to be able to apply for citizenship after two years but they have ended that for security reasons and citizenship takes 5 years. The thinking being, that those undesirables refused entry to Australia could apply to NZ, live here 2 years, obtain citizenship and be entitled to enter and live in Australia through the back door. Very clever, but not everyone wants to be Australian.

Permanent Residency allows just that, it allows you to live in NZ forever....hooray. You can still support England and cheer when the All Blacks lose but this is your home and I wouldn't really advise the latter if you want Kiwi friends.

Space For Your Research

www.jobfastrack.co.nz/tegindex.php

The Immigration Group website. We used this company for our application paperwork and they were excellent.

www.immigration.govt.nz

NZ immigration department (again). If you decide to do the visa process yourself, this is your main resource.

www.britishexpats.com

Pretty self-explanatory but with a good discussion forum and lots of practical advice.

www.emigratenz.org

A useful website to check out many aspects of life in New Zealand including house rentals prices in the regions. It offers a balanced viewpoint on many aspects and is a good starting point for serious research.

Once in New Zealand

Well done. You've made it to a great country, whether it is as a migrant, a holiday maker, to reconnoiter things or escape the mafia. You deserve a cup of tea. I hope you brought some PG tips? You didn't? Never mind they sell Twinnings here.

If you are here to work at some point there are a number of things you might like to do first.

- Without wishing to sound like Ned Flanders, visit the IRD to register and receive a number and tax code that allows you to get paid by your employer.

- Swap your phone SIM cards for New Zealand SIMs so that you don't have to phone the UK to speak to someone in New Zealand two streets away. These don't cost more than $30, but hang onto your UK SIMs and the UK number of your phone if ever you need to go back to the UK. However, we have found that the UK SIMs stop working after a year of no use at all, so it may be worth making the odd call to keep them "active".

- Think about sorting out any visa applications that may need to be made as illustrated in the earlier section. The sooner you can do this the better and cheaper it will be for you.

- Think about converting your driver's licence to a full New Zealand one. More on that in the section on driving.

- Hire a car as you will need it for a lot of the running around that needs to be done in the first few days. We hired one for ten days until we had a chance to research and buy a car of our own.

Physically leaving New Zealand

Now I know this passage looks out of place in a section on "once in New Zealand" that is barely a page long, but I need to warn you that when you leave New Zealand, (for instance to check if you did unplug the iron), you will be charged $25 departure tax per person over 12 years of age. And you thought you'd use up the last of your Kiwi dollars on a nice tattoo? (Actually you need to be 18 to have a tattoo or any sort of piercing done here). Depending on when you are reading this there are plans to move this tax to the airline, so you'll pay it anyway as your ticket price will go up. In the meantime you have to pay it separately and have your boarding pass stamped to prove it has been paid before customs release you to travel.

This is applicable even if you have residency and leave to go on a foreign holiday. **You are allowed to be in NZ for 3 months without a visa but your passport must be valid for at least three months after your intended departure date**.

If you have incurred any fines or defaulted on student loan repayments, indeed anything like that, while resident in the country and they haven't been settled, you will not be allowed to leave New Zealand. This includes holidays to Australia as well. Remember the population here is small and it is far easier for the authorities to track people's movements and how naughty they've been.

Thinking about going back to Britain?

This is a perfectly natural feeling, it seems everyone has these thoughts at some time, often after the honeymoon period or after some sort of crisis or even saying goodbye to visitors from home. We have had these thoughts several times.

The worse times were when we had to have our cat and dog put to sleep. I was ready to jump on the next plane out of here. The Evey talked me down. She put her negotiator training into action telling me to stay calm, put down the passport, **slowly**, and move away from the suitcase. It was the sense of isolation and the knowledge that if ever we went back we would be two members of our team down. My Foreign Legion training, which I did with Jean Claude Van Damme, is very clear, you never leave a comrade, your weapon or a pet behind.

Here are some techniques that I use to remind myself that Britain isn't as rosy as I remember it.

- Read the BBC news website daily and check out the murders, sexual violations, child abuse, criminal activity, antisocial behaviour and unpleasantness. Of the 25 English news stories listed on the website today 12 of them are murder, rape, shooting or organized crime related. The other 13 are just as cheerless but they aren't criminal in nature. I know that bad news is the stuff of news agencies, and the same things happen in New Zealand as they do anywhere, but the small population base makes such horrors less frequent.

- Check out the weather, both in Britain and New Zealand for the same time of year. The BBC site is good for summarizing average weather conditions for all the main centres of habitation including Christchurch . Compare these summaries with London or Edinburgh. Please note the average number of hours of sunlight midwinter each location receives. I firmly believe that humans are outdoor creatures and evolved to need sunlight, so is it any wonder we feel glum in winter shut away in offices and missing any available sun February might give us.

- Remind myself there are fewer losers in NZ. I read that a British motorist who lost his human rights case in The European Court was reported saying "The fight for freedom goes on. We can't allow the tyrants, who are taking away our rights, to succeed. They have to be stopped." Considering he was caught doing 47 mph in a thirty zone he has a distorted view of his rights and even less understanding of his responsibilities. I say throw the book at him and lynch him on the nearest speed camera, preferably the one that caught him speeding and leave him there to rot as a message to all motorists. I know I am repeating myself here as I mention this punishment later on but at least I am consistent. I know what you may be thinking with me over here there's one less loser in Britain and one more loser in New Zealand. I agree I can be a loser about some things, but that story deserves an entry to remind me there are bigger losers than me in this world, but at least that one I am referring to is twelve thousand miles away and will probably have to catch the bus from now on.

Space For Your Research

http://news.bbc.co.uk/1/hi/uk/
    The BBC's news home page read by Moira Stewart.

www.metservice.co.nz
    Check whether the weather be good.

www.bbc.co.uk/weather/
    Is it sunny in Britain? I bet it's raining in Manchester though.

www.bbc.co.uk/weather/world/
    Check the weather in New Zealand's cities.

Chapter 5

Driving in New Zealand

I am going to spend some time and a more patronizing tone for this section purely because it can take a bit of getting used to and I will illustrate the pitfalls with some of my mistakes which aren't often and almost unheard of behind the wheel of a car. But then every day is the dawn of a new error.

Driving here can be an absolute joy. Imagine the stereotypical commercial. You are behind the wheel of the latest model of car, the open road ahead, lots of bends to test the latest safety technology and nothing else. Even the road kill has been airbrushed out of the final advert. Outside of the cities and large towns this is what driving can be like, though chances are it won't be free of squashed animals, and you won't be watching anything but the scenery, which is probably why there is so much road kill.

I am not a car enthusiast but I do notice the large number of older "classic" cars running about on the roads. A few decades ago people here would not have been able to afford cars and those that did would have probably bought British models and looked after them. Today these can be seen still running with some in immaculate condition. Every time I see one I get a blast from the past, usually the 1970s. I have witnessed in Christchurch alone various Wolseley models, several Triumph Dolomites like my grandmother drove, Hillmans, Morris Minors and more Austin 1100s than Basil Fawlty can shake a tree branch at. And so on.

In town, roads are wide and many work on the American grid system which makes finding alternative routes easier and lightens congestion. When we first visited Christchurch and tried to get our bearings we always seemed to end up on Montreal Street. We'd cross it in the south of the city, drive for 15 minutes and end up on it in the north. It was like that scene in The Matrix Revolutions where Neo runs through the pristine underground station only to end up back where he started. It caused arguments and accusations of pompous male arrogance and being too proud to stop and ask someone, and that was just the children shouting at me.

There are over 2.5m cars and vans in NZ in a country the size of the UK and with just over 4 million people. While most families will have more than one car the roads are not congested in the way we would understand. As mentioned the roads are wide in town and you can usually perform a U turn without it being a three point turn. It is rare to have to pull in behind a parked car to give way to oncoming traffic.

That other bane of British urban driving, parking, is not usually a problem, though I cite the incident where two days into migrating here I dropped The Evey off at a shop and pulled into a space across the road so I was facing the on-coming traffic. I got out of the car and a Kiwi walking his dog greeted me with a good morning and "You must be English". Astounded by his clairvoyance I asked him how he could possibly know that. For a fact I knew I wasn't wearing the English national dress, a number ten Rooney shirt and Manchester United tattoo. He advised me that it is an offence to park against the flow of traffic and I risked an $80 fine if caught. There is nothing like the state stealing your money to concentrate the mind and thanking him I pulled over to the other side where a little further along there was ample parking.

So don't get caught out by thinking you can pull the same tricks in New Zealand that you can get away with in the UK. Here are some very important things you need to know about driving in New Zealand.

- If you are indicating to turn left and an oncoming vehicle is wanting to turn right where you are turning, they, I repeat, **they have right of way**. This is known as the courtesy rule. By all accounts it took a bit of getting use to when it was introduced in the 1960s, probably with a lot of discourteous language. It is a quaint sort of road chivalry, completely alien to the British. Your fellow road users will be expecting you to conform, and good luck putting it into practice as it takes some getting used to. Get it wrong and it's a bloodbath waiting to happen.

- If you are turning right into a junction that has no road markings and someone is wishing to turn from that road onto the road you are on, it is they, I repeat, they that have right of way. **This is known as the right hand rule.** Essentially give way to the right.

To my embarrassment I have engaged in several tirades of discourteous language and reverse victory signs, only to be told by my daughter who was learning to drive that I was in the wrong. This is hard to accept for us males who have carried the driving gene ever since the wheel was invented. So for those people who I shook my fist and swore at, I am truly sorry. Especially the incident with the white haired old lady driving the church bus full of orphans and nuns.

- When turning at a laned intersection stay in the respective lane you just left and don't drift across without indicating for a few seconds and then moving into the far lane. Lots of people get caught by the Police doing this and are fined. The Police run purges once in a while for this sort of flagrant, irresponsible and outrageous defiance of the Road Code.

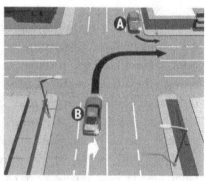

You can learn to drive at 15 years of age. NZ has one of the lowest driving ages in the world. I suspect this is because there are large areas which are very rural, with little in the way of public transport and young people would be much less mobile. While everyone acknowledges the sentiment behind giving the youth, adult responsibilities it does cause problems. A twenty minute test can secure you a restricted licence and within the hour you can be down the New Zealand equivalent of Halfords and be fitting the largest sports exhaust you can afford to the back of your Japanese import. Though, they may be better buying a cushion to see over the steering wheel. There have been some terrible accidents where young people have been killed and age has been a factor. Calls for raising the age to 16 are made all the time.

Hooners, or boy racers to us British can be a complete pain in the afore mentioned exhaust. I have a hypothesis I am working on that there is an inverse relationship between the size and amplitude of the exhaust of such accessories and the size and circumference of the driver's God given "tailpipe." Fortunately most lads grow out of the phase, and although other parts have probably stopped growing long ago there are operations you can have to at least give the appearance of size. Anyway I am told size doesn't matter, in fact I am told that all the time, and yes that other thing can happen too and "it's OK, but if it happens more than twice you're going to the doctors, alright?"

My point is boy, and girl racers can be a real nuisance. In South Auckland alone, 76 cars are being seized each week for either being unsafe or being driven in an unsafe manner and while most of the cars are handed back to them after 28 days, the chances are the driver's aren't insured which conveniently brings me to my next point.

You do not have to have car insurance, even third party cover. Apparently there are 800,000 new Zealanders who drive without car insurance. This is because the ACC system covers injury and costs due to accidents. It is probably very wise to get car insurance and I always get fully comprehensive as it is relatively cheap here compared to home. Incidentally, if you buy your car on finance you do have to have insurance, it is mandatory. Over 20,000 cars are stolen in New Zealand each year. So for this reason alone it is well worth getting insurance.

Do not speed here. **New Zealand is metric**. Speed limits are in kilometers per hour. The authorities are very hot on speeding. As we all know speed kills and there is a great deal of public information and education attempting to prevent speeding near schools and drink driving. I am of the opinion that people who speed near schools need to be pulled from their cars and lynched on the nearest tree in front of the children. The authorities will fine proportionate to the speed. There are only 45 speed cameras in New Zealand. There are no warning signs like there are in Britain.

Unmarked police cars or "mufti cops" will catch you, and anyway if you are going too fast you will miss some of the most stunning scenery in the world. More than half the accidents happen on bends where people travel too fast and the laws of physics take over. There are a lot of bends in New Zealand between towns and cities.

I have to admit that I recently got pulled for exceeding the limit while driving through Arthur's Pass Village. I am not a speeding type and have never been pulled by the police in 25 years of driving. I am really embarrassed about the whole incident. I didn't realize I was speeding but just as The Evey was chastising me for not slowing down we saw the cop car.

He did a "u-ey" and before he could blue light me I had pulled over and got out the car. I then admitted to him I had been a bad boy, fumbled for my licence, which I couldn't find (an offence in itself), went into Mr Bean mode, did a nervous little jig on the spot, a bit like the Mexican hat dance, and played the air piano with my hands and fingers.

I think he was more than a little shocked and after he'd quizzed me and I'd acted even more peculiar, he just let me off with a warning, not before leaning into the car to tell The Evey to make sure I kept to the limits and to get me some help for whatever it was I was suffering from. I use this to illustrate how "hot" they are on speeding. I also wait to be strung from the nearest tree as befits the punishment I advocated earlier in this section.

Fines for speeding start at $30 for 10 kmh infringements all the way up to $630 for speeds of 45 kmh over the limit. Licence demerit points go hand in hand with these tariffs. Despite there only being 45 speed cameras in the whole country they are extremely productive. Taking over 700,000 stills a year, 455,000 of these pictures result in fines. At the cheapest level of fine that's a nice little earner for the government.

New Zealand driving licences

As stated, NZ drivers get "demerit points" removed from their licence for infringements. One hundred or more points over a two year period results in a 3 month suspension. New Zealand operates a graduated licence system awarded in three stages regardless of your age (over 15 years of age).

Stage 1

Learner. You can't drive on your own. Your supervisor must hold a full NZ licence and have done so for over 2 years. You must display L plates front and back and carry your licence with you when driving. When you have passed the test you receive a restricted licence.

Stage 2

Restricted. You must not drive on your own between 10 pm and 5 am unless supervised. If tested in an automatic you can only drive an automatic. You cannot carry passengers unless one is a supervisor and holds a full licence.

Stage 3

Full. You can apply for this after 18 months of holding a restricted. (less if you are over 25 or have completed a defensive driving course). You have to sit a practical test too.

Your UK driver's licence will cover you for 12 months, after which you have to sit the NZ conversion test or lose the right to drive. This is done at one of the AA centres and involves an eye test, a photograph for the licence taken in the AA centre and a 40 minute multiple choice questionnaire where you scratch off the silver foil to one of the four answers. The eye test is performed by looking through a device and reading Snellen's test letters on a card and reading them out to the AA staff. If English is your first language and you have read through the Road Code book you should be ashamed of yourself if you don't get all of the questions correct. All the questions they use are in the Road Code and they are unbelievable in their simplicity. You are allowed to get three questions wrong and no more. This allows most house bricks a chance to drive.

Mind you when The Evey was doing her test a young lad in the cubicle next to hers cried out "Dad I need another sheet I've got four wrong". At $84 dollars to convert your licence and do the test you need the parenting skills of a saint to stop yourself beating the answers into a child who quite obviously never opened the Road Code. Though The Evey, naturally achieving 100%, never found out if he passed the re-sit, my guess is with enough goes and several thousand dollars he probably did and is now cruising around Christchurch with the biggest exhaust from Repco he could find and driving like Mario Andretti but without any of the skill or intelligence. Scary isn't it?

If you don't sit your conversion test within 12 months of arriving you will have to sit a practical driving test as well. Now that *is* scary as most of us probably would fail such a test just adjusting the wing mirrors.

Other driving information

- The highway code is known as the Road Code here and is available at bookshops or from the AA shops dotted around the big cities. Second hand copies can also be purchased from www.trademe.co.nz.

- Half of the New Zealand car fleet is Japanese in make and model.

- Sunstrike is a problem especially in winter where the sun is low in the sky and the days are brighter than we are used to.

- Snow chains are a sensible investment if you are going to do a lot of exploring. Indeed all vehicles using the Milford Road in the South Island are required by law to carry chains for their vehicles over winter months. You can see the Milford Road on the podcast link below.

- Don't expect vehicles to stop and give way to you as a pedestrian about to use a zebra crossing. Many drivers don't stop as they are too busy texting or staring past you blankly. Therefore cross with care as eye contact is no guarantee they have clocked you.

- Some town roads have very pronounced cambers meaning low slung cars can scrape on the Tarmac when pulling out of driveways for instance or opening the car door when parked.

- Traffic lights sequences are different to the ones we are used to but they are stacked in the same order with red at the top. I did warn you this was a patronizing section of the book. However the difference is the lights go straight to green from red, none of this "ready, get set, and ......stall".

  NZ lights: RED to GREEN to AMBER to RED and so on.

- The first commercially available biofuel is now available with the government insisting all oil companies offer it for sale from April 2008. A 10:90 ethanol mix called Gull force 10. (Incidentally Air New Zealand are running trials on a biofuel for their fleet.)

Before you come out here arrange for your car insurer to issue you with a letter or no claims certificate stating how many years "no claim" to prove you are not bad risk for insurers. We didn't come with one and had to phone our insurance company from NZ to arrange one. Having said that they took my word for it when I got insured, even though my "Live to road race" skull tattoo was clearly visible (on my forehead).

You have to keep your driver's licence on you if you are driving as it is an offence not to produce it when a police officer pulls you over. Mind you, one of The Evey's friends did not have hers on her in that situation but the officer was happy for her to prove her identity with her firearms licence instead!

You won't ever integrate into New Zealand if you can't drive a car and use your mobile phone at the same time. The world and his wife drive one handed here. Younger people will text while driving. I am amazed there aren't more accidents. It used to really upset me at home when people used their mobiles and drove at the same time. I would mouth "get off the phone you bleep, bleep, bleep", unless they looked bigger than me and then I'd just glare. I must have really chilled because it doesn't bother me half as much now.

There is a constant battle between the two big car brands here. Ford and Holden. Like the never ending battle between good and evil, alien v predator and Jason v Freddie these two manufacturers fight it out for sales and the very popular V8 races. You are either one or the other. A bit like the chariot races of ancient Byzantium, you are either for the blues or greens, Ford or Holden. I am for the reds: Honda, but then no one takes any notice of me.

Alcohol and driving

One in every one hundred motorists may be drunk according to a recent report. There are two legal alcohol limits. One limit is for licenced drivers over 20 years. The other is for all drivers under 20 years and those with learner or restricted licences.

The upper legal limit is:
80 mg of alcohol per 100 ml of blood or 40 microgrammes per 100ml of breath.

(Compare this to 80 in blood and 35 in breath for the UK)

Drivers under 20 years the upper legal limit is:
30 mg of alcohol per 100 ml of blood or **150 microgrammes per litre** of breath.

Being pragmatic the NZ Police Association give the public guidance on how to stay under the limit:

"Male drivers should have no more than one 375 ml can of beer (4.5% alcohol) or two cans of low alcohol beer (2% alcohol). An average-size woman could go over the limit even after a double nip of spirits or a small glass of wine, or a can of beer."

Penalties are severe and include prison, fines and disqualification. Adverts with catchy tag lines like "If your mate's pissed you're screwed" and "If you stop a drink driver you're a bloody hero" run all the time. Despite this 30,000 Kiwis are convicted of drink driving each year.

Space For Your Research

www.aa.co.nz

The Automobile Association of NZ, a wonderful organization with a long history. If you are an alcoholic you need the AA not the AA.

www.hoof-it.co.nz

A department of Transport website about speeding and excuses given. Reminds me of Nick Park's creature comfort commercials.

www.landtransport.govt.nz

For fact sheets and some of the most important road rules.

www.ltsa.govt.nz/roadcode/

Everything you need to know about the New Zealand highway code.

www.nerdsinnewzealand.blogspot.com

Catch a look at some motoring shots of the scenery.

www.repco.co.nz

NZ version of Halfords for shocks, exhausts, mags, paper, pens and other bits of stationery.

---

i-Tunes do a series of New Zealand video casts free to download from their i-Tunes store. Search for "New Zealand Podcasts" to watch views of NZ at spectacular places including the Milford Road mentioned above. Once you've seen this clip you'll understand why it might get a bit icy in winter.

Buying a vehicle

These are some general points to be aware of when buying a vehicle. Most of it applies to cars but if you were buying say a lorry or bulldozer or something that ran on recycled chip fat then it becomes a bit more complicated so check with the Land Transport NZ website.

Most vehicles are purchased through finance unless you deal drugs then you probably pay cash. For a vehicle to become yours you need to ensure the person selling it has paid off all their finance owed. You can register and search the Personal Property Securities Register. Searches cost $3 and can be done by the vehicle identification number or registration plates. The vendor should be able to prove to you that the full ownership has been transferred to them. The owner is responsible for transferring ownership and paying any costs to do so. They lodge a form (MR13B) with Land Transport New Zealand within 7 days of the purchase date. Did I mention NZ is very bureaucratic?

It is worth having an independent vehicle inspection unless you know what you are doing. I ask to see the engine and then pull a few leads, wobble the odd pokey out thing, check under the car for oil leaks, and find that is enough to convince the seller I know one end of the car from the other. I also ask to see if the drinks holder is functioning. That usually settles it without doubt in the vendor's mind and their thought bubble reads "twat".

The vehicle ought to have a current road licence and make sure it has a Warrant of Fitness (WoF) that is no more than one month old when you take possession.

To confirm a vehicle is not reported as stolen and is properly registered and licenced, you can complete a "request for motor vehicle details" (form MR 31) at a Land Transport NZ agent eg the AA. The fee is $2.25. And did I mention New Zealanders like filling out forms?

I think it is a lot simpler to buy from a forecourt dealer than a private purchase, but check that the dealer is a member of the Motor Trade Association. The Automobile Association gives you a good synopsis on how to buy a car.

Any car 1.8 L or over will almost invariably have a tow bar. Kiwis love towing things, usually on a week day it is a trailer with something in it or a boat if it is a weekend.

There is an A4 sized paperback book available from bookshops called "The Dog and Lemon Guide" which describes itself "...like a lonely planet guide to the world of cars". It offers impartial advice on all makes and models from 1988-2008 and tells you what can go wrong and what a model should cost both to buy and resell. It costs $25 and is worth buying if only for the humorous way it is written.

Space For Your Research

www.mta.org.nz
> Motor trade association members would be preferred to non-members.

www.autotrader.co.nz
> This will give you an idea of what is available and what it costs…

www.autobase.co.nz
> ..so will this….

www.turners.co.nz
> …and so will this if you like auctions.

www.consumerguideauto.howstuffworks.com
> U.S. site but gives good reviews on cars you might be considering to buy here. Remember the cost are American dollars not Kiwi dollars.

www.ppsr.govt.nz
> Personal Property Securities Register to check there is no outstanding credit.

www.aa.co.nz
> I recommend you join for peace of mind and the AA offer all sorts of help. Use the AA site to find the manufacturers' price of new cars in NZ. Standard cover costs from $77 a year.

Vehicle registration and road tax

Not so much a tax disc as a tax oblong. Six months costs $95.39, twelve months costs $183.22 but you can also buy just 3 months. You can pay on line at "transact.landtransport.govt.nz" or at the AA shop, post shops and vehicle inspection and testing centres.

Warrant of Fitness

The Warrant of Fitness is the Kiwi version of the MoT certificate only less pretentious. A good idea they have here is the WoF is fitted to the inside of the windscreen with the expiry date clearly visible. You can get your WoF up to 2 weeks before its expiry date. It is an offence to drive a vehicle without a current warrant of fitness. Vehicles older than six years need a WoF every 6 months.

Trailers require a Warrant of Fitness and require registration too. This will cost around $26 as will a motorcycle's. The test is a set of basic safety checks including brakes, lights, exhaust and some others including:

Tyre tread and condition
There must be a tread of 1.5 mm minimum. (You can never have enough m's in a sentence).

Safety belts
Buckles and overall condition must be good. A 20 kg dog unrestrained in the back will hit you with the force of a polar bear in an accident. However global warming would have to be pretty bad if you had a 200kg polar bear in the back of your car. Plus if a 20 kilo dog does that, think what your mother-in-law would do.

Doors
Do you have them and do they open or do you have to climb out the window like Daisy Duke?

Exhaust
There must be no leaks and not be too loud or smoky, and be inversely proportional to the size of your manhood (if male).

Windscreen integrity
Less than 30,000 insects per square metre.

In Summary

My grandfather's advice was stay out of dentists, solicitors' offices and garages. True advice today as it's ever been. A good, reasonably priced mechanic is as good as my father's saying "always buy a good bed and a good pair of shoes because if you're not in one you're in the other". I have yet to formulate any advice of my own to pass on to the next generation except stay out of the underwear stock market as the bottom is about to fall out of it. In Christchurch we use a little side street business. It is run by a couple of Brummies but their sexual persuasion of course is none of my business.

Space For Your Research

www.landtransport.govt.nz

The Kiwi's version of the Ministry of Transport.

www.plates.co.nz

Make up rude words for a number plate and buy them here. You are limited to six characters though which cuts out all but the most obscene words. I saw a terrific Tottenham Hotspur FC plate that said YID R ME. They can also be bought for your business vehicle as I have seen a lorry delivering spuds with the plate POT4TO. I have also followed an erratically driven car with the registration 2DEPUB. The permutations are endless and I am easily entertained.

www.vtnz.co.nz

Vehicle Testing New Zealand. An independent testing company originally formed by the government but now privatized. Use it to check out more about motoring. They are open on public holidays, which is handy.

www.onroad.co.nz

"On Road New Zealand". Another group of testing stations to get your car assessed for its WoF.

Chapter 6

Schools and Schooling

Schooling of New Zealand children follows a typical pattern, but what we would understand as secondary school is known as intermediate and high schooling.

· Primary school	5 -10 years
Intermediate school	11-12 years
High School	13-17 years

Because of the intermediate schooling the first year of high school is actually the third year of secondary school if that makes sense? Students starting at high school become known as Thirds which is corrupted obviously to Turds. Please don't be alarmed if your 13 year old child comes home upset at being called this.

Typical School terms

		Approximate Dates	Duration
Term 1	Autumn Term	7 Feb–5 Apr	9 weeks
Term 2	Winter Term	23 Apr – 29 Jun	9 weeks
Term 3	Spring term	16 Jul – 21 Sep	10 weeks
Term 4	Summer Term	8 Oct – 20 Dec	11 weeks

Pre-school

A large not for profit organization that helps families with children under 5 years of age is the Plunket Society. Run by volunteers and trained nurses it provides a point of contact and support network for anyone with small children. It does lots of other good stuff like hiring out car seats to families who can't afford to buy them.

95% of children between three and five years of age are entitled to twenty hours of free childhood education in teacher led centers. In reality parents do end up contributing towards the cost. The Labour government was criticized for rolling out a plan it could not sustain. Now that sounds depressingly familiar doesn't it?

Primary school

I came across a survey (2007) that showed one in seven teachers reported being physically assaulted by students in that year. A sorry state of affairs and shows that NZ is up there with the rest of the world for poor discipline at home and even worse role modelling for poor little Johnny who really didn't deserve being put on the naughty chair because he was being creative (making pipe bombs) and expressive (setting light to the Wendy house).

I could have been a teacher but I have a medical condition that precludes me. Known as Fawlty Syndrome I have an elbow that inadvertently hyper-extends my open palm. I just know it would engage the back of little Johnny's head if he was disruptive (or if he was ugly).

Now the most sensible advice you can give your child starting school is "If any of the kids give you any trouble just tell them your dad's got an axe and he'll come and chop off their heads"

I remember a kid at school who told me his dad was going to do that to me and I was so scared I had the rest of the week off sick. The thing was I knew this boy's father was a fireman so understood, quite reasonably, that his dad had free access to axes.

Even now when my daughters go baby sitting I say to them if the kids give you any trouble you must say "my dad's got a saw and he'll come and saw off your head if you don't go to bed right now". I then back this up by making sure at some time, I always get seen by these kids, holding a rusty old handsaw.

NCEAs

These are the National Certificates in Educational Achievement. Exams are in November. They are divided into levels 1, 2 and 3 and are the equivalents of O, AS and A levels respectively. I think to be fair, level 1 is a little below an O level and level 2 is above an O but less than an AS and so on. This is not to undermine the qualification but it is worth bearing in mind if you are transferring your education back to Britain.

An excellent aspect to the courses is the ability to accumulate credits towards achieving the certificate before you sit the final exam. Students can achieve between 2 to 6 credits per assignment. There is the criticism therefore, that the students don't push themselves at the exam if they are close to achieving the required number of credits.

You need:

80 credits to achieve Level 1 (roughly O level)
80 credits to achieve Level 2 (20 carried over from level 1)
60 credits to achieve Level 3
(roughly equivalent to A level in the UK)
(or the Higher School Certificate in Australia)

Credits in turn reflect the standard or ability of the student, with course work and internal tests being allocated one of the following grades:

Not Achieved, Achieved, Merit or Excellence

A record of what you attained for each credit accompanies you through your education and beyond. In theory two students can achieve level 1 NCEA by earning 80 credits in the year but one student may have all "achieved" status while the other earns over 80 credits all with "Excellence". The national education authority now issue the certificate with the standard of the pass, so it may read "Level 1 NCEA with Excellence" or "Level 1 NCEA with Merit".

In 2006 only 110,000 students in total sat the exams and only 5.2% gained Excellence in level 1, 3.8% in level 2 and 4.2% at level 3 and in 2007 more than a third of the students did not achieve level 1.

School tables show the number of students sitting each level of NCEA and the percentage achieving, so it is not hard to work out the failing schools in the place you choose to live. If you live in the rural areas there will only be one school for your children to go to. The impression I get is these schools are educating the farmers of tomorrow and many of their students go into the family business after learning how to count the cows in and out at milking time. Overleaf is a snapshot of exam results for Christchurch.

	Level 1	Level 2	Level 3	
National average of students passing each NCEA level (2006)	**56.5%**	**60.7%**	**51.2%**	**Comments**

Top and bottom schools in Christchurch

Christ'sCollege (boys)	96.2%	92.8%	93.3%	Fee paying.
Christchurch Girls' High School	90.0%	89.5%	83.8%	State School.
Aranui High School	29.6%	41.5%	9.9%	Co-ed state school in poor area.

There has been criticism of the NCEAs as one school was bought to book for giving a large number of credits at NCEA level 1 for getting their students to pick up rubbish. Credits can also be attained for fork lift driving and hospitality so the courses can be vocational, depending on the school.

Entry to University here and abroad is achieved by collecting a set number of credits at level 3. This is where it sounds complicated. You need 42 credits at level 3. Twenty eight in major subjects (14 in each one) and 14 credits between any other two. Plus you need 8 level 2 credits in English and 12 level 1 mathematics credits. In the absence of the necessary credits a student can sit bridging papers to meet the standard required.

NCEA exam fees are payable in June and cost $75 for all exams sat, per child entered.

Zoning for schools

In general you go to the school for the zone in which you live. The best schools are often in the areas of expensive housing. If the school cannot fill its roll it will accept out of zone students. Talents and academic recommendation are worth including in the application paperwork. Certain schools excel at different things. You may find a child who lives in the zone for one school goes to a neighbouring school because there is a strong emphasis on sport, music or dramatic arts at that school.

"The trend (*...of spurning your nearest school...*) is often derided as white flight. While there might be a racial element to some of the decisions being made about school choices–as in white parents wanting to avoid schools with a large number of brown students–it is far too an emotive and charged label for it to be used safely or sensibly. Snob appeal is a surer way of describing the situation. Some parents will go to all sorts of lengths to avoid sending their offspring to the local high school, if its prestige is not considered to be high enough."

The Press Newspaper Tuesday, 17 July 2007

Shocked and amused in equal measure at the above I agree there is more than a degree of snobbery or resentment felt about the schools your children go to. This may just be a regional thing. We have had some nice friendly conversations with strangers until the question "where do your kids go to school?" Suddenly the tone and friendliness drops ever so slightly. You could blink and miss it. Often the conversation ends shortly afterwards. It is almost as if I have asked them to wipe my anus with cotton wool soaked in warm water because I'm a little constipated.

My daughters go to a school that is only 85% full, but out of a roll of 1057 pupils there are 452 students from out of the zone. What happens is the parents have moved the family into the catchment area, enrolled precious Molly and her sister Davina in the school and have then moved out of the rented accommodation and actually live in the wop wops. While I cannot condone this I do understand it. One school in the city is only 59% full, while another is 113% full. Schools are obliged to take the children in zone first then they will open the doors to out of zone applicants allocated via a ballot and they will keep back a number of places in each year. I think it may be as high as 20 to cover anyone who moves into zone after the academic year has started. The out of zone places are heavily oversubscribed for the good schools.

Grundy run

There is a highly amusing tradition at single sex schools across the country as the final term ends. My children's school is twinned with the local boys' high school. You can imagine the sexual tension after a certain age. Each year in the last weeks of the final term a handful of boys from the neighbouring school will sneak onto the girls' school grounds during lunch and streak in their underwear in full view of all. Identities are protected with stockings over faces as the punishments following identification and capture are severe. To the imaginary tune of Benny Hill the moment these boys are spotted someone lets out the cry of "Grundy run" and teachers, and some students, attempt to rugby tackle the trespassers to the ground and apprehend them.

There are obviously many stories that accompany this tradition. One year the invaders wore the stripy uniform underwear of Christ's College the very posh fee paying school, in an attempt to frame someone else. Unfortunately someone at the girls' school recognized one of the gangly youths in silhouette and they were rumbled.

Another year there was a girls' Grundy at the boys' school where some brave, and one would have to say "extrovert girls", ran in their underwear and chanced their luck on "away soil" so to speak. Unfortunately (depending on your point of view) one girl was caught and tied to a lamp post with cling film and, by the sounds of it, sexually assaulted. It has not been attempted since by any girl.

High school japery has been known to happen all year. Just recently one classroom was put out of action when it is believed at least four boys from another school crept into the girls' school, crapped and crept out again. I don't know, boys will be boys!

Hidden costs

Expect a number of hidden costs in sending your child to school. For instance we have had to pay for Internet use, printer use (a wopping $1 a sheet), stationery, the Parent Teachers Association and so on. I have asked to be exempt from donating to the PTA if I don't have a cup of tea at parents' evening. I was told it doesn't work like that, you still have to pay for refreshments. The bill comes in the post and includes "compulsory donation to PTA" which is a lovely oxymoron.

Extra curricular activities like basketball and soccer will cost you per season. You will have to buy stationery and work books and some textbooks each year. Pens, pencils, pencil cases and furry gonks are extra as are paints and crafty equipment.

Uniform

The vast majority of schools enforce uniform, which is something I am in favour of as it stops the fashion race and spitefulness of children who are into that sort of thing. I was the child from C&A and BHS (and I still am).

Do not choose your school on uniform look alone, they are all much the same. The downside to uniform is it looks very old fashioned. Girls wear ankle length kilts with T bar sandals. Boys wear short trousers up until they leave school at seventeen or eighteen. Blouses, ties and blazers finish the winter wear. Voluminous summer dresses complete the warm weather look. The whole collection is most unflattering and my children hated it.

There is however pride in the uniform and you can collect badges of achievement to be worn like medals on the blazer lapels. "Peer leader", "academic colours", "house captain", "map reader" "overfriendly with boys" are just some of the badges in the series. This pride in the uniform continues long after school ends. A recent Air New Zealand advert showed a girl in her school uniform embarking on an emotional journey and there were numerous complaints about the fact that the blazer had red piping and was clearly an upper school blazer but it was being worn with a blue tie from the lower school instead of a red one. Clever marketing because everyone now remembers the advert.

Sports at school

School playing fields haven't been sold off for development here yet and besides, the students actually seem to like sports. Even my children have engaged in sport, something that the UK government has been trying to get teenage girls to do for years. It's hard not to do sport in NZ as the climate is right for outdoor activities and the national psyche is one of fanatical sports madness.

Most schools offer a huge range of sports to suit all interests including some highly unusual ones like underwater polo? While rugby is the sport to follow, more Kiwi kids are playing soccer. This is because parents get a little concerned about the risk of a rugby injury. This is understandable when you realize that some Pacific Island kids at ten years of age weigh twelve stone or more and are solid as rock so the spindly little white kids don't stand a chance. There have been moves to separate the leagues children play in, by

86

weight and size so you have pale sticky little lads playing against equally anaemic looking skin and bone.

Sport is taken seriously and school sports teams are disciplined. If you don't turn up to an organized match against another school and there are not enough players to make the team you are fined $100 as a team, forfeit the match and face the discipline of the school.

Driving to school

With a letter from your parents you can take your car to school. My mum refuses to write me a letter so I have to walk, but many do take advantage. If you want to run your friends home you have to have letters from their parents too. This little formality doesn't seem to bother most kids as they park away from the school buildings and at the end of lessons lifts home are offered and accepted and they all pile into their cars. Most drivers of that age only have a restricted licence so the practice is illegal. No one cares though.

Now if you wondered how many people can really fit into a classic mini (and you missed Roy Castle and the McQuirters testing this on Blue Peter in the 1970s) you only have to watch and learn at the end of the school day. There is a girl at my daughters' school who has a mini and numerous students climb into this little car, more than you could imagine is safe or comfortable. The suspension drops and there is a mass of squashed bodies, faces and kilts pressed against all the internal glass surfaces. Screams of delight and possibly cramp fill the air as the car races off down the road tooting its horn. Truly amazing but if it was biologically possible you'd be having kittens if that was one of your daughters inside the vehicle.

Space For Your Research

www.nzei.org.nz
New Zealand's largest education union.

www.ecd.govt.nz
Ministry of Education early childhood education website.

www.minedu.govt.nz
Ministry of Education main website.

www.nzqa.govt/ncea
More detail on secondary education qualifications.

www.plunket.org.nz
Sounds like Kerplunk, that "fast, exciting game and fun for all ages", but is actually much more useful and has a complete set of marbles.

www.peace.net.nz/coolschools.htm
As old as the hills, I am sad to say bullying is alive and well in NZ, but good stuff like this is always welcome.

www.porse.co.nz
A network for providing in-house child care. As opposed to looking after children outside or in the coal bunker.

www.careers.govt.nz
A site offering careers advice.

www.teachnz.govt.nz
Sufferers of Fawlty Syndrome need not apply.

www.chch.school.nz
For Christchurch schools and their websites. Not all schools are listed.

www.finda.co.nz
To locate schools and their websites. Be warned school the sites vary considerably in quality and the information offered.

Chapter 7

Weather, Climate and The Environment

New Zealand occupies a similar latitude in the southern hemisphere as Portugal does in the Northern, but being surrounded by sea it has a maritime climate and the weather can be quite changeable. Locals in Christchurch say "four seasons in one day". Being British we know all about that. This climate allows the British to grow some things, that are a bit exciting, without the need for a greenhouse. Things like apricots, lemons, avocados, grapes, kiwi fruit and melanomas.

Weather forecasts in New Zealand

Unfortunately weather forecasts appear not to be as accurate as we are used to in the United Kingdom. I guess that the reason for this is that the country is surrounded by water and sea. The difference between the British Isles and NZ is that their sea is the huge Pacific Ocean and is influenced by the Antarctic with few other large masses nearby save Australia.

The poor accuracy that the forecasts predict is often criticized by farmers and tourist operators. A recent study suggested that the forecasts were only 50% accurate. This really isn't good enough if you are a sheep farmer needing to know if you have to get your sheep in before snow is dumped or a balloon or helicopter pilot. All these people rely on an accurate forecast for business. Regardless of these poor auguries the Kiwis are more obsessed than we are about the weather and you are on safe ground in opening a conversation on this subject. In the south there is a special weather system that is a great topic. The Nor'wester.

The Nor'wester in Canterbury

This is an interesting wind. It is a warm northerly blast that originates from warmer climes and becomes a Nor'wester as the Earth rotates on its axis. It is most common in the spring when the temperature differences between the Equator and South Pole are greatest. Collecting lots of moisture as it crosses the Tasman Sea the wind then hits the Southern Alps and drops all that moisture in an attempt to dissolve the mountain range. Hence the west coast gets very wet and is very green. The great thing about this wind is, as it comes down the mountain on the eastern side of the Alps it is dry and warm giving a gusty blast which is electrically charged.

Many locals hate the Nor'wester as it makes them crabby and gives them headaches. To be fair it can be very destructive and in 1988 tonnes of topsoil from the Canterbury plains were blown out to sea. And in 1975 a number of chickens were blown into the Pacific. If the Kiwis were more sentimental about animals, it would have been a great opportunity to rename the ocean the Pachickic in memory of those poor, stupid creatures.

The Nor'wester makes me feel like we are on holiday and as I am crabby anyway no one sees a mood change and what was paracetamol invented for if it wasn't to treat wind-induced headaches?

I welcome the warnings of the Nor'wester coming and I want to get out in it. I like to face the wind head-on arms held out in crucifixion. The scene is almost perfect save having Leonardo DiCaprio hold my waist and whisper in my ear.

Early on I attempted to paint the outside of the house during one Nor'wester because I thought the paint would dry quickly but chickens kept ruining the finish.

It is also worth investing in some decent pegs if you don't want your lingerie ending up in the hands of that filthy pervert next door, though I've wasted hours waiting for some of it to end up in mine.

The wind is pre-empted by an interesting cloud effect, the "Nor'wester arch". The air off the Alps displaces any cloud in a gently curving arc. The appearance is of mountains with a semicircle of clear blue sky above them, and bunched up clouds above this. The headache follows shortly afterwards.

Does it need to be said that weather patterns are the reverse of the UK's, in that Nor'Westers bring warmth and Southerlies herald the cold snaps off the Antarctic?

90

Winter in New Zealand and Christchurch

Likewise I am sure I don't have to tell you that the seasons are the reverse of home, but for completeness I will say June, July and August are the cold months, so very much like the UK then? As I have mentioned New Zealand summers are hot and long, however, given the alpine geography of the South Island it is not surprising that the winters are pretty cold. These days are sunny, crisp and bright but the price you pay for great winter sun are cold nights. Living on the coast here I find the cold isn't any more than the icy blasts the UK gets over winter. This would not be a problem if Kiwis had heard of double glazing, central heating or even insulation. Apparently Swedish homes are so well insulated they don't need heating so can we have some of that here please?

I was talking to a lady in Christchurch who came over here from Minsk in Belarus. They are used to pretty cold winters (-25 degrees) and she and her fellow Russian migrants have never felt so cold as when they came to NZ. In Russia they are prepared for the cold, in NZ the locals just put up with it.

Old houses leak water and draughts and as I have mentioned double glazing and central heating are not installed in them. Under such circumstances Kiwi advice would be if three extra sweaters don't keep you warm then do some star jumps. Sometimes their stoicism just gets on your nerves.

Now I can't stand the reputation we have as winging poms, but sometimes you just have to give into your genes. In winter it can feel so cold I have to go to bed with a wooly hat on, so I guess I am the worse sort of winging pompom.

I include this paragraph because, although I write this section in deep mid-winter and have another five weeks to go until spring officially starts, we have experienced a Nor'wester and the temperature reached 19 degrees today. Locals were walking around in shorts and t-shirts, their standard attire for all weathers. But it truly felt like summer, an amazing day. The Nor'wester is set to stay for a couple more days and then we return to winter at the weekend of course, but it has been a welcome break and we haven't needed the fire on. At 9 pm it was 15 degrees on the outside thermometer.

Having dissed the winter I have to say there aren't that many days when we haven't been able to hang the washing out to dry naturally on the line, not that my thongs need too much drying. I can't help noticing on crisp sunny mornings when I hang the washing out, it steams. Praise the Sun!

Cold days yes, miserable days yes, but midwinter doesn't have as many of those dank damp days where clouds of battleship grey hang just out of reach and you don't see the sun for weeks, as we seem to have in a British winter. New Zealand skies have a certain high light intensity about them, but then maybe that's the hole in the ozone?

Clear sunny days in winter come at a price in that they cool down quickly when the sun goes down. (Haven't I just said that above already? Just reinforcing the message then). I have a set of solar garden lights that run off rechargeable AA batteries and there is enough power in the sun to keep them charged and working through winter. This is something that a dull December day in Britain can't do. Neither can you BBQ in the equivalent of late February which we did only this week. I suppose you could do it in Britain in February but it might set the fire alarm and sprinklers off. It's funny because you get a run of some sunny days particularly in early spring and it catches you out. T shirts and shorts becoming the order of the day then the weather turns and it's back to five layers again plus beany hat.

Smog, aggravated by wood burners is a perennial problem in Christchurch due to its geography. The winters of 2007 and 2008 however threw up fewer smoggy days than average. Proponents of the clean air lobby put this down to the improvements in wood burning practices while others say it is down to unseasonal weather conditions and fewer settled days.

The Press newspaper lists the air pollution in Christchurch over winter along with ski field snowfalls, and a UV index and pollen count in summer months. Each local newspaper is different in what it reports along these lines. Rather quaintly The Oamaru Mail gives a daily blue penguin report telling you when they will be coming ashore so you can be there to p..p..p..pick up a Penguin.

Don't be fooled into thinking NZ is just chilly in winter. Twizel in the centre of the South Island recently went to minus 11 Celsius.

In some ways the South Island cold snaps in winter are welcomed as some economies rely on the snow for skiing. As usual the stoicism shines through with "so what if Queenstown is completely cut off?" Just to illustrate how isolated New Zealand can become in bad weather or disaster, McDonald's in Queenstown had to shut for 24 hours because supply lorries could not get through. The famous Kiwi stoicism was surely tested that day. The riot police were stood down only when there was a break in the weather. Kiwis do love their Big Macs and Kiwi Burgers.

There are areas deep in Central Otago in the South Island that, in winter, develop hoar frosts. These are sub zero temperatures that leave icicles on everything from trees to the end of your nose. A hoar frost is beautiful to behold, but not if you have to live and work through it. Conversation for instance is spoken, snapped off at the mouth, brought indoors and defrosted before it can be heard, all very time consuming.

The upside of brutal winters like this, are equally brutal summers. Alexandra one of the main fruit growing areas of the country, gets clobbered by minus ten or more, or is that less? I never have understood negative integers. In summer it regularly gets temperatures into the "thirties". A right little sun trap. Despite such high summer temperatures the lakes in New Zealand stay cold all year round which in itself doesn't stop Kiwis swimming in them. To borrow a favourite NZ joke "you enter the lakes as Angus and come out as Agnes".

Environment

New Zealanders are rightly proud of their environment and want to protect it. October 2006 saw 200 climate change experts from 46 countries meet in Christchurch to discuss reducing greenhouse gases. I don't think they will be invited again because after they finished it was found they had left all the lights on, the mini bar door open and the hot tap running.

Talk about pot calling kettle all black, New Zealanders waste $100 million of electricity a year, produce 1 tonne of landfill rubbish per person per year and have a carbon footprint of 9 tonnes per person per year. All this makes them some of the world's worst polluters. In fact they are the twelfth highest carbon emitter. This is higher than Japan and Germany despite only housing 0.06% of the world's population.

Most foods are imported into New Zealand which in turn means higher costs and lots of travel miles behind them. In fact only last week I bought a tomato that had collected so many air miles it was planning a trip to the Gold Coast, Australia. Well not any more it isn't.

Renewable power

New Zealand is in a good position in that two thirds of its electricity is produced from renewable sources, mainly hydro and some geothermal. Most of this sort of power is produced in the South Island. Wind turbines are springing up around the country but this contributes only about 3% of the production. The remaining third is met by more conventional methods namely gas, coal and oil. There are 240 wind turbines in the country which is nearly one per person. More are in the consent stage so the country must be expecting more people to arrive?

Meridian Energy is New Zealand's first carbon neutral electricity provider. For that reason we signed up with them, plus they sweetened it with an offer for a Soda Stream and all the CO_2 we could drink for free.

Saving Energy

If every New Zealand household installed just five energy efficient light bulbs, it would save enough energy to power every home in Christchurch. Also if every New Zealander gave me just one dollar I wouldn't be cold next winter, I'd be somewhere warm.

Kiwis love their beer fridges but if all of them were turned off it would mean the South Island's Coleridge power station could be decommissioned. That is an outstanding fact. To put it another way it takes a whole power station just to give New Zealanders cold beer. We may have been mocked and ridiculed, but proof if it were needed that warm British beer is good for the planet.

Given all this consumption and waste it is not surprising electricity prices in New Zealand have risen 50% in the last 6 years. However if you pay your electricity bill early or as soon as you get it you receive a discount.

Household waste

It's your rubbish you pay for getting rid of it. Sounds fair enough and it is. Your council rates entitle you to one black bin bag a fortnight. The council gives you a voucher when you have paid your rates and you cash it in at the supermarket, receiving 26 black bin liners in return. This happens once a year. Most people generate more than one sack of rubbish a fortnight so use up their allocation from the council in no time and have to buy extra bin bags from the supermarket. These cost in the region of $1.20 (or 40 pence in our money) per bag. I throw whatever I can over the fence into next door's garden and they don't seem to mind.

You cannot use any old bin liner and place it out for refuse collection, it must be a council stamped bag. They will not collect anything that is not official. A family of four's non-recyclable rubbish for <u>one week</u> can easily fit into <u>one</u> landfill bag. You may need a size thirteen to squash the air out of a <u>fortnight's</u> rubbish and then you may be able to get the bag to last its intended two weeks, in which case you are laughing. Whether the Kiwi's large carbon footprint means they have a large carbon foot to help squash down the bags and make them last longer I am not sure. Be careful as the bags break easily and the week before last's chicken carcass is likely to be after revenge.

Bags should not weigh more than 15 kg, so a dead body would use up four or five of your allowance. Rubbish bags which are not collected are given a sticker noting the reason for rejection. The householder is responsible for removing any rejected bags as soon as possible. Bags must be on the kerbside by 7.30 am on the day of your collection.

In Christchurch if you miss the collection you are allowed to take council bags to the dump free of charge. You are also allowed to take up to three council rubbish bags per week free of charge to Barry's Bay Transfer Station. Three is the number and the number shall not exceed three. Four is unacceptable and five is out of the question, three must be the number. Rule, rules and more rules. Welcome to New Zealand.

The rules also state that the bags are issued to the household not the individual. If you move house you are meant to leave sufficient bags for the new occupier at the rate of one a fortnight until the end of April, but of course no one does.

I have read that wheelie bins are on their way for Christchurch (2009). Being a bureaucratic city there will be three bins per household. An 80 litre one with a green lid for green rubbish, a 140 litre one with a red lid for red rubbish and a 240 litre yellow lidded one for yellow things. God help anyone who is colour blind. I can see tears over this. For instance there is a block of flats over the road from where we live and they will need to store 18 wheelie bins on the ground floor. On Thursday night when the bars chuck out, wheelie bins will be all over Christchurch.

Hazardous waste

There has been a big push on low energy light bulbs but this comes with an environmental price in that the bulbs contain mercury so become a problem for safe disposal if they break and at the end of their natural lives. Such waste is considered "hazardous" and can't be sent to landfill in your black bin (not that there will be any room for it). You can find your closest "hazardous waste centre" by contacting your local council.

I liked the story of a local Canterbury couple who, in 2007 started the country's first commercial scale nappy composting service. It can handle up to 2000 disposable nappies a day and produces rich organic garden compost which it sells to gardeners. John Innes Number Twos I believe?

Footnote: Huggies liked it too and recently went into partnership with them and they stepped up production as opposed to just stepping in it.

Council Recycling Centres

A trip to the local tip will also cost you if you are disposing of material that cannot be recycled. Most centres have a layout where you drive in to an area where you can dispose of cardboard, glass, metal and certain plastics for free. Currently Christchurch can only recycle plastics numbered 1 and 2 on the container. Types 3-7 have to go in landfill, though this is set to change.

A weighbridge on the way in and again on the way out measures your load. The difference in the two weights is what you pay for. The cost in Christchurch per metric tonne is $143. Last time I went I had 20 kg and it cost me $7.50. I don't quite know how they worked that price out. May be there is a minimum charge, either way I think it is money for old rope. You would imagine there is a great deal of fly tipping as a result of paying for your rubbish handling but there does not appear to be a huge problem. There are some black spots around the city, mainly in the poorer areas or in parkland outside, but on the whole the city is rubbish-free.

A resourceful Kiwi in Christchurch has set up The Paint Exchange. In the nine months since it opened he has already recycled 20,000 litres of paint and rescued 15,000 litres from landfill. Another example of how Kiwis make use of what they've got.

Yet another example of recycling big time is the waste exchange run by the organization Terranova, a not for profit organisation set up by Christchurch Council. It aims to reduce waste and as we know one man's rubbish is another man's treasure. One of its outlets is the Supershed where you can buy furniture, kitchen stuff even computers that have been recycled.

I have had a look at this outlet and while it is a good place to pick up door handles, cheap paperbacks and magazines it is a little bit "jumble saley" in its nature. A really sad thing hit home while I was there. Apart from being very popular, judging by the people, there was a big sign announcing that the management reserved the right to inspect anyone's bags. Obviously they get a bit of shop lifting but believe me you wouldn't want to touch some of the gear there let alone pinch it. This is all very rude of me I know and sounds terrible but I didn't miss the fact that some New Zealanders are very poor and some may resort to stealing second hand goods.

Garden Waste

Local companies will collect your biodegradable garden waste, branches, cuttings and grass clippings in wheelie bins for a charge. The councils will take garden waste for composting but our council states "we are not happy composting newspaper, old compost heaps, soil, animal waste, string and toys." I would agree with most of that policy leading me to comment just how do you compost a Scalectrix or a climbing frame?

Residents are encouraged to engage in home composting and I have gone down this route. However it can encourage vermin. I have gone to tip waste in our compost bin and found a mouse staring up at me. I don't know who had the biggest fright. I think I might have screamed in a girlie way. All garden waste that you won't compost or can't handle must be taken to the transfer station where you will be charged for dumping it.

In Christchurch there is a fire ban throughout the winter months because of the contribution bonfires make to the air pollution and quality. There used to be open season for burning garden rubbish outside the winter months but it is now a year round ban. If you have to burn garden waste you have to get special written dispensation from the council to do it. If you see a bonfire it may have a permit but likely as not it won't so dob your neighbour in with the fire brigade and enjoy the repercussions.

Plastic bags

Plastic bags are becoming a thing of the past. Hang onto them they may be collectable. Many stores are plastic bag free shops now, but do you think I can remember that every time I go to them. Stores charge 10 cents for each one. I end up either buying a woven recyclable bag for 75c or come out with my arms brimming with gear that looks like I've been on a shoplifting high. And another thing as plastic bags are phased out I am not sure I would be wanting to shake hands with a dog owner any more.

Space For Your Research

www.mastagard.co.nz
> A Christchurch company offering wheelie bin hire.

www.ecodepot.co.nz
> Refuse stations in Christchurch.

www.meridianenergy.co.nz
> Offers free CO_2 with everything.

www.lgnz.co.nz
> Local Government New Zealand.

www.lgnz.co.nz/lg-sector/maps/
> All 85 local councils are listed here. Handy to link to where you might be living.

www.terranova.org.nz
> A sort of recycling swap shop. Another of its outlets is a retro store for stuff from the 50's 60's and 70's. Nuclear weapons, washed out singers, old All Blacks, that sort of thing.

Chapter 8

Health

I think this is a big issue for any migrant, young or old, whether you have given it any thought or not. The NHS has its faults, but at the end of the day you are swapping one of the best health provision services in the world for another country's health system and that can be an unknown entity.

Going to the doctors

You have to pay to see the doctor. Consequently you can get an appointment very quickly but it will sting you for $30 and then any medication prescribed is extra too. It used to be $55 until quite recently but the government brought it down to $30 to encourage people to go to their GPs and not crowd the accident and emergency departments of the few hospitals in the country.

You do not have to register with any particular doctor as you can choose to go to any doctors' practice where you live but it costs you more for a consultation if you aren't registered with the medic you see. However the visit will allow you to have a proper chat to the doctor and not always on your health; rugby, politics, life in general are all acceptable. I like to talk existentialist philosophy or the early works of Solzhenitsyn to ensure I get my money's worth, unless the doctor likes soccer, then I will talk Premiership Football.

I recently had a suspicious mole removed by my GP and it cost me $150. Expect all minor procedures to hurt you in more ways than one.

Discounts can be achieved through circumstances like age or disability but there is still a charge. For this reason people choose to die at home rather than see a doctor. This helps reduce the burden on the health system. Actually it does help to focus the mind. You find yourself asking "Shall I go for that minor ailment that would give me a day off work, but I could live with it or shall I soldier on and save it up until I get something else or a life threatening disease and then I will be quids in but be dead before the weekend?"

Many people go to the local A&E department (called the ED here) which is free, but puts considerable pressure on the acute services. Radio adverts encourage people to go to a GP rather than crowd the hospital emergency department, but who wants to pay $30 for an experienced doctor when you can be treated by a student for nothing?

Be aware that if you are taken ill in a small community while travelling and there is no public hospital present in that place there is unlikely to be any government subsidy for treating you in the private clinics that operate in those towns. A couple of hours treatment there and you are clocking up several hundred dollars. Always carry some sort of health insurance.

Hospitals

Teaching hospitals and the public sector hospitals have many of the problems we, who have lived with the NHS, have come to expect, including winter deadlock, bed blocking and unfilled positions for health professionals. There are private hospitals here too. Over a million Kiwis have health insurance. That's 1 in 4.

The public hospitals have that nasty bug MRSA but not to the same extent as British hospitals. They do however seem to be fond of Norovirus, that vivacious little fellow that causes the gastroenteritis that lays low whole wards. Your guess is as good as mine about what happens in the private hospitals.

As stated above, too many patients use the ED (Accident & Emergency) for treatment as they pay less. Authorities try to discourage this as it leads to bottle necks and long waits. These delays aren't helped by the fact that over 2,000 Kiwis attend A&E each year after attempting to open beer bottles with their teeth as the government recently informed us. Chances are the wait you are experiencing is due to the bloke in front with the toothless grin. Japery (© 1923) makes way for blatant buffoonery (© 1883)?

Please note it is fair to say that only the big centres of population have large acute public hospitals. Serious illness or injury outside of the cities often warrants transfer some considerable distance to these larger hospitals.

The Community Services Card

A Community Services Card can help with the costs of health care. For instance lower consultation fees for your doctor and lower prescription costs. Receipt of the card is based on income. If your family (of four) brings in less than $56,096 a year you may be entitled to receive a card. Waving the card is like the American Express ads of the 1980s. If the doctor charges $30 a consultation you wave the card and the receptionist says "that will do nicely" and only charges you $15. What I don't understand is that a child over 6 years will cost you $20 a visit?

The card **does not** subsidize visits to private health professionals such as osteopaths, podiatrists, acupuncturists and dieticians. See the link later on to check you own personal circumstances.

Medicines

You can get many of the medicines you may be using in the UK, though they may have a different trade name. There are some European preparations and combinations that don't exist in Australasia and your doctor may have to put you on an equivalent. There is a very big difference between the UK and New Zealand in terms of medicine funding and that is Pharmac.

Pharmac

Medicines that are not funded or partially funded have to be paid for in full by the patient. For instance if you are on Tramadol you have to pay the full price for this medicine otherwise make do with codeine, which incidentally is considered a "controlled drug" here.

Pharmac is responsible for funding medicines for patients in the community. It was set up to keep control of spiraling drug costs. Depending on where your viewpoint sits it has largely achieved this. Where other countries have escalating drug budgets each year to fund treatments New Zealand has managed to put the brakes on such expenditure. Don't forget the country is trying to run a health service with taxation from a population of 4 million (and probably much fewer tax payers than this).

Some medicines require a "special authority", "discretionary community supply" or "exceptional circumstances" application to be completed and approved by Pharmac in order to be funded. Hoops, jumping and forward rolls to a standing position through said hoops, all spring to mind.

Prescriptions and their charges

You will most likely pay something for your medicines on prescription. Most prescription medicines are subsidized by the government so the most you will pay is $15 per item or the full cost of the medicine, which ever is cheapest.

Adults.	pay up to $15 per item.
Children up to 17 years of age	pay up to $10 per item.
Children under 6 years of age	get free prescriptions.
Oral contraceptives are not free	pay $3 or fake a headache.

These charges can be reduced further with a high user card or a community services card or a subsidy card. Charges may then be nil or in the region of $3.

If you are on a number of regular prescription medicines or you know them to be expensive, they may not be available in New Zealand and you have to: swap to something else, pay the full cost if they are not subsidized or explore one of the reduced card options listed above.

Like the UK you can buy certain medicines from the chemist without prescription. If the medicine is a Pharmacy Only medicine your details have to be recorded by law in their system. So if you are a bit bashful about buying Canestan for instance be prepared for them needing your name and address.

If you take a medicine even intermittently, bring the empty packet out from the UK when you come. It will help them this end. I asked for Piriton (chlorpheniramine) for hay fever and they'd never heard of it. They eventually sold me Dexchlorpheniramine, which is just three letters longer but does the same thing. However I suppose Arsenal and arsenic differ by just two letters with one being a panacea and the other a poison. So that argument doesn't always follow.

Dentists

You may need to do some running around to find a dentist who has not closed their books on new patients. You can always say they were recommended to you and that may get the books to open. Flattery is universal currency. I rubbed the side of my nose with a rolled up $50 bill. It didn't work and I got a skin infection. The government pays for one dental check-up a year for children under 18 years and in full time education otherwise:

A consultation may cost you	$60.00–$ 90.00
Digital x-ray imaging	$30.00–$ 50.00
Composite Restoration	$230 per tooth
Micro-abrasion treatments	$50 per tooth

To be fair, being essentially private, dentists can offer state of the art treatment, more advanced than NHS providers in the UK. Our dentist drives a Z4 series BMW soft top and I like to give him a full tank of petrol or a contribution to a weekend away in Queenstown every six months, but then he is a very good dentist.

Other services
Giving Blood

Don't bother, they don't want it. If you are British or lived in Britain you are a CJD time bomb. They don't mind giving you blood if you need it, they just don't want it back in return. There is a funny little cartoon mascot who is the New Zealand Blood Service's trade mark. He is a tear shaped drop of blood with a face and trousers, except, on a permanent advertisement on one of the routes into the city his trousers are round his ankles and the caption reads "Don't let us get caught with our pints down". A memorable way to encourage blood donation.

The service needs 162,000 whole blood units a year to cover NZ's requirements and that's without a major disaster happening. The service operates out of permanent centres rather than visiting church halls or from a large lorry in a car park. This makes the tea taste better. The blood group in demand is on display on the sign outside the building. Today it was "O negative". If supplies run low tomorrow it may read "Oh-Oh negative".

Physiotherapy and other services

These can be found in the yellow pages. Some practices are attached to doctors' surgeries. Some of the treatment may be funded by ACC but expect to pay otherwise. Chiropracty, osteopathy, acupuncture and Chinese medicine are also available from clinics for a fee. Cervical Smears also cost.

X rays

The public hospitals will have x-ray facilities for use by their patients otherwise you have to pay for x-ray services. You will see big signs outside the clinics that offer x-rays. Some of these centres will have been contracted to provide services by the local District Health Board. For example breast screening x-rays are free under the "Breast Screen Aotearoa" national breast screening programme for eligible women aged 45 to 69.

Childhood vaccination program

New Zealand has a slightly different vaccination scheme for its young people. If you are a parent you will take an interest in this sort of thing otherwise you can skip to something else as other people's children are about as interesting as watching grass grow.

There are differences between New Zealand and the United Kingdom when it comes to their respective vaccination programmes. Most notably, out here, they don't bother with BCG for teenagers but vaccinate against Hepatitis B from infancy.

A baby born in New Zealand and having all of its vaccinations would be covered for the following diseases: Diphtheria, Tetanus, Whooping Cough, Polio, Haemophilus influenzae B, Hepatitis B, Measles, Mumps and Rubella.

The Government also does special offers and the last programme was to cover for Meningicoccal B (Meningitis). Old people over 65 years of age get yearly influenza jabs and 45 year olds can get a booster for some diseases that they would already have been vaccinated against. If you are not a 45 year old or own any old people that last fact will be as inspiring as knowing the grass you have just watched grow needs cutting.

Many of the vaccines are combined ones and it is very difficult and expensive to have the single vaccines. I strongly recommend bringing a summary of any childhood vaccination history with you to make it easier for your doctor to gauge where your offspring are in the vaccination scheme.

New Zealand health risks

Mental illness

Despite the winter sun people still suffer from seasonal affective disorder here. However I do feel the locals get out and about more than we British do in the equivalent winter months. One in five New Zealanders experiences mental illness ranging from depression to bipolar to psychoses. There are regular ads with a thought provoking tag line "Know me before you judge me" to highlight the prejudice that can exist in the population. Well known Kiwis who have suffered mental illness are often used in these adverts. I think this is a good example of what Kiwis do well.

Obesity

In thirty years Kiwis have gone from outdoor people to couch potatoes, but then telly can be addictive. One in three New Zealanders is overweight and one in four is obese.

I wonder if the 1.4 million New Zealanders who are overweight doesn't have something to do with New Zealand having the highest number per capita of McDonald's outside of America? But then again it may not, depending on who might be trying to sue me.

New Zealand ranks 6th fattest nation in the western world, just behind the rather large **behind** that is Australia, showing that they can't even beat the Oz at that either.

Selenium in soil or lack of it

There is not a lot of the trace element selenium in the soil here so potentially there is the risk of running deficient which can lead to thyroid, heart disease and cancer. I take selenium when I can remember but most people don't, preferring thyroid problems, heart disease and cancer. Brazil nuts from abroad are a high natural source, but avoid Chinese sourced nuts as there have been a number of food scares from there.

Campylobacter food poisoning

The country has one of the highest rates of Campylobacter infection in the world. 14,000 people a year contract it mainly from contaminated chicken. Always operate safe food handling techniques when dealing with chicken. First make sure the chicken is dead and wipe the knife you've just slit its throat with on your jeans before making a salad with it. Where is Edwina Curry when you need her?

I saw this really interesting thing on the television the other day. It seems all our understanding of food safety comes from NASA's space programme in the 1960s. They didn't want their astronauts shitting rusty water in zero gravity so they developed a risk management strategy for food handling and we follow those guidelines to this day. Fascinating what came out of the space race. My favourite story is the millions of dollars that NASA spent in developing a writing implement capable of delivering ink to paper in space. The Russians saved a fortune and took pencils with them.

Other food scares

It is not a legal requirement here to label food with the country of origin, so you can buy a branded item thinking it comes from New Zealand and its ingredients actually come from China. This sort of thing has been in the news for a while. NZ does a lot of business with China but some and I stress some of the food stuffs have been contaminated with cadmium, magnesium or lead. Peanuts and shellfish, not to mention Fisher Price toys have all been implicated. If they are going to add things to this sort of stuff can we please have some selenium contamination which would be more welcome and useful to New Zealanders.

Maori and pacific islanders

Some ethnic groups are at a high risk for developing diabetes, heart disease, obesity and smoking related diseases. Much effort has been put into tackling the problems of these New Zealanders.

Cancer of the colon and skin

New Zealand has one of the highest rates for bowel cancer in the world. This is hardly surprising considering they eat a lot of beef and lamb. In fact they eat twice the amount of red meat of any other country in the developed world. The male attitude is it is manly to eat half a cow a day. The fact that it gives them breasts seems to be overlooked.

Dermatologists recommend wearing sunscreen everyday even in winter. I can vouch for that, my nose burnt in August (late winter) at sea level not on the ski slopes. I now have a sack with eye holes like the Elephant man had for going out in. The upside is I got a seat on the bus with no trouble.

Other health risks for budding hypochondriacs like me include:

Leptospirosis

This is the infecting organism that causes Weil's disease and is the most common work related disease in New Zealand. Scary! It comes from working closely with livestock. This is why I won't touch the urine of cows or sheep, let alone rub it into open wounds.

Cryptococcal Meningitis

If you are in NZ and soaking away your aches and pains in a thermal pool somewhere in the country you may wonder why the little sign says do not put your head underwater. The Cryptococcus bug that lives in thermal springs can get into your body through your tear ducts and then into your brain. You wouldn't want to be entertaining this fellow or any of his mates as it is a complete bastard to treat, so do as the sign says and don't put your head under the water unless you want Monday off work (probably for the rest of your life).

Giardiasis

This is a nice little gut parasite you can pick up from sheep and cows by drinking contaminated water. Infestation results in foul smelling greasy stools and diarrhoea. Nice. The reason I include this one is because the town of Geraldine in the South Island, and I dare say other places too, has had outbreaks of this disease. It is likely that it is due to farmers sinking their own wells and the run off from infected livestock entering this water source. Potable tap water is perfectly safe and is actually some of the best in the world. Treatment for this condition is antibiotics. The message I suppose is, if you are staying in isolated B&B farms you should gently probe the origins of the water you may be given to drink. A simple question like "is drinking this going to make me sh*t for England?" would probably be enough to endear you to your hosts and set up a pleasant overnight stay.

Drowning

New Zealand has numerous waterways, lakes, rivers and access to beaches, not to mention swimming pools in many a back garden. Consequently, and very sadly, drownings are far too common. Always respect water here. My advice would be use it to wash in or to dilute your scotch but never swim anywhere unless you know it is safe to do so and then be sensible and know your limitations.

Space For Your Research

www.everybody.co.nz
Consumer health information for Kiwis.

www.immunise.moh.govt.nz
Get that lawn mower out and start oiling its moving parts.

www.immune.org.nz
Good luck getting your head around the immunization schedule.

www.likeminds.org.nz
> A mental health organization.

www.moh.govt.nz
> The Ministry of Health.

www.feedingourfutures.org.nz
> A Government site aiming to help parents feed their kids right. "Do you want batter blobs with those fries mate?"

www.foodsafe.org.nz
> Advice on avoiding food related illness. "Clean, cook, cover, chill" and "Don't eat yellow snow".

www.pharmac.govt.nz
> Good luck with government bureaucracy, you may need to read this site in triplicate, before filling out form C1922837(a).

www.pharmac.govt.nz/interactive/index.asp
> Use this link to check to see if your medicine is a runner or not.

www.weightwatchers.co.nz
> Jamie Oliver pops up here, and like the Jehovah Witnesses you can't escape him so don't try.

www.workandincome.govt.nz/get-assistance/csc/
> Information on the extremely useful Community Services Card.

www.everybody.co.nz/page-03e7c39d-01a8-4f00-a4ad-51e3f8d983d7.aspx
> Allows you to search for hospitals in the country. Maybe just try www.everybody.co.nz.

www.weka.net.nz
> New Zealand's disability information web site.

www.watersafety.org.nz
> Advice on staying safe in water in NZ.

Drug Culture

I may have said this before but Kiwis are pretty resourceful. The country is quite a long way from the drug scene experienced by other countries. Being an island separated from any drug supplying mainland the New Zealand party scene has to fend for itself. There is a bit of cocaine and a bit of heroin in the country but smuggling this gear onto the islands is a bit tricky. A bit tricky is not enough to stop the resourceful Kiwis from being excluded from drug fun.

Can't get a regular supply of cocaine? No worries, we'll manufacture a synthetic version of it using what we can get our hands on. Called "P" on the streets, this is not a bladder void on the pavement after a late night booze up, but "P" for "Perfect". While not unique to NZ they make it in home labs using decongestant remedies as a base for the clandestine chemistry involved. If you want technical it is the hydrogenation of the hydroxyl group pseudoephedrine to yield a methyl group or methamphetamine.

Not without its risks the noxious chemicals used to purify the product and the very practice of rearranging chemical bonds, often results in explosions and fire in residential dwellings where the labs are sited. Ram raids of pharmacies to steal Sudafed tablets and the like are not uncommon.

Christchurch police have been concerned, because by the August of the year 2007 they had busted 14 home "P" labs in the city, while in the whole of 2006 they had only found three. This worrying trend may be due to several reasons which could easily be:

- The police are getting better at finding shoddy labs as they burn down, probably by simply following fire engines?

- Police dogs are getting hooked on the smells and are constantly looking for their next fix?

- A new chief executive has taken over in the world of organized crime and is pursuing an aggressive expansion model rather like Superdrug or Tesco's?

- Possibly organized crime is diversifying by selling off franchises?

110

If hard drugs like P are not worth the risk, then why not "BZP" (Benzylpiperazine), which forms the active ingredient of most party pills here. It is a synthetic sympathomimetic of approximately one-tenth the potency of dexamphetamine. In other words a substitute for Ecstasy. Originally synthesized by the pharmaceutical company Wellcome, it was marketed as a worming treatment for livestock.

I suspect what happened was a young cowhand from hickville New Zealand, somehow managed to ingest a dose intended for Daisy and felt good on it. I can only assume from then on, Daisy's dose was collected up every Friday night when he went out with his mates and the rest is history. Meanwhile the nematode population never had life so good.

A healthy commercial market existed until April 2008 with specialist shops selling various presentations of "cow drench" openly to anyone over 18 years. Following a number of high profile poisonings of young people in recent times it is now illegal to sell or possess BZP. Fines of $500 and 3 months in prison have been endorsed by parliament. Of course BZP is still available, it's just more expensive now as it has been driven underground.

Amazing isn't it what young people will put into their bodies in pursuit of a good time or to help score some action? In my day it was six pints of Shepherd Neame and a joint, the combination of which often resulted in someone's carpet being written off or in my case the best pair of dessert boots I ever owned; light suede with a crepe sole.

Mind you that was Guinness and white wine come to think of it. I do remember lying on my back in a field with sheep bleating all around me. Whether they had had their BZP I was far too crapulent at the time to care, but I do remember I never got any action that night. Well unless you include the back and forth action of a mop and bucket on my mum's best carpet.

Alcohol

Most shops are strict on selling and serving alcohol to young people, but young people still get access to booze, though the impression I have is it is less of a problem than in the UK. Anyone attempting to buy alcohol and who looks under 25 years old will be asked for identification to verify they are over 18, if that makes sense?

My feeling is kids in NZ play sport and have other things to do outside, like graffiti fences, rather than hang around in gangs on street corners.

In 2005 New Zealand consumed 458.8 million litres of alcoholic drinks and the trend appears to be on the increase over recent years. Not bad for a country with a population of 4.1 million and where a number of ethnic minorities, like the Asian population, often don't drink. If you are nerdy enough to do the math like I have it is 112 litres per person, man, woman or child per year. Remember a litre is a pint and three quarters.

Various TV and poster campaigns hit the message home hard about overdoing the bottle or drink driving. The ads are very good and make you think so all I can add to this is the very practical advice of not mixing Guinness and white wine.

Smoking

Smoking is especially high in young Maori women. Health campaigns target these groups as it is having a big impact on life expectancy and smoking related diseases.

From 2004 many places became smoke-free, including the grounds of schools and childhood centres, putting pay to the quick fag behind the bicycle sheds enjoyed since Sir Walter Raleigh's day. Only public schools are allowed a quick fag behind the sheds but then that doesn't have anything to do with smoking.

You can't smoke inside licensed premises so bars, restaurants, cafes, sports clubs and casinos are now smoke free as are workplaces including "smoko" rooms. This is interesting because where I worked everyone went on "smoko" at 10 am and again at 3 pm. No smoking went on but the name "smoko break" still exists.

Herbal smoking products have also been included in smoking bans so it's goodbye to the little bits of carpet and cut grass we all tried to smoke as kids. And you can't buy cigarettes if you are under 18. I suspect you can, you just need to know where. Probably the same guy you buy your "P" from. Most kids under 18 who want to smoke and drink have fake ID anyway.

It is funny in a figure of speech sort of way but the Health Boards have banned smoking on their premises even outside on their grounds. So you

112

see all these health professionals from the hospital behind, huddled around the bus stop on the pavement just off-site, having a quick fag on "smoko" break. So, pretty much the only place left to smoke is by the swings at the local park.

No Space For Your Research

www.alac.org.nz
>   The Alcohol Advisory Council of New Zealand.

www.alcoholdrughelp.org.nz
>   In researching this topic I am more than a little concerned at how much drug taking is going on here.

www.ash.org.nz
>   "Action on smoking and health".

www.cads.org.nz
>   Community and Alcohol Drug Service.

www.moh.govt.nz/smokefreelaw
>   Use this link to check where you can smoke but I tell you it is only in the car with the windows up and the children safely strapped in the back.

www.newzealand.govt.nz
>   "Find out all that you need to know about everything that Government has to offer". Now there's a challenge.

www.nzna.govt.nz
>   New Zealand Narcotics Anonymous.

www.quit.org.nz
>   Stopping smoking, easy really.

www.wikipedia.org
>   If you want to look at "P" for pure.

Chapter 9

Property in NZ

One of the first things to strike you when you first come to NZ is the eclectic mix of house designs. Some are old with heaps of character and others, much newer, often from the 1980s with 'things' stuck to them. These 'things' are often bedrooms or "sleep outs" and will poke out to spoil the flow of the building. Imagine what a hard time the Chi energy in Feng Shui has in flowing around such properties. They look horrible especially if painted in 1980's colour schemes browns, dark reds and oranges. On the other hand there are some fabulous looking properties but there is one thing that almost all properties have in common, rich or poor, well designed or visualised under the influence of drugs or alcohol, and that is they nearly all have wrinkly tin roofs.

We British know wrinkly tin as corrugated iron. That wonderful utilitarian material used to make Anderson shelters, aircraft hangers, pig sties, garden sheds and out-houses. It doesn't matter that it comes in a range of colours, profiles and treatments to stop it rusting it's still corrugated iron sheeting. Having said that, it has some wonderful properties and can look really nice, in colours other than 1980s brown and orange. Corrugated iron gives a colonial feel to the place. I am now a convert and being the nerd that I am I can recommend a thoroughly good book on the subject. "Wrinkly Tin:The History of Corrugated Iron in New Zealand" by Stuart Thompson. A really clever title I think you will agree. I enjoyed it immensely as it covered all aspects of the production including, manufacturing machinery, thicknesses available and finishing coatings plus a real bonus, some of Stuart's own poetry on corrugated iron.

> In winter a little tin house
> Let in the cold quite a lotta
> But then when the summer came later
> It got hotta and hotta and hotta
>
> The answer came as they do
> And it made the house a lot grander
> A Kiwi spectacular vernacular
> The corrugate bullnosed verandah!

114

Thanks Stuart, that was great. Actually the fact that corrugated iron is light and strong means the roofs have very little in the way of trussing so they can, and are, often converted to make more space. You do have to get up there every few years to make sure the nails haven't shifted in the weather. When I checked our roof I was amazed we hadn't lost it in one of the regular high winds as every other nail head needed banging down. You see it is the wrinkly nature of the product, the wind can get under the wrinkles and then with the metal expanding and contracting in the sun it all contributes to loosening. The truth be known, I just like getting on the roof and it has nothing to do with living next door to a sorority house.

The Kiwis like the Australians embrace the open plan living style. Kitchens, with the ubiquitous breakfast bar, are an integral part of the living space. Family room, dining room and kitchen all share the same space. This cuts out the need for walls, which after all most people only use to hang things on. A little strange to poms, this set up reminds me of the old communal spaces found in Neolithic through to late medieval dwellings. It's not completely like having a cooking pot right in the middle with a hole in the roof for the smoke to through but it's not far off. Unless you have an extractor fan over the cooker expect your cushions to smell of fried onions. There are a lot of adverts for air fresheners.

House numbering

Many people with big gardens, especially in the cities, have in the past sold them off for townhouses or smaller properties to be built on. You often see many letterboxes at the roadside showing that there are properties behind the roadside one all sharing the same house number. This accommodation can be numbered in one of two ways. The way we are used to 78A, 78B, 78C etcetera or as 1/78, 2/78, 3/78 and so on. Verbally they are described as unit one, unit two, unit three.

House prices

There had been strong growth in house prices despite high mortgage rates in recent years, up until 2008 that is. There are now some real bargains out there. A house near Dunedin went on the market for $30000 about £10,000 to £12,000. Though to be fair it needed a little work like four walls and a new roof.

Property price rises were reminiscent of those in the UK back in the late 80's. A single space car parking slot in an Auckland car park was sold in 2007 for $100,000 (about £38,500). My first house in the late 1980's didn't cost that much. The market is "readjusting" as of mid 2008.

Heating and insulation

Older homes often have little insulation and integrated heating. Our first home here had no heating at all and condensation would run down the inside of the walls in the morning. Some of the poorer housing or lower end of the renting market is responsible for "sick home syndrome" which is not to be confused with Stockholm syndrome. I discuss Stockholm syndrome in the section on leaky homes and sick home syndrome in the section on "successful kidnapping, ten ways to boost your income in NZ".

Most homes are heated by electricity delivering hot water and warmth in the following ways:

Plug in electric fires and heaters
Night storage heaters
Heat pumps
Electric radiators
Underfloor electric heating

Additional heating can be achieved with:

Wood burners	Raw wood or 'pelleted' fuel.	www.cleanheat.org.nz
Diesel burners	Look like wood burners but run off an outside tank.	www.ecan.govt.nz
Gas fires	Run off LPG cylinders located outside.	www.lpga.co.nz
More electric fires or oil filled radiators	Expensive to run	www.dimplex.co.nz
An extra jumper	Eco friendly and simple.	www.thetinshed.co.nz

As in the UK electricity is expensive. The typical usage per household is 10,000 kWh per year. This is perhaps twice the UK average annual consumption. Just to be different we used 14,700 in our first year, but then we had lots of guests and a poorly insulated and uncontrolled immersion heater. By 2007 (our second year in NZ) we had used 13,661 kWh. This was because we'd fallen out with all our friends rather than lagging the hot water cylinder.

The average cost of electricity is 19 cents/kWh plus a daily fixed charge of 63 cents.

Due to the earthquake risks piped gas isn't popular here. There is some mains gas around but not the infrastructure you'd see in the UK. In other words roads aren't being dug up every few months. Cooking and heating with gas is achieved by LPG bottled gas. Some newer houses have central heating from bottled gas which can look unsightly but it does mean you have paid for all your fuel up front, which is also the case for wood burners. A "9kg bottle" of gas for our gas hob (refilled from any petrol station out here) costs us about $30 and will last us between five and six months. A smaller bottle on the BBQ, lasts us forever.

As the sun is available for much of the year a lot of properties top up their hot water heating with solar water heating systems. There are many designs on the market and how they all work is a nerd's idea of heaven. Government grants are available to the tune of $500 and it makes sense because such systems can provide 75% of your hot water in summer and 30% in winter. These figures are higher than is achievable in Britain so payback times are shorter and they become more financially viable.

Heat pumps

The most efficient way to heat a New Zealand house appears to be what they call heat pumps. Essentially these are highly efficient refrigerators in reverse, taking heat from the outside cold air. Heat from cold air how does that work I hear you ask? The refrigerant collects the heat in the outside air and is then compressed where it gives off the heat which is fed to your rooms. They can take 20 to 40 minutes to reach the temperature you set so they are often left on over winter. In summer they can cool your living space acting like air conditioners, by reversing the direction of the hamster inside. They can deliver up to 4.5Kw of heat on just 1Kw of electricity or $3 of heat for every $1 spent. Not as efficient as perpetual energy devices but not bad.

117

Renting a house

One in three Kiwis rent. Renting in New Zealand is much like the UK with a couple of differences. The deposit for a rental property is called a rental bond and like a deposit is refunded in full at the end of your tenancy or in part if there are fewer doors than when you took up the tenancy.

Your bond will probably be 4 weeks rent. A Bond Lodgement form is completed by the landlord or agent and it and the money is held by the Department of Building and Housing, a third party which I think is a good idea. When we rented we negotiated a lower bond because the landlord could see we were responsible and mature. First impressions can be so wrong. You will also have to sign a tenancy agreement which forms your contract with the landlord. Tenancy is terminated through either a "notice to leave" or a "notice of intention to leave" form, depending on who dips out first.

Many rentals accept cats, but be warned many landlords do not let to dogs. Maybe they default on the rent more than cats? New Zealand dogs often live outside, but the dogs don't mind because they are also stoic. What it does mean to you is you may have to push your case for having the three Alsatians, bullmastiff and Australian Labradoodle as lap dogs inside or even on the property.

The tack we took was we had to spend a great deal of money having the pets flown over and consequently we were responsible owners and would therefore not allow them to bury their bones in the living room carpet.

You and the landlord both have rights and these are laid out in the Residential Tenancies Act 1986 and the Privacy Act 1993. Tenants who rent a property don't pay rates as it is included in the weekly rent so effectively you get your rubbish collected for free, but you still only get one black bag a fortnight.

In Christchurch the rental listings along with houses for sale are published twice a week in The Press newspaper (Wednesdays and Saturdays). Most agents prefer to list on "Trade Me".

We found it very hard to live in a small two bedroom unit with a cat and dog and a bike in the hallway. We were very grateful for being given the let because we had pets and no one else would entertain a cat *and* a dog.

118

We paid extra a week in rent for the animals (about $35 above the usual rent) and although we had signed a 6 month lease (usually they are 12 months) we were able to leave it providing the landlord could find someone quickly. We paid for some weeks advertising in the newspaper and cleaned the carpets professionally. Most landlords are obliging because if a case, for whatever reason goes to tribunal, invariably they find in favour of the tenant provided the tenant is a decent type.

Kitting out a new home

When shopping in bulk for a new home ask for further discount on any deals as retailers often play ball. Cash Converters is a chain store that will buy gear off you for cash often a third to a quarter of what it cost you and sell it on to the public. A sort of up market pawn shop. This place is worth checking out for bikes, some electrical stuff, ski, sports or exercise equipment. Be aware that it may be a lime green ski suit or a purple guitar, but the 1980s were a great time. I had hair then.

It is worth having a cash supply for essential house ware until your possessions arrive in NZ as this can take up to 12 weeks and you will need at least a knife, fork, spoon, cup and kettle. We bought seconds and cheap ranges of these sorts of items.

Space For Your Research

www.dbh.govt.nz/tenancy-index
Information for tenants if you are considering this route.

www.minhousing.govt.nz
Grab a look at a blank tenancy agreement form.

www.mrrental.co.nz
Why not rent those essentials household items rather than buy them. I rent 3 teaspoons, a footstool and some unused exercise equipment.

www.cashconverters.co.nz
To be honest I find them a little expensive for what they offer.

Buying a house

Like the British it is every New Zealander's dream to own their own home. Like many a Brit they have been finding it hard to get on the property ladder because of all the bloody poms coming in and buying their houses, pushing prices up and raising inflation. I feel pretty bad that we did the same thing but I take comfort in the fact that, that was three years ago and all those bloody poms that came after me were the ones who have caused all this misery. The other thing that comforts me is that buying our house made one Kiwi pretty happy and quite wealthy. We mustn't be too hard on ourselves because in migrating here we did bring money into the economy.

Most houses (but not all) are marketed by "open home". This means everyone interested can invade your house at a weekend, say Sunday between 2pm and 2.45pm. No appointment necessary, just roll in off the street. Just remember to take your shoes off and leave a false name on the register. This sort of practice has its advantages. It means you tidy your house once, disappear and come back an hour later and everyone who may be interested in your house has seen it. However it makes your estate agent's life far easier than yours, plus there are security issues. All my clothes and even my toothbrush came from open homes I've been to.

Many houses are sold by auction. Again estate agents like this as they have potential for more commission. They also like auction because the vendor has to pay for advertising. However there are a few who still market by an offer price. Coming into the market from Britain where we don't buy at auction to any extent, it can be a mystifying way to purchase the most expensive thing you will ever own. Always be sure to ask the guide price at the open home and if you are really keen get the survey done before the auction day. Go to a few auctions before you buy to see how they work and for goodness sake trim your nostril hair before you go so that you don't keep touching your nose.

Without wishing to sound hysterical if you are thinking of buying a house whose interior has suspicious yellow or red stains on the walls and doors or has a lot of dead grass outside or smells heavily of chemicals, check out its history with the council, real estate agent or even the police. It may have been used as a "P" lab in its last life. Now these scenarios are not very common but the property may be vacant or going below market price and this has caught a few people out. They then get clobbered with a large clean up bill for the professional decontamination needed to make it habitable again.

120

Equally there may be a perfectly harmless explanation for these things. For instance the previous owner may have had a large dog which killed the grass, while the stains and chemical smell could be due to a violent murder and subsequent pickling of the body parts.

Legal and surveying costs

Our costs for buying a house in late 2005 are summarized below:

Land Information Memorandum LIM Report	$150
Solicitor costs (including GST)	$675
Search Fees and photocopying	$30
Bank cheque	$5
Registration fee transfer	$50
Agency disbursement	$15
Property check (including GST)	$390
Total	$1315

There is no capital gains tax in New Zealand or Stamp Duty on property as there is in the UK and Australia. Having said that if the Inland Revenue think you are flipping houses for a living and haven't declared it....

Buying a house is relatively easy. You see a home, like it, speak to the agent and buy it. New Zealand's housing contracts are designed by the Law Society of New Zealand and are standard across the country. They exist as a pre-printed A3 sized form folded into A4 size, with all the clauses, legal bits and penalties are typed out already but where the space for the vendor and buyer's name and the price and completion date are blank. It is the estate agent who fills it in, it doesn't come from the lawyer. They get you to read through and sign the contract with your offer in words and figures and this is presented to the vendor for counter-signing if they accept the offer. Within a short period of time (hours usually) they come back to you with a yes or no. If another offer is made the contract is amended and countersigned with the new offer and re-presented.

We were told, this contract is one of the tightest in the world and once you have signed it you can't get out of it without forfeiting your deposit. For this reason make sure that the offer you make is subject to survey which will give you an escape route. You can also negotiate the deposit. We were still sorting out our finance so could only commit $20,000. Be absolutely sure

121

you like the place. We know of a woman who signed contracts and pulled out because she liked another house more. She lost an $80,000 deposit. Two years on I would love to know if her husband is talking to her yet. Always insist on including the statement "subject to finance" in the contract. If you are refused a mortgage but you have signed the contract without this caveat you will be selling both kidneys and your blood to fund a house you HAVE to buy.

There is little in the way of property chains and property falling through. Once you have signed that contract you buy that house. It is much simpler than the UK, but you have to make sure your finance is in place because you may need to pay for it within a fortnight. We could have moved in, in two weeks but we asked for a month as it was all going too fast.

The national median price had topped $350,000 in May 2007 but as with everywhere else by early 2008 the property cycle started to turn. Be careful when using median prices though as they may not reflect local changes.

Below are the various regions showing rough median house prices to give you a ball park figure of property values, from May to June 2007 and possibly at their highest?:

Northland:	$330,000
Waikato and the Bay of Plenty:	$325,000
Hawkes Bay:	$268,100
Manawatu and Wanganui:	$248,000
Taranaki:	$265,000
Wellington:	$375,000
Nelson and Marlborough:	$335,000
Christchurch	$330,000
Otago:	$230,000
Southland:	$177,750

Be aware of the following when buying a house. If the garden has been sectioned off and developed the land may be cross leased especially if it involves sharing a driveway to access the house. Check with the agent whether the property is freehold or cross leased.

DIY New Zealand

Once you have your house you can join the legions of Kiwis who trundle down to the large number of local DIY stores, paint shops and tile centres on a Saturday. Once there you will be amazed at how many bargains and gadgets there are available. More than I have ever seen at B&Q. An 18 volt cordless drill for less than a tenner? Bargain. It has lasted more than two years but the irritating thing is the forward and reverse button is the opposite to the one I had in England which has led to some bad language.

A big word of warning if DIY flicks your switch or stirs your paint. Always drill a pilot hole if you are screwing anything into wood here, especially in old houses. If you take on no other advice in this book than this I will be pleased. I have lost count of the number of drill bits and screws I have broken in holes not big enough or deep enough to take them. The wood that they made their older houses out of is very hard indeed. We are used to nice soft pine back home where a watch maker's screwdriver provides enough torque to throw a three inch number 10 screw up to its head with no trouble. The bit of wood may even be straight if you were lucky enough to find such a piece in any UK superstore. No chance here it's like screwing into concrete.

The law does not allow a "DIY-er" to engage in electrical work. You can rewire a plug, change a fuse or the element in a kettle and they allow you to change light bulbs. Anything outside these exceptions needs to be done by a qualified electrician. You can lay your own circuit (radial) but it must be thoroughly checked and certified by a sparky. Whether Kiwis abide by this I don't know. Most of them have a mate who is an electrician who will sign off the work for a cold beer. The same is true of plumbing work.

But the law is the law and must be obeyed.   Yeah Right!

There is a building code which was introduced to raise standards in housing manufacture. The building and refurbishment legislation is constantly being updated and added to. The authorities are extending this to roofing work in the next couple of years. A lot of work requires building consent from the local council before it can start and has to be signed off. If you ignore these regulations you will have trouble when it comes to sell your house. Some work can go through on the nod with written consent from the neighbours it affects, but bureaucracy has its cost and resource consent costs seem to start at $400. I have tried to make head or tail of the process reading the rules but got lost by the second sentence. If you are keen to find more then contact the delightfully bureaucratic sounding Planning Administration Environment Policy Approvals Unit at Christchurch Council on the internet link displayed later on, or far easier, employ an architect.

Buying a section

Land is still a sound investment as they aren't making any more of it and with global warming they are probably losing it. In 2005 the median sale price for rural lifestyle blocks was $247,000 in 2006 it had risen to $375,000. With Kiwis returning home and interest from foreigners "the South Island in particular is seen as a safe haven and solid option for investment"(The Press newspaper). Expect to pay upwards of £50,000 for a plot in suburbia.

If investing in a rural lifestyle block you need to check the following:

Water quality and supply
Proposed land use and soil type
Will your plans be contiguous with the local council zoning
Existence of any covenants
Fencing, standard and suitability
School and bus runs
Local Infrastructure
Neighbours: smells, noise and country activities.

Building a house

Most houses are wood framed with the finishing material over the top. There are permanent material buildings, brick or block to you and me, but there are preformed and poured concrete designs too.

Old houses were built on concrete piers to support the joists but new builds seem to be on concrete slabs which presumably are the most efficient and safe kind of foundation with the earthquake risk that exists here.

Kiwis who go down the self build route buy a section and then the plans which are often built by the same company who sold them. We have seen some great looking show homes that come with loads of extras included in the price. Things like spa bath, double shower (sexy, unless you are sharing it with your spouse's granny), under floor heating, heat pumps, double glazing and those vacuum cleaners that is just a tube you plug into outlets in the wall

124

and empty from the unit in the garage. When we investigated, a 5 bedroom home like this would be about $315,000 (about £120,000) but you could pay another $250,000 for the section of land to build it on. Then there are consents needed from the council and soon you are looking at a money pit.

All new builds and many existing properties come with the ubiquitous double garage or even triple garage. These essentials are not for storing the car in. The typical Kiwi will store his boat or trailer in one side and have a workshop, den, pool table or drum set in the other. Hence a double garage is a big buying and selling point with NZ property.

If you go down the build route or even just to modify a house be sure to engage a Masterbuilder, the federation that registers craftsmen. These guys are all the business, cordless this, cordless that, pneumatic nail guns and so on. If you don't use one of these blokes you may end up getting someone who uses a hammer to bang in nails.

You can buy a four bedroom kit home with en suite and double garage for $80,073, but obviously you have to buy the nails and a piece of land to build on. This is not something you can do while the wife and children wait in the car. This option is only for those who truly love flat pack furniture.

Leaky homes

There has been a lot of controversy about the so called "leaky homes" problem. In fact some state housing is among the worst, but who cares we'll just put poor people with no education or voice into these properties. Christchurch has some 2,600 social housing units making it New Zealand's second largest provider behind Auckland.

These sick houses impact most on the children and those with pre-existing conditions like asthma, quite apart from the psychological aspects of living with condensation, mould, unpleasant smells and the cold. Kiwis are tough and most migrants are tough but there is a limit to what anyone can endure. Research has shown it doesn't take much, just a one or two degree increase in daily indoor temperatures will raise 40% of subjects into the comfort zone.

Cheap, unqualified labourers, poor materials and rubbishy DIY can all contribute to the problem. It also sounds like my CV. Unless you are good at this sort of stuff always go for a licenced building practitioner with Certified Building Association registration.

If you do end up in a leaky home all is not lost as the government is backing a grants initiative to help individuals with leaky houses get sound repairs done.

Standard of homes

The standard and design of homes can vary considerably. I have to generalise here because I have been to a number of open homes across the city but often you can tell the quality of the build and upkeep early on (as you take your shoes off at the front door). The older villa types with weather boarding and character are well built but unless they have undergone a refurbishment they are very cold. This is a pom's perspective, one who has been reared on double glazing and central heating. The upside of having houses with no radiators is you are not limited to where you put your furniture. Look for heat pumps in the main living areas and ask about insulation in the walls and check the loft for Pink Batts. This is a popular brand of itchy, scratchy, carcinogenic glass fibre insulation and funnily enough it is pink in colour and nothing to do with flying mammals gay or straight.

As a rule newer built homes are likely to be well insulated as New Zealand embraces sustainable housing. Solar hot water systems are also a bonus as 40% of your electricity bill will go on heating water. Look also for housing with big North facing windows which quite apart from being light and airy will trap all that passive solar heat even in winter and help fuel bills.

In between newer housing and the older weather-boarded properties are an eclectic mix of dwellings. I am afraid you will have to judge for yourself what you think of the way the building is put together and ask the right questions before you rent or purchase as standards will vary.

Fencing

I have included this topic because the approach to fencing is different to the UK's. The Fencing Act of 1978 lays down certain rights and responsibilities about fences that separate you from your neighbour's property. You can't just pull a fence down and stick up what you like. Apart

126

from the obvious considerations like height, which is up to 2 metres maximum, you have to reach agreement with what goes along the common boundary because the costs are split 50:50. This is where taste and finances are added to the melting pot and notices can be served and arbitration and tribunals all add to the fun.

House Sitting

Obviously you will want to explore this beautiful country but you may have pets or a house you don't want left empty for a length of time. There are several home-sit services available. Last time we went to England we filled the bath up with dog food but by the time we came back it had dried in places and it was very difficult to clean. We have used a home sitter this time.

Actually this is a very good way to get the feel of a suburb, city or even the country itself. If you have the time and flexibility you could enrol yourself from the UK with one of the home sit companies out here and become a house sitter when you come over. Obviously you will have responsibilities but you get paid for staying in a house that you would have to have paid to rent. The down side is they will be short term tenancies (like a week). This would be an ideal way for a retired couple wanting to see New Zealand, or for someone relocating and wanting a feel for an area to buy or rent in.

Space For Your Research

Some abbreviations used by agents in adverts

Osp	Off street parking	As in it has a drive so no one can key the side of your car.
perm mat	Permanent materials	As in it's made of brick or block and not straw or wood.
Ver	Verandah	As in probably bull-nosed wrinkly tin.
Pvt	Private	As in private c/yard (courtyard).
Dble int acc gge	Double internal access garage.	As in you can go into the garage in your nightie and you won't be seen.
y/o	Year old	As in only two years old, owner going bankrupt.
ENS	En suite	As in a place to have the three S's.
WIR	Walk in robe	As in somewhere to hide a lover in an emergency.
Nthn facing	This is what you want	As in North: the sunny side of the world here.
O/plan	Open plan	As in nowhere to hide from fried onion smells from the kitchen.
CBD	Central Business District	As in cafes, bars and coffee shops to be seen in.
Sep	Separate eg Sep lounge.	As in somewhere to get away from the fried onion smells.
Lge	Large	As in subjective and it probably isn't at all.
U/F	Under floor	As in heating not bodies.
BBO	Buyer Budget Over	As in "offers over ".
SHS	Summer Hill Stone	As in a soft pink brick. Tacky looking if you ask me but obviously a selling point. I suppose it is a perm mat (see above for details).

CHRISTCHURCH specific abbreviations

BHS or CBHS	Boys High School	As in the better schools in the
GHS or CGHS	Girls High School	city and as in, expect to pay a
BHS	Burnside High School	premium on the properties in these zones.

Notes

For any abbreviations you may come across in property advertising just think text speak, insert the missing vowels and use a little imagination.

> Easy acc, sunny 700m² Sctn 6 bdrm t/house. Nelson bound.
> Fantastic in/out flow. Dble gging.

> becomes

Softly spoken, jovial but large Scotsman seeking sex in the boardroom of his restaurant. Into wrestling and bondage. No bladder problems, discretion absolutely assured.

Equally it could mean

> "Easy access 700 hundred square metre section, six bedroom town house. Owners Nelson bound. Fantastic indoor outdoor flow. Double garaging."

Zoning means the density of housing and industry that can be placed in an area. For instance:

"L2 The Living 2 (Inner Suburban) Zone, provides principally for low-medium density permanent residential accommodation. In most cases there is potential for infill and redevelopment at higher densities than Living 1 Zone."

1 hectare is approximately 2.5 acres.

Expect lots of corny alliteration and cheesy puns in the estate agents' adverts. Eg "Fabulous for Families", "A winner for the beginner" or with beachside property "Shore to impress". How about the advert for a real estate company I saw

"He sells, she sells by the sea....sure".

Bring me a bucket please and forget the spade.

Size certainly does matter

Any section over 1000 square metres in the city is a pretty good size plot and garden. A comfortable living space for a family of four would be about 160 square metres or more. Be aware a property may be described as total floor space and include the space the double garage makes up. There is a subtle difference between total floor space and living area. At the end of the day I suppose it makes no difference because Kiwis live in what we would call garages but they call houses (block construction, tin roof, no heating).

Suburbs and Christchurch's suburbs

Most cities as expected are divided into suburbs and it is worth checking with the locals which are the better ones. You can gauge this to an extent by comparing property prices between suburbs. Names on paper sound like nice places to live. New Brighton sounds like it's a happening sort of place while Merivale sounds a bit down market?

In Christchurch the east of the city is poorer than the rest and it must be one of the few places in the world where the poor people live by the sea and the rich people live near the airport.

The Coriolis Effect

I include this rather odd section in the property chapter because I don't know where else it could go. I am sure deep down you have a bit of a niggle about which way down the plug hole or toilet the water goes now that you are in the southern hemisphere. My immediate response would be: did you notice which way it drained when you lived up north? Probably not, so why are you worrying about it now? Having said that it worried me enough to find an answer.

The Earth's rotation gives rise to the Coriolis effect, discovered by a French scientist in the 19th Century. It is the spinning of our world that influences things like cyclones and hurricanes and which way they spiral and even shells fired by battleships in combat, and is dependant on which hemisphere you are in.

In reality the water goes down the hole any way it likes. The Coriolis effect should influence it in a perfect situation but factors like how the water is designed to leave the cistern, whether there is inherent movement in the water, (which there will be as you pull the plug) and the shape and volume of the water involved all impact more readily. The Coriolis effect exerts most influence over big distances and large volumes of water. Now get on with living your life in New Zealand and leave this sort of thing for sad old nerds like me to worry about.

Space For Your Research

www.bayleys.co.nz

A large estate agent. They have a nice feature on the site where you can search for property in pounds sterling.

www.ccc.govt.nz/planning

Everything from residential zoning to overhanging and protected trees.

www.century21nz.co.nz

Century 21 the NZ franchise of the American Real Estate company.

www.consumerbuild.org.nz

Building law and responsibilities Let battle begin, with how to upset your neighbour with a new fence.

www.cowdy.co.nz

A Christchurch based real estate agent who also market with property prices and not by auction.

www.dbh.govt.nz
> Department of building and housing. Advice for tenants of properties too.

www.ecan.govt.nz
> The agency attempting to protect water and air quality and promoting sustainability. Complete with rules for keeping warm in Canterbury in winter eg you can't burn old carpet in your hearth.

www.eeca.govt.nz
> Energy Efficiency and Conservation Authority.

www.guthriebowron.co.nz
> Paint and ideas shop and not the sound of the cat with fur-balls.

www.harcourts.co.nz
> 400 offices throughout Australasia. One of the big boys in the market they seem to sell everything by auction.

www.homesell.co.nz
> Home owners selling their houses without estate agents. The top sale package is only $2250 so agent savings are passed on to purchasers.

www.homesit.co.nz
> A service we have used and found to be very good.

www.linz.govt.nz
> Use this site to check property details before buying a home or land from someone you just met in the pub.

www.masterbuilder.org.nz
> Been around since 1892, but still waiting for them to pop back to finish that last little snag they promised they'd come and do.

www.nzbskitsets.co.nz
> Kit homes, but you don't have to be called Kit to buy them.

www.powerswitch.org.nz

Find out if you are paying too much for your power and see whether another plan is worth switching to.

www.qv.co.nz

Subscription site that offers full market evaluation and ability to check local sales in the area you are interested in. Impressive amount of information supplied.

www.ratesinfo.ccc.govt.nz

Check the rateable value, land value and improvement value of a property in Canterbury. Better still check what your neighbours' house is worth.

www.raywhite.co.nz

A good website because it has many prices displayed, certainly for the lower end market but it has a school zone search facility which you can exploit.

www.realtor.co.nz

A glossy freebie listing NZ property for sale. One of the top publications.

www.reinz.org.nz

Real Estate Institute of NZ. Professional governing body for estate agents.

www.resene.co.nz

Paint and wallpaper shop.

www.shf.co.nz

Diesel heating supplier in Christchurch.

www.smarterhomes.org.nz

Information on designing and building homes.

www.townandcountryhomesit.co.nz

They will water your dog and feed the plants or even live in your house.

Chapter 10

Finance and Money

The Currency

In 1967 decimal currency was introduced. Prior to this they used pounds, shillings and pence. Decimalization brought in dollars and cents. Such is my mental wiring that whenever I hear dollars and cents it reminds me of a text someone sent into Radio 5 some years back. They were discussing hip hop ganster rap of the day compared to the music of the past. This really quick thinking guy texted in with his feeling that "50 cent is only half as good as Dollar was in the 1980s". Very clever, I laugh all the time about that one as it works on several levels, but then I am a nerd.

The paper notes aren't paper they are plastic. They have a little plastic window you can see through and they melt when you put a naked flame to them. I wish now I hadn't used a $100 bill to test that out with because technically I have only $75 dollar bill left and finger burns as they melt very fast. These kind of bank notes have the advantage that they can be laundered better than most currencies, if you leave them in your jeans I mean; just don't use a hot wash unless you want to weld your pockets shut.

On a more serious note, be aware that new money drawn from an ATM (usually $20 bills) can stick together when you count them out to someone. Always double check what you hand over. Having said that the vast majority of Kiwis are very honest and don't expect a tip so will give any overpayment back to you, as has happened to us on several occasions.

Converting sterling and indeed other currencies to New Zealand dollars is always fun. Bill Gates is 34% richer in New Zealand as his net worth would be 72.9 NZ dollars. Sorry that should read 72.9 billion NZ dollars. I always forget that billion bit. I guess it is quite important.

Banking

Now I know I have approached this book in a very garrulous way at times but this is one chapter you need to assimilate and if like The Evey you are what I call a "Mrs Thrifty Bun Arms" you will understand why.

If you want to know the best place to eat while abroad you ask the locals. I see no reason why you shouldn't do the same for banks. Customers rate the small banks best. The Consumer's Institute annual banking services survey in October 2006 put TSB and PSIS at top. Each of these institutions achieved 98% approval ratings. The average approval rating for all banks was 84%. HSBC was at the bottom with 47%.

The main players in the New Zealand banking system include:

ANZ
Australian owned being the third largest bank in Australia has been part of the ANZ National Bank Limited since 2004. Has the advantage of having over 700 ATMs around the country.

ASB
Established in Scotland (England) now owned by Commonwealth Bank of Australia.

Bank of New Zealand
Australian owned by the National Australia Bank Group who also own Yorkshire Bank. God's own bank right in t'heart of God's own county. All y' chosen ones who bank with this un may find a BNZ account offers y' more. Aye, but y' knew that already cos ya can't tell Yorksh' man nowt.

HSBC
We had an HSBC account in England but in 2005 we couldn't open one in NZ from the UK despite them being the world's local bank. We went somewhere else.

Kiwi Bank
100% New Zealand owned and a very popular bank with Kiwis, offering lower mortgage rates.

National Bank
Looks very like that thoroughbred bank we had. It is also part of the ANZ National Bank and like the ANZ bank, Australian owned.

PSIS
Originally founded as a low cost co-operative to help Kiwis working in the public sector.

<u>TSB</u>

Another 100% New Zealand owned bank and popular with the natives.

<u>Westpac</u>

Was the Bank of New South Wales until 1982, and has had more name changes than the artist formally known as Prince. It sponsors the Westpac helicopter that most Kiwis, if they haven't already, will eventually get a ride in and they are affiliated to Barclays Bank in the UK.

NZ bank charges

Don't kid yourself, that we UK nationals, have free banking in Britain. At least in New Zealand they are honest about the charges. They stick a few cents on everything you get the bank to do. Standing in the queue waiting to be served? "That'll be 5 cents please madam". Please be aware bank charges exist at every step of the way. They are becoming more competitive even in the time we have been here, but it pays to shop around for the best deals.

I used my Eftpos card seven times in a month of shopping madness and it cost me $2.10 of charges.

A useful tip we checked out before leaving England was to see if our UK banks had any sort of reciprocal agreements with New Zealand banks where we could draw our UK money out from ATM without being charged.

We banked with Barclays and a Westpac ATM will not charge you for the transaction. We also know this works with the Nationwide.

Services

Internet banking is popular and we run a small account using this system. As in the UK make sure your firewall and anti- phishing software is up to date if you want your money to stay in your account.

Phone banking also exists, but I have never been a fan as I don't own a phone which might be important.

Building Societies

Building Societies also exist, so if you like putting your money in these rather than a bank, check one of the search engines for building societies in the region you are thinking of settling in. I like building societies and have had a building society account since I was 8 months old when I realized that to be a mutual society really did work in favour of the customer rather than the shareholder. I also hate carpet baggers having lent some money to a friend in need two weeks before the Woolwich became a bank and forfeited any compensation. The lesson to be learnt is don't lend anyone, any money, ever so don't even think about asking me for any because I am as mean as mouse sh*t.

A word of warning:

In the sixteen months (up to September 2007) eight finance companies had collapsed. In the last week three companies have entered receivership. One poor woman invested her husband's life insurance payout in two companies both of which went under within four weeks. These companies are the people who want your money out of the bank and into their schemes by offering higher returns. There is obviously nothing wrong with what the companies are doing, except going bust of course, but it is wise not to give them any spare cash you may have until you get to know who the big players are and you have a feel for New Zealand finances.

In my humble opinion there isn't the same scope of protection here that the FSA gives back home, particularly in the case cited where the poor woman, and she is poor now, was sent a letter assuring her that the two companies' finances were sound and it had been a good year. Two weeks later she is struggling. Disgusting. However when interviewed on the telly she said she was relieved as she had been worrying about the second company going under and now she knew that to be the case. One word once again springs to mind: stoic.

It seems that NZ was not immune from the 2007 sub-prime market in the USA and when the NZ equivalent of the FSA wrote to all the finance companies asking them how they were fairing in the present climate, many held their hands up and said that they weren't. We wait to see the long term fall-outs as the world enters uncharted territory.

Footnote: By 2009 over twenty finance companies had either folded or were experiencing difficulty.

Moving money to New Zealand

We keep a bit of money in our old English bank account and have been known to bring it over via ATM when the dollar is weak against the pound. In the meantime it sits in an "e-account" earning a little interest, but we are aware it is depreciating.

In fact if you can keep a bit of money in England using a family home as a postal address for the account it can give you some extra buying power if you bring it over when the exchange rate is right. You will have to declare any UK assets to the NZ Inland Revenue as there is dual taxation in place. Yeah Right.

Set up an internet banking account before you leave the UK and you can use the web to keep an eye on it. Don't worry if you forget to check on it. Someone in Nigeria will probably do that for you.

We keep a UK credit card active for emergencies using my parents' address as our billing address. We notified the credit card company saying we would be in NZ for several years. If we stay longer I will keep phoning them to extend it. Having some other potential pot of money even though it is basically an unsecured loan with high APR gives extra piece of mind.

We did a little experiment here recently taking some cash out of a Westpac ATM. As I have mentioned, we bank with Westpac because they are affiliated with Barclays and we were told there was no charge taking money out of an ATM with British debit cards. However The Evey took out $600 with her Barclays card and $600 with her Nationwide card. When we checked on line how they compared the Nationwide transaction cost us £215.65 and the Barclays £221.58. A difference of £5.93. I won't now be sending my Barclays bank manager his Christmas box this year. The lesson being the differences in exchange rates offered by each establishment and a further example of how charges are levied in the UK's so called free banking system.

We have found that Kiwi Bank also accepts a Nationwide card and seems to give a better rate of exchange than the banks whenever we have used it. It also has the added bonus of showing you your balance albeit in dollars which the other ATMs do not for British bank accounts.

There is a limit to what you can withdraw in a day. If you access a UK account via a New Zealand ATM and intend to draw out more money over several days you need to leave a full 24 hour period between withdrawals and not "calendar days". The machine will enjoy displaying "Sorry you have insufficient funds". This does not mean the Russian mafia have cleared out your account but that your daily limit for withdrawals has been reached.

Calculating the exchange rate

I go to the Westpac homepage or maybe the BBC business pages for currency rates. Obviously one gives you the rate in pence and the other in dollars and cents. It took me a long time to work the rates out, which is why I include it in the book.

If the rate for one dollar is **0.3776** pounds:
To work out how many dollars will buy a pound divide 1 by **0.3776**.
So you get **1 / 0.3776 = 2.648** or 2.6 dollars buys you £1

If the rate for one pound is **2.648** dollars:
To work out how many pounds will buy a dollar divide 1 by **2.648**
So you get **1 / 2.648 = 0.3776** or 38 pence buys you $1

A bit on the side

A bit on the side is always handy and my grandfather and great grandfather always lived by this adage (in more than one way come to think of it).

As I have said earlier, we keep a little pot of money in our account to exploit the differences in the money market. The aim is to buy sterling when the dollar is high and sell when the dollar is low. The New Zealand dollar is a floating currency and the Kiwi can fluctuate all over the place. It has been as low as 32.8 pence and as high as 41 pence since we have been here. That's a twenty to twenty five per cent swing depending on how you look at it.

139

We have had a letter from George Soros' attorneys in a thinly veiled attempt to intimidate us out of the currency markets, but we aren't frightened. To us he's just small fry. He may have broken the Bank of England but we aim to break the Banks of England, Scotland, Wales, Northern Ireland, Rutland and the Channel Islands.

Westpac have an international currency account from which to operate such a scheme. It is legal but you will have to pay those nice people at the Inland Revenue some of any profit you make because after all they've worked really hard for it too.

You could try the not so legal way of currency dealing. In August 2007 two burglars in Christchurch made off with a biscuit tin they found under the bed which had $80 000 US and NZ dollars in it. The police believe they were small time opportunists looking for a quick steal, the burglars I mean, though I guess the victims were opportunists too. With any luck they will be caught because you couldn't help bragging about such good "burglar luck" could you? Poor consolation for the victim. It is much safer to let the Government steal it, because they don't brag so much.

Spending money in New Zealand as a visitor

Think in dollars not pounds. Think "what is my hourly rate?" and "how long will it take me to earn the cost of this…(insert item here)". A work friend told me this very early on and it has taken a while to apply it, but it is absolutely true.

You look at something that is $30 and at its highest exchange rate it would be £12 and it might seem cheap. Alternatively you need to think the dollar price as pounds to impress the value of something, then it starts to make sense.

Be aware you will be charged some commission by your UK credit card company on a transaction if you use their card to buy something in dollars. Barclaycard for instance charge 2.75% commission on a purchase in a foreign country. Do not use a credit card to withdraw cash from an ATM unless in an extreme emergency. Cash withdrawals via a cash point machine accrue interest at 27.9% APR per day and they add insult to injury by stinging you with a 2.5% handling charge for the privilege. In an emergency I would prefer to use the £50 note tightly folded into a little glass fronted locket I keep around my neck. Very popular in the 1970s.

Do not get $50 or $100 dollar notes from your bank to bring out here, request your money as $20 bills. It just smacks of Tourist with a capital T or worse still a drug dealer. You rarely see these denominations and the locals don't know what to do with them. We paid the $8,000 deposit on our car with $20 bills and overpaid by $40 because the bills were new and stuck together, but got two of them back, just to illustrate the honesty of the folk out here.

When we paid the deposit for our house our finance was all in the UK and we hadn't been able to set up a SWIFT transaction to bring it over before the deposit needed paying. So we withdrew $20,000 in $20 bills from the ATM to put into our bank account here, so we could write a cheque for the solicitor.

ATMs only lets you take out $800 on a card in a day, so we withdrew it using all four of our debit cards. It must have looked like we were fleecing an account. No one batted an eyelid though, but we couldn't help looking and feeling furtive about it and it was *our* money. With hindsight it would have been wise to set in place something with our bank before leaving the UK so we could move money over on a nod and a wink. Something like a SWIFT transfer perhaps, which is an electronic money transfer between countries and accounts you hold.

Depositing money

Bank charges vary but it will cost you to pay your money into your account. Gone are the days when I could get paid in cash and take it to the bank to be changed into pennies then bring it back a day later to be paid into my account free of charge. It costs to pay money in. It depends on the type of account you have and your bank. Ours is pretty bad about it and we get charged $3 (or a pound) for any cash we pay into our account through a manual transaction. If we pay more than $15,000 into our account in a month (hardly likely I know) we get charged a percentage of the total amount you are depositing.

I have often thought about the remake of the film Brewster's Billions where Richard Prior has a month to spend 1 million dollars in order to inherit 1 billion dollars and learn the value of money. Bringing his money to New Zealand would be a good idea. For each deposit transaction it would cost him $3 so he would only need 330,000 trips to the bank to do it. Of course he'd have to be quick and do it continuously as you wouldn't want the interest accrued on one million wiping out a good plan.

Writing a cheque costs you money before it is even cashed. I know this can seem alien to us British as it is our money we are handling but as I have mentioned many of the banks have shareholders in Australia that need to maintain their lifestyles.

Make as few transactions as possible or check what the service charges are each month. Westpac charge $3 to process a cheque you write. Kiwi bank offer the same service for fifty cents a cheque. So it is worth shopping around. Stamp duty is payable on a cheque which contributes to some of these costs.

Credit cards

You can't apply for a credit card in NZ unless you are a permanent resident. Fair enough, they don't want you hopping out the country owing millions. We chose a "Visa debit plus" card from our bank which acts like a credit card for internet shopping for instance but removes the funds directly from your current account. All credit cards at the time of writing have annual fees and interest rates of 17% or more. For more information of Kiwi credit cards check out the "consumer.org" and "interest.co.nz" links below.

Even if you are financially independent it can be worth buying something on HP just to get you a credit history here as with most developed countries you can look odd with no credit history and it can work against you because there is nothing for agencies or individuals to check up on. It's like you never existed and you don't want CSI or NCIS New Zealand coming after you do you?

Credit Fraud

Just as likely to happen here as anywhere else so the same safety measures apply. There is an organisation that you can subscribe to annually for a small fee and they notify you whenever credit is applied for in your name. Obviously if it is you, you will be aware of it. If it is your husband, wife or some other thief you may like to know your identity has been stolen and then you can block it.

142

Space For Your Research

www.anz.com.au/nz/

The Australia and New Zealand Banking Group Limited. ANZ is the largest bank in New Zealand.

www.asb.co.nz

Since the year 2000 , it has run an award winning series of *really irritating* TV commercials following the exploits of Ira Goldstein a fictional American banker. Whether *he* caused the current crisis isn't clear, but he could easily serve as the scapegoat we all want.

www.bnz.co.nz
: Bank of New Zealand but with an Australian parent company.

www.consumer.org.nz
: Many of the reports are subscription only but some are free to any surfer. There is some information on NZ credit cards.

www.hsbc.co.nz
: HSBC the world's local bank. Yeah Right?

www.interest.co.nz
: Check out the interest rates across New Zealand financial products.

www.kiwibank.co.nz
: Owned by New Zealand Post.

www.mycreditalert.co.nz
: Keep tabs on your credit habits. Costs $40 but offers peace of mind.

www.nationalbank.co.nz
: Part of The Australia and New Zealand National Bank Group.

www.psis.co.nz
: PSIS, careful how you type it. Public Services Investment Society. A financial services co-operative.

www.sbs.net.nz
: Southern Building Society which then became a bank in late 2008, d'oh.

www.tsbbank.co.nz
: New Zealand's favourite bank (according to a survey).

www.westpac.co.nz
: Westpac Bank formally known as Westpac Trust, previously known as Bank of New South Wales.

New Zealand Economy

NZ is a small economy and can be at the mercy of the world's other economies when things go belly up. The NZ$ is fully floated so can show big swings. There have been calls to peg the currency with another to stop these swings. Might I suggest the Zimbabwean dollar?

In 1987 share prices plummeted 59% in four months. Now I am not an expert but that doesn't sound good. The old joke goes: economists have predicted seven out of the last three crashes.

Up until 2008 people here, like most places in the developed world were spending more than they earned because they were feeling secure in their jobs. Indeed they appear to buy on credit all the consumer goods a confident economy offers.

Approximately 500,000 cargo containers enter New Zealand each year. I know this isn't a conventional economy marker and it probably doesn't sound much but this is one container for every 8 people. These things are big so that's a lot of pickled onion Monster Munch they are importing.

New Zealand has one of the highest interest rates in the world making it an attractive for people to invest here. It has been suggested it is the Japanese housewife who controls the economy. Japanese rates are ridiculously low so eight, nine or even ten per cent yield is very enticing. I can imagine Mrs Taranaka finishing off the housework before settling down to upset the balance of trade in New Zealand. I guess they have to be industrious with their day because they don't have The Jeremy Kyle Show to watch, like we do.

The New Zealand economy has been growing faster than other developed countries including the European Union, the United Kingdom the United States and Japan. (I bet it ain't any more). Not so good is the fact that by mid 2008 inflation was at an eighteen year high.

Overleaf is a summary of some of the New Zealand economic markers from April 2007 to indicate what the economy was doing at that time when things felt good in the country. They can also act as a benchmark for future trends, when life had to restart after the sub-prime and credit crunch fallout.

I have included some footnotes to illustrate the rapid increase in some of these inflationary indicators.

145

Unemployment figure (March 2007 quarter)	265,000
2.158 million of 4.1 million are in jobs.	Up 3.8% on previous quarter

Petrol (per litre)	156 cents
(footnote: Jan 2008)	176 cents
(footnote to footnote: Mid July 2008)	219 cents

Interest rates for savers	7.4%
Interest rates for mortgages	9 to 10%
Interest rates on credit cards % APR	17 to 24%

Exchange rates	
Australian dollar	85c buys $1 Kiwi dollar
UK pound	37p buys $1 Kiwi dollar
US dollar	70c buys $1 Kiwi dollar

Migrant numbers	-1,260 Permanent/long-term

NZX 50 (the top 50 shares)	4230 (Sept 2007)
	3510 (Oct 2007)

Median rents (depending on where you live)	$270-370 per week

Median salary	$47,000 to $50,000 per year

These are ball park figures, collated from a number of sources to give you a comparison with the UK and an overall feeling for the economy. They are not to be used as an investment guide unless you are a big risk taker and have more money than sense.

146

Space For Your Research

www.rbnz.govt.nz/index.html
   The Reserve Bank of NZ for nerdy types.

www.stats.govt.nz/top-20-stats.htm
   See you there mister square!

www.abnamrocraigs.com
   NZ share-broking firm offering commentary on the share market.

www.nzx.com
   NZ stock market. Lots of numbers and abbreviations which mean
   something to some people.

Chapter 11

Work

Income tax

What a terrible legacy from the Napoleonic Wars. Raise a tax for a scrap with the French and then forget to abolish it when it's over. They must have seen us coming. Napoleon was stopped in Egypt and never got as far south as New Zealand but the founding fathers managed to bring this unpopular tax with them along with Polio, TB and a few lifestyle diseases too I suspect.

Currently Income tax is raised at 19% for most people. Children have to pay it as well if they are in employment, whether they work down a mine or not. At the end of the financial year they are able to claim a proportion back.

One of your first jobs should be to call into the nearest IRD office (Inland Revenue Department) and register your details. You will not be paid by your employer until this has happened. You also need the tax code to avoid being taxed at the higher rate. This will also register you for any financial assistance you may be entitled to.

Income tax is charged as follows at the appropriate thresholds:

Basic rate	15% up to $ 9500
Then	19% from $ 9501 up to $ 38000
Then	33% from $ 38001 up to $ 60000
Then	39% above $ 60,000

Interest from savings in a NZ bank is taxed at a rate of 19.5% and everyone pays it man, woman, beast, pensioner or child. The IRD "withhold" tax at source so by the time you get any interest the Government has efficiently removed their bit. Charities, Trusts and Maori Land Trust under The Treaty of Waitangi can claim some tax back.

Donate to a charity and have some paperwork to prove it and you can claim a third of it back on your tax return which they give to you as cash rather than tax relief. Careful who you approach, I asked the old boy selling Poppies for a receipt and he spiked me with the pin.

148

Parliament has recently introduced a mandatory four weeks paid annual leave. It is the first increase in 30 years as most people have survived on just three weeks paid annual leave a year, plus the public holidays and some sickies. Take care pulling sickies as this strategy only works once you have been with your employer for 6 months otherwise sick leave is unpaid.

Rates of pay

Most full time work is based on a 40 hour week. The average rate of pay (2005) in New Zealand is $19.30 an hour (about £ 7-8) with many earning much less than this. There is a minimum wage dependant on age. For an adult it will be $12 an hour from April 2008. So you won't be getting rich here. In fact workers are paid pretty poorly here.

A young person delivering free newspapers could expect to earn $10 (£3.50) for a 220 household round. I ask my daughter "do you want to deliver newspapers or own the newspaper?" "But dad I want to be an architect."

The median salary in New Zealand is around £17,000 (assuming rate of 34p to dollar). For comparison the median salary in the UK is of the order of £24,000 or about $70,000. For technophobes the median is an average. If you lined up all the salaries in order of size the median would be the one right in the middle and is about £2,200,000 below any one of the UK's 10 highest-paid bosses.

There are regional differences and if you work in healthcare the rates of pay are negotiated locally. For instance a nurse in Auckland will earn more than one in Invercargill. Speaking to people who have strong opinions suggests that district health boards in the South Island can keep the rates of pay low because there aren't many hospitals to work in and people who want to explore the South will use Christchurch as a base and will therefore take what they are given. I am sure this is the case for other professions and trades.

As usual some women earn less than men by a couple of dollars per hour. This is more apparent in the older workforce where it seems older women earn less than the men. However both sexes below 35 years of age earn roughly the same hourly rates of pay for doing the same job.

Many people get paid every two weeks as opposed to monthly. This works well for budgeting. You can also pay your mortgage off every two weeks which means you get 26 repayments in a year as opposed to 12 if it is monthly. This way you pay your mortgage off quicker.

Maternity leave

Pregnant mums are often allowed to work up to two weeks before the birth. Not because they want to but to give them longer maternity leave after baby arrives. In the UK we get 28 weeks maternity leave in NZ it is only 14 weeks. Dads get a week paternity leave at the birth to allow them time to finish all those computer games that need completing before they never have a chance to play them again.

Maternity pay is funded at the average national wage. That will be two thirds of nothing then?

Space For Your Research

www.ird.govt.nz

The Inland Revenue (boo, hiss etc), though to be fair we have found them to be very helpful (so maybe just boo and not hiss).

www.ird.govt.nz/calculators

Check out the personal tax summary calculator if you haven't got a life of any sort.

www.winz.govt.nz

Work and Income New Zealand. The Kiwi equivalent of our Department of Social Security.

Some Recruitment Specialists

www.canstaff.co.nz

www.advancedpersonnel.co.nz

www.enterprise.co.nz

www.manpower.co.nz

www.ryan.co.nz

www.teamreliance.co.nz

www.skilled.co.nz

www.nzrecruitme.co.nz

www.0800labour.co.nz

www.tradestaff.co.nz

www.coverstaff.co.nz

www.dkw.co.nz

www.drakeintl.co.nz

www.extrastaff.co.nz

www.greenlightrecruitment.co.nz

www.icg.net.nz

Classifieds sites for job hunting

www.jobstuff.co.nz
www.jobweek.co.nz
www.trademe.co.nz
www.seek.co.nz

Some sites for Entrepreneurs

www.newkiwis.co.nz
> This is a free resource for employers and job seekers.

www.biz.org.nz or www.business.govt.nz
> Information and tools designed to help you start, manage or grow your business.

www.b-vital.com
> Auckland Chamber of Commerce.

www.investnewzealand.govt.nz
> A trade and enterprise site. Beam me up Scotty.

Accident Compensation Corporation (ACC)

ACC is unique. It is a body run by the Crown to provide 24 hour personal insurance injury cover on a no blame basis to New Zealanders. In fact it also covers temporary visitors and residents (who don't have citizenship). Basically, everybody and their dog. It covers road traffic injuries, home injuries, injuries as a result of criminal activity done to you, sports injuries and not just work-related accidents. The funding is levied from your salary, employer and road tax. A sort of National Insurance?

The organization also tries to prevent accidents and injuries using various methods like workplace inspections and advice. The cover includes accident and emergency costs, reasonable medical, rehabilitation costs and most of your lost earnings (up to 80%) and provides compensation to your family if you are killed. It can also help to prepare you for a new post-injury job while topping up your salary if it pays less than your old job did before the accident. In return for all these benefits you can't sue for personal injury.

As you can imagine it has the potential to be a horribly complicated system and much more detailed than I have let on. Having said all that, it is reasonably simple to enter the scheme within hours of your injury. If you injure yourself and go to the doctor with it, you fill in some paperwork and you are in the system. You will then get some of your injury associated charges waived or subsidized including doctor consultation fees and medicine costs. I was in the doctor's waiting room once when a young male student type came in needing to see the doctor with an injured right wrist, so I guess ACC even covers *that*.

Space For Your Research

www.acc.co.nz

> Accident Compensation Corporation. The personal injury insurance for New Zealanders, temporary visitors, people who once saw a programme about New Zealand on TV…basically everybody.

Kiwi saver and Pensions

You may hear people refer to something called "Super". This is New Zealand Superannuation which offers financial Assistance for people 65 years or over. You must be over 65 (obviously) and a New Zealand citizen or permanent resident. A little bit like Harry Potter and the Goblet of Fire where age charms operate to protect its misuse. Satisfy "the Goblet" at Work and Income New Zealand and you may be entitled to $500 a fortnight.

New Zealand has one of the poorest savings rates in the world it has been said that on average households spend $1.15 for every dollar earned. In an attempt to encourage saving the Government has introduced of the "kiwi saver" acting like a top up pension.

From April 1 2008 your employer will contribute 1% of your gross salary increasing this by 1% each year to reach 4% by 2011. Employees contribute 4% of their gross salary although you can contribute 8% and this is done through the PAYE system which operates here.

All New Zealanders or permanent residents between eighteen and 65 starting a new job are automatically enrolled in the kiwi saver scheme and the scheme moves with you when you change your job.

You can opt out the scheme after two weeks and before the eighth week in your new job by telling the Inland Revenue. If you are already in a job you can join at any time but you are not automatically adopted into this scheme. **The government will contribute $1,000 to kick start the saving for you.**

Your contributions can only be accessed if you are a permanent resident reaching retirement, "permanently" emigrating or seriously ill or under significant financial hardship. However after five years of being in the scheme you can withdraw the money you have paid for a first home purchase and the government will give you $5,000 towards your deposit or $10,000 for a couple. The government contributions vary depending on your salary. The lowest earners can receive up to 12%.

A recent poll of New Zealanders showed only 35% would join. Not surprisingly it was the two extremes of society who would not be joining. The wealthy because they already belonged to a retirement savings scheme and the poor who felt they couldn't afford the deductions.

An example of how it may work for someone on $40,000 a year paying in for 30 years and electing to contribute 4%.

The government deducts $133 a month at source and puts it into the kiwisaver for you. Your employer contributes $33 a month increasing annually to $148 a month by 2011. The government gives you $1040 tax credit a year. So by 65 years of age you will have $198,153

If you opt for the 8% contribution you will have $282,950 in your pot at the end, then you'll find out who your friends are.

Space For Your Research

www.kiwisaver.govt.nz
        More information on pension contributions.

www.workandincome.govt.nz/get-assistance/main-benefit/nz-superannuation.html
        This page of the Work and Income site offers information on Super plus some stuff on Terrific, Excellent and Marvellous.

New Zealand Public Holidays

New Year's Day	Jan 1st	Celebrate this before anyone else back home in Britain.
New Year Holiday	Jan 2nd	Bonus!
Waitangi Day	Feb 6th	To celebrate the signing of the Treaty in 1840.
Good Friday	varies	Observed more religiously here than UK.
Easter Monday	varies	It feels odd to celebrate the birth of Mother Earth in autumn. Feels odd that they have less chocolate too. Again observed more religiously here than UK.
Anzac Day	Apr 25th	Commemorates forces landing at Galipolli 1915 and is NZ version of Armistice Day.
Queen's Birthday	Jun 5th	Celebrates the monarch's official birthday.
Labour Day	varies	"Power to the people" or workers' holiday like May Day but on the 4th Monday of October.
Christmas Day	Dec 25th	Open your presents before anyone back home.
Boxing Day	Dec 26th	Take those presents back for a refund before anyone else too.
Regional holiday	Varies	Each part of NZ has a separate day. Christchurch's is also called Show Day (November) which is the local agricultural show.

Those of you who keep a close eye on annual leave, which is most of us, will have spotted that there are three more bank holidays here than in the UK. Bear in mind that the average NZ full time job is a 40 hour week with 3 weeks annual leave and that only recently a bill put through parliament sanctioned 4 weeks paid annual leave. A lot of employers will make their staff take their annual leave at Christmas. Bear in mind also that the best summer weather seems to be January and February.

On religious public holidays (Christmas Day, Good Friday and Easter Sunday) shops do not trade and you don't get the endless TV adverts as there is an embargo. Shops do open on the other holidays but on some days like Anzac they don't open until the afternoon. New Zealanders support this policy of "closed all day" for Easter, though Easter Monday is busy as the shops have been shut a full 40 hours.

There is a 15% surcharge imposed on food bought in cafes and restaurants on Public holidays to cover the staff's increased rate of pay for those days. MacDonald's does not charge this.

Part of the new holiday legislation means that if you work a Public Holiday you are entitled to time off in lieu.

Space For Your Research

156

Chapter 12

New Zealand Culture and other bits and bobs

ANZAC Day

I include a section on Anzac Day because it is worth being aware of the real sentiment and respect that the New Zealand public hold for their fighting men and women, past and present. While we remember our fallen on Armistice Day the Kiwis use the first day of the battle of Gallipoli to honour theirs. I am labouring the point a bit because I think if you come to NZ to live it is only fair to stress this is a big day for them and while the Kiwis are very similar to us Brits in so many ways this is a part of their culture that is very important to them. Not that our remembrance day isn't to us, but in NZ the day is embraced by everyone and dominates the news. For this reason I think it is worth looking at the history behind the day.

The Australian and New Zealand Army Corps or ANZACs engaged the Turks in 1915 landing on the Gallipoli peninsular. 8450 kiwis landed with 7473 being killed and wounded or put another it way; an 88% casualty rate. No community, town, city suburb, village or hamlet seemed to escape without losing someone to the carnage of World War I, all those miles away.

A Kiwi blogger called Kara-Leah's states in her blog "New Zealand sent 10% of it's population to serve in WWI—more than any other country. Our casualty rate was 58%—giving us the dubious honour of having the highest per capita death rate of any nation involved in the war. 42% of men and women who were of military age (and some who weren't) served."

Paraphrasing the late Rod Donald (NZ Green MP and co-leader of the party) in one of his speeches "The percentage of eligible manpower recruited was 19% second only to Britain. 100,000 left to go to war and of these nearly 17,000 were killed and more than 41,000 wounded."

Given that the population of New Zealand in the early twentieth century would have been in the region of only one million this would have had a major impact on the small farming communities of the time. Britain felt the consequences of WWI to the point that a generation was said to have been lost, how much more did New Zealand lose?

Passchendaele was the other big ANZAC engagement and the country lost ten All Blacks among the 1330 New Zealand who died in that battle. The horror of it can only be imagined when you read that aerial photography of the battlefield showed one million shell holes in 1 square mile.

There is a national pride in what all those young men did for their country and the Commonwealth in both World Wars. All these years later, the sacrifice is regularly remembered in the news, and not just around ANZAC day. I find this sentiment very moving and I wish we had more of it in Britain.

ANZAC day is commemorated on 25th April, and is a public holiday, with dawn services at War memorials all over NZ. Dawn remembers the time the first troops landed in Gallipoli. Young and old all make the effort in rain or shine and usually cold, to be at these ceremonies at dawn which is about 5:30 am at that time of year.

I may be British but I am grateful to all those young men and women from all over the Commonwealth who in many wars who have lost their lives to keep the world free and make it a better place. Whether they would approve of today's world and the freedoms we take for granted is something else.

Many Kiwis on their overseas expedition make the effort to visit the battlefields where their compatriots fought, and pay their tributes to them at dawn on ANZAC day. The memorial at ANZAC cove offers some beautiful words that are very moving.

"Those heroes that shed their blood and lost their lives… you are now lying in the soil of a friendly country. Therefore rest in peace. There is no difference between the Johnnies and the Mehmets where they lie side by side here in this country of ours… You the mothers who sent their sons from far away countries, wipe away your tears. Your sons are now lying in our bosom and are in peace. Having lost their lives on this land they have become our sons as well."

Mustafa Kemal
(first president of the Republic of Turkey but at the time the
Commander of the Turkish counter attack at Anzac Cove)

The Victoria Cross

Kiwis have earned more than their fare share of Victoria Crosses when you look at the award per population and the most recent was made to a very modest Maori soldier, Corporal Willy Apiata, for his conduct in saving a wounded soldier in Afghanistan in 2004. A great achievement when you know there haven't been that many VCs awarded since WWII.

A section like this cannot mention one of New Zealand's greatest heroes, Charles Hazlitt Upham. Indeed a local hero as he was born in Christchurch, and one of only three men to have been awarded the Victoria Cross twice (which, by convention is cited as "VC and bar"). He was the only soldier of World War II to win it twice. He also worked his way through the ranks achieving the rank of Captain.

He won his first Victoria Cross in 1941 during the withdrawal from Crete. In close quarter fighting he was injured badly by mortar fire not once but twice and was suffering from dysentery when he saved an injured man carrying him to safety. Eight days later he fended off a German attack felling twenty two of them.

His second VC was won at El Alamein in 1942. He had been promoted to captain, and was again wounded twice during the fighting, but his company achieved their objective and along the way he personally destroyed a German tank and several other vehicles all with grenades before heading to a forward position and bringing back some of his men who had become isolated. He got patched up but upon returning to his men was overrun by the enemy and became a prisoner of war.

He ended up in Colditz because he tried to escape while rehabilitating from his wounds. Even here he continued to try to escape. On liberation from Colditz by the Allies, most of the POWs made their way home. Not Captain Upham, he broke into an armoury stole guns and went out hunting Germans. Sorry if you are German reading this but this guy was amazing and a true hero. I think I would have given up at the dysentery bit.

When King George VI had to sign off the recommendation of VC and bar, a most unusual and rare event, he was believed to have asked if Upham really deserved it. I have never been a great fan of Royalty. Many Kiwis love the Royals, even today, and the House of Windsor should feel very privileged to have such a loyal colony.

Watch out for the film being made about him. I only hope that "Hollywood" doesn't embellish it as I think you'll agree it doesn't need it. If you check out the Wikipedia entry for him he sounded a decent, honourable man with integrity which he observed throughout his life. A model Kiwi he is buried in Christchurch and I visited his grave one rainy afternoon. He died in 1994 and is buried with his wife. The plaque on his unusual tombstone is simple and modest.

Incidentally his unusual middle name probably stems from the NZ tradition of keeping family surnames alive by making them middle names.

Space For Your Research

www.wikipedia.org/wiki/Passchendaele
> Any battle in any war is truly awful but this has to be up there with the worst.

www.greens.org.nz
> Sometimes the Green's do say the right things.

www.nzhistory.net.nz/culture/the-memorials-register
> To see pictures of the memorials. Some must have cost fortunes in their day. A very touching thought.

Television

There aren't many terrestrial channels here. Maybe five or six if you include local telly and Moari stations.

TV One
TV Two
TV 3
C4
Prime
Maori TV

TV One broadcasts many British shows both BBC and ITV productions. The other channels, TV Two and TV Three show mainly American programmes. Viewers are always warned about the language and sexual content of programmes to avoid offending sensibilities. Unfortunately they never mention the whiny and tearful nature of American productions that offends my sensibility.

New Zealand only has two regular home grown dramas; Shortland Street and Outrageous Fortune. August 2007 saw the arrival of a new TV station, World TV which broadcasts in Mandarin and Cantonese.

I hope you won't be coming to New Zealand to watch television, but I'm sure like most of us you will watch it if it's on. There are some things to be aware of before you push that button and hear the cathode ray tube click into life. The first one is you don't have to have a TV with a cathode ray tube. Flat screen televisions are popular here and, if like my neighbour you don't have net curtains or blinds you may not even need a TV of your own. My neighbour has Sky but he isn't sentimental and doesn't have TCM or Sky movies, which is a real shame.

He has rugby on the whole time, and I don't understand rugby. I'm a football fan through and through. I see no point in watching thirty muscular men rolling around on the ground in the all weathers chasing an egg that has a mind of its own when you can watch twenty two men rolling around on the ground in all weathers chasing a pig's bladder that has a mind of its own.

There are some things you need to know about New Zealand television. I will attempt to summarize these below.

- Do not bring your telly out here. It will not work (well not without some effort to get it working). You may love your British telly. It may have bells and whistles and a remote control that is so impressively complicated that you only understand the programme change, volume control and standby buttons, but it stands a good chance of being impotent here.

- Get yourself a New Zealand telly. They have all types of TV here that we have in the northern hemisphere, high definition, flat screen and so on. I know for a fact all come with remote controls equally discombobulating as your UK one. Have I mentioned that Kiwis love technology?

- You do not need a TV licence here. New Zealand television is funded by advertising. If you like adverts you will be in telly heaven.

- Though there are only about six terrestrial stations, and one of those is in Maori. There is however no shortage of programmes. You must expect to revisit Hollyoaks, Coronation Street and Eastenders episodes as these run behind the UK. In fact I hope I am not spoiling the storyline but did you know that Dirty Den is the father of baby Vicky? On the other hand you will be on top of Home and Away and Neighbours episodes. If like me you can't get enough of Alf Stewart calling the latest low life "a flaming mongrel" then you will be very happy here.

- Watch out for crafty American style programming. You will be twenty minutes or half an hour into a film or favourite series and then there is a commercial break. Fine, this sort of interruption can be handled easily enough. However once you have invested a decent piece of your life in the programme the adverts come thick and fast after that, with commercial breaks at ten minute intervals then what seems to be at an exponentially reducing rate until all you want is to order a pizza or to clean the bathroom. New Zealand television buys a lot of BBC productions, but it can be disconcerting to have Fawlty Towers or Life on Mars constantly break for messages.

- This is Murdoch country him being Australian by birth, though I think, ironically less Murdoch country than the UK. Sky is available on subscription here. Many people subscribe monthly, though not at the expense of feeding the family as can be the case in the UK.

- Freeview was launched in New Zealand in May 2007 but there are currently only the terrestrial channels and a couple of radio stations. Other channels are promised in the future. What the nature of these channels will be remains to be seen, but it is safe to assume there will be more of the same adverts.

- Leave your Friends videos and DVDs at home. Friends is on TV2 at 6.30pm everyday or so it seems and then when episode 18 of series 10 is over ....they repeat them all over again......aaaaaaaaaahhhhhhhhh. The Simpsons is on 365 days a year but who can ever tire of them?

- There are some HD TV broadcasts but these are limited (mainly to those with a HD TV).

Be warned adverts are recycled. From where I am standing and see it, New Zealand is small, companies are small and advertising budgets are small, therefore adverts are recycled, season on season. It makes for reinforcing the message and is sort of quaint, if not a little irritating. Adverts are banned all day on Easter Sunday and Christmas Day and on every Sunday morning from 6 am. The 2007 rugby world cup sponsors got round it by broadcasting from abroad ie France.

At times live programming can be a little unpolished with reporters stumbling over their words or forgetting lines, but this just adds to the quaint nature of TV here.

I was stunned only the other day when the mischievous presenter of Breakfast TV attempted to read out a fax sent in by a viewer. It made

163

reference to a line from "The Sound of Music" where a character says in a German accent:

"What is it you can't face?"

It took perfect comic timing from the anchorwoman to defuse the situation but the camera bopped up and down as the support crew sniggered off stage and there was a quick cut to the newscaster who tried hard to keep it together. All this at eight thirty in the morning. Incidentally if you are interested in a TV watershed it is supposed to be 8.30 pm though the above example suggests that it might be 8.30 pm *UK time*.

I cannot talk about television without mentioning Kiwi adverts again. There are some real beauties out there. New Zealanders do not take themselves too seriously and this is evident in the nature of their commercials. Adverts on the whole, anywhere in the world, are irritating, though a good one is always worth watching again and again and again six months later.

Corporate America and Australia are here advertising in their subliminal …mmmmmm trans fatty acid way. There are also some UK brands here like a certain milk chocolate in a familiar purple and white wrapping. Made in Dunedin it is chocolate but not as we know it, so if you want the lardy, fatty version we British like, get someone back home to send some out or just get use to the Kiwi Cadbury's, which is an acquired taste.

Radio

You can get a feel for NZ radio by listening live or replaying shows via the internet.

Stations will play the current hit music. At least I think it is current, I can't tell, being over here and trying to work out what is in the charts in the UK. Debbie Blondie and Leo Sayer are new artists at the moment. That isn't true, I made that up, but there does seem to be a large amount of older material. I think it is fair to say that soft rock rocks here. Toto, Air Supply, Chicago, Bonnie Tyler and Fleetwood Mac all air regularly in what feels like an endless loop. Maybe the royalties aren't much or like Dickens or Austen there aren't any royalties to pay on older artists like Supertramp and Neil Diamond.

164

You do however, realize you are in the twenty first century when the frequent adverts offer medicinal help for your impotence or rub it in (no pun intended) with the latest offers from the local sex shop.

DAB digital radio isn't here yet so your digital radio will not work here.

For Your Research

www.freeviewnz.tv/ and www.freetv.co.nz/freeview.html
Information on free to view digital television in NZ.

www.maoritelevision.com
The Maori language station.

www.tvnz.co.nz
One of the state owned channels.

www.skytv.co.nz
Where have you been if you don't know this company? Oh you've been in a coma........sorry. Well you haven't missed much.

www.tv3.co.nz
TV station 3's website.

www.radionz.co.nz
Get a feel for what pushes a Kiwi's buttons or twiddles his knob.

www.theedge.co.nz
The Edge FM. A station for young, trendy, hip, cool and happening people like me to listen to with my Horlicks.

www.tvnzondemand
The name says it all. Learn to speak with the Kiwi accent before you come here by watching their TV on the internet in work time.

www.therock.net.nz
"Music….it's about the only thing we take seriously" Says it all.

www.thebreeze.co.nz
Lionel Ritchie and Celine Dione style music.

Swearing

Warning: Those readers easily offended were warned about the book in the disclaimer at the beginning. I cannot be held responsible for raised blood pressure and blustering speechless affront experienced with the following section.

"Bloody","bollocks", "bastard" and "bugger" are all perfectly acceptable words and should be liberally sprinkled into conversation if you want to integrate.

I read in the paper of a young man going missing in the bush up in the north of the South Island and the local constable leading the search described the missing man as "a bloody good bastard" and it was quoted in newsprint. He also received kudos for getting more than one in the same sentence. The man turned up a few days later so he was probably referred to as a dozy bugger as well.

The word wanker has been broadcast on the six o'clock news without being bleeped out and the word means the same here as we understand it in Britain, although a shag is a type of bird here. So technically not the same as our understanding?

Meaty swear words reserved for drunken brawls, finding your thumb with a twelve pound club hammer or being caught out by unpredictable homemade fireworks are the same the world over. As for "For Unlawful Carnal Knowledge" and "see you next Tuesday" these words are best left to the all male audience, though given the multicultural nature of New Zealand you can always learn the Korean, Japanese or Chinese version and then safely use it in front of the vicar, as long as he isn't Chinese, Japanese or Korean.

Swearing is not bleeped out of recorded programmes after the watershed which starts surprisingly early to me as I mentioned earlier. I heard the c word in all its horrible glory only the other day and the f word regularly pops up and down more frequently than you would perhaps like, but then I have never been a great fan of Songs of Praise.

Space For Your Research

If you are wishing to research profanities used in NZ you are as sad as me.
166

Regional differences

There is a joke that I think sums up Kiwis and their regional differences quite nicely though in a very clichéd way.

If you meet an Aucklander the first thing they ask you is in which suburb do you live? If you meet a Cantabrian (Christchurch) the first thing they ask you is which school did you go to, and if you meet someone from Wellington the first thing they want to know is which cafes have you been to.

There has always been a bit of rivalry between Christchurch and Auckland. The Southerners see Auckland as a sprawling metropolis with a population of over a million so anyone from Auckland is called a Jafa (Just Another *ucking Aucklander). What the Northlanders call the Cantabrians, heaven knows? Something equally derogatory along the lines of being tight fisted, one eyed and with one long eyebrow. What makes you laugh is the TV news will refer to Aucklanders as Jafas. "Mummy what's a Jafa?" I hear echoing around the country's living room "Oh just another fu........." comes the reply.

Kiwi names often reflect the historic nature of the settlers who colonised the country 150 years ago. Names like Dougal, Hamish and Campbell keep the Scottish heritage alive while the Australian influence is represented by names like Duane, Brent and Ross and they are just some of the girls' names. You may think this is a cheap swipe at the locals except that Bryan is girl's name and is pronounced "Bree Anne". Sorry but from where I come it's Brian, albeit a bit posh, but Brian nonetheless. As I may have mentioned I have a real disability when it comes to differentiating the Kiwi accent to the point that Ellis and Alice could in fact be the same person.

The Red Light District of Christchurch

Like any other medium to large sized city there is an active adult industry that appears to provide enough support for the world's oldest profession. The red light district is focused around Manchester Street in the city centre. The street looks respectable enough to me and isn't run down. In fact it is only a couple of streets or blocks east of Cathedral Square, the tourist magnet. Maybe it's Manchester Street that is the tourist magnet and the square is somewhere to go to kill time until it is dark?

167

There are other support industries dotted around the city. Several sorts of dancing girl clubs located in old fire stations by the look of the hardware involved, a couple of adult boutiques which I think sell adult sort of things like pipes and slippers and a healthy looking classified section in the paper.

In early 2007 there was a "Boobs on Bikes" parade through the city centre that drew condemnation and condonation in equal measure from both sides of the argument. It happened on a work day around lunch time. A bloke from my work was going to have a look during his break and we all had a laugh about how it made him seem seedy and "pervey" and how you wouldn't catch us at anything like that, but we all wanted to know what it was like when he came back. He described the "glamour models" as all a bit ropey. Pot and kettle sprang to mind as he wasn't exactly a Johnny Depp himself.

I have my own experience of this side of Manchester Street. The day before that memorable soccer world cup final between France and Italy. I met Andy from work on the slopes of Mount Hutt. Andy is an affable guy in his mid twenties from the Blackburn area, but he couldn't help that. He suggested meeting up before work early Monday at a bar on Manchester Street to have breakfast and watch the first half of the match. Fair enough by me, though it would mean a dark cold early start in midwinter but this is football and we would lay down our lives for the glorious game. I don't get out much and certainly not to the pubs, bars and clubs that dot the city centre. He explained to me where we would meet and at what time. The Evey and the kids weren't interested so it would be just me and my mate Andy. How "expat" is that to watch the World Cup in a country dominated by rugby?

Boy was it a cold dark early start to the morning. Did I mention it was midwinter? I kissed The Evey goodbye, well I kissed the little bit of hair that was all there was sticking out from under the duvet (or it might have been a hot water bottle cover I couldn't be sure), and pedaled off to watch the game. I had no idea where The Loaded Hog was on Manchester Street, what it look like, which side of the road it was on, or how big it was. I rode up and down Manchester Street four times trying to find it as I squinted through my myopia and the early morning cold. By the second circuit I had noticed her. She was hanging around the traffic lights at the intersection of one of the blocks and I guess things were a bit slow as she was eating what looked like a bag of Monster Munch. With hindsight I suppose she was hoping to catch the shift workers clocking off so maybe she hadn't been there long. It had been a very cold night and her skirt was very short.

168

She had clocked me probably on my second circuit too. By the time I had failed to find the place for the third time I groaned inwardly, even I was feeling I was acting suspiciously like a perspective punter. I took a deep breath and resolved to pass her one more time. I built up a good 30 kmh in an attempt to scoot past, when the traffic lights changed to red. Noooooo! I was stuck in the cycle lane not six feet from her. I fixed on a distant object and thought of the nuns with their moustaches who had taught me as a child. I could see her out of my peripheral vision doing all the alluring body language thing as she thought she might have a transaction in the making. I mean I don't blame her. I had after all in my naivety, cruised up and down the red light district before anyone was up and about looking for action and had done so for twenty minutes. Although I was not in a car, at least from her point of view it wasn't a tandem bike she had to get onto.

The only action I was after involved men: at least twenty two of them.

The light stayed red for longer than I have been alive on this planet and when God had finished sniggering He changed it to green so quickly I forgot I was in top gear and pulled a tendon in my groin and screamed out. She said something to me as I pulled away...I never heard what it was, probably "I could massage that for you if you like for $20" but it could have been doing her an injustice and she might of said "would I like to join her Bible reading classes". What I should have said if I was a worldly wise, ducking and diving geezer is "no thanks love I don't like pickled onion Monster Munch".

I found The Loaded Hog and kicked myself for not noticing the big signs all over its frontage the first time I scooted past it. Andy the bugger blew me out and never turned up saying he overslept. Bastard.

Space For Your Research

Do your own research I'm not getting involved.

Politics

The political system was originally based on the British one and indeed The Bill of Rights 1688 is still part of NZ law. Election of MPs is by proportional representation based on the German system. Some MPs are elected "first past the post" others on the proportion of the national vote. Elections are held every three years so it's amazing anything gets done or stays done. Indeed they have minority governments here so lots of bartering goes on, meaning even less radical policies which I suppose is a good thing, as it keeps the country moving in the same direction, albeit at about two knots.

In 1950 the Legislative Council was abolished meaning New Zealand is ruled by an elected single-house legislature with a speaker and is one of the few democracies in the world with only one House. There is no second chamber for old fogies to nod off in. All the nodding off goes on in the one tiered political system. This abolition occurred because it was felt that membership was by selection and not election and was therefore undemocratic and not what NZ was all about. The country's politics was then dominated by just two parties without anything to curb it. Whoops. So in 1996 New Zealand switched to Mixed Member Proportional voting.

The parliament building, or at least the modern bit, is known affectionately as the "Beehive". Not because it is a hive of activity with an army of worker politicians removing a continuous supply of policies and legislation, until recently, from the cloaca of queen bee Helen Clarke, but because it looks like one of those bee hives from when Moses was a boy.

Parliament is televised and what a revelation that is. Now I know our politicians fall asleep in the graveyard shift debates, or as a result of postprandial hyperglycaemia, or even just debating the rights of the latest minority cause. New Zealand politicians do the same, but to see an elected representative give his opposite number the middle finger albeit behind a sheet of A4 paper so the cameras or the speaker doesn't see it was an amusing revelation. Or maybe a government minister mouthing "F**k you" to his opposite number and then have the audacity to pretend he said something different when he realized he'd been caught on camera. I think most people have a lip reading vocabulary of at least three words of which the F word is probably top of the list. Last year two overweight, middle aged, balding MPs threw punches in the corridor. Who says politics can't be interesting?

170

If only I was one of those people easily offended I could have spluttered and stormed incandescent with rage all the way to Beehive. The first thing I would do if I was ever elected as a political leader is make sure my MPs all understood camera angles. Some of the behaviour here puts Heseltine's swinging the mace incident right down with crossing the road when the red man is flashing (and I don't mean Ken Livingstone).

The Governor General is the de facto head of state, appointed every five years, and signs off any legislation as the Queen's representative. They also open village fetes, supermarkets and hospitals. The current boss is Anand Satyanand, who replaced Dame Sylvia Cartwright in 2006 who went to Australia to replace Dame Edna.

Political parties

ACT party
> Liberals or possibly right wing liberals if that isn't an oxymoron?

Progressive Party
> A real heavyweight lefty party with one MP.

National Party
> Broadly equivalent to the Conservative Party, they are for low taxes, small businesses, free trade, and criticizing Labour.

United Future
> Centre right Christian party more tub thumping than guitar playing tambourine types.

Maori Party
> Promotes rights and interests of Maori and courted by Labour.

Labour (in power until November 2008)
> Were tax and spend, tax and spend, tax and spend. Nothing new there then. Centre left at the moment. Having said that they were $9 billion in surplus until the recession so they aren't very Labour at all.

> Footnote: by March 2009 the international fallout of the sub prime markets had eaten a big chunk of this.

New Zealand First

> Centre nationalist party, reducing immigration. Its leader was Winston Peters an interesting character who was Foreign Minister under a coalition deal with Labour. He was a right laugh and just what you need representing your country abroad. Not.

Green Party

> Greeny, lefty sorts, tried (and succeeded) to get smacking banned. Didn't go down well, they got spanked by the public over this but the legislation is in place. Any defense of "reasonable force" has gone now and you can't slap the back of a child's hand at all let alone lock them in the coal bunker with snakes.

Other political facts

Number of Parliamentary seats	120-122 (due to the MMP system)
Last three parliaments	Labour, Labour, National
Current majority	59 of 122 seats won
Next general election	November 2011
Last Prime Minister (3 elections)	Helen Clark (Labour)
Current Prime Minister	John Key (National)
Finance minister (Chancellor)	Bill English
Immigration minister	Jonathan Coleman

There is a recently adopted practice in parliament where the MPs have prominently displayed folders whose spines show their party's name and logo in large fonts. This is great for us newbies who can place a name to a face to a party. I wonder if on camera they inadvertently line up and make a subliminal message as in that Simpsons' episode ("yvan eht nioj") let's try…?

New Zealand First, Act, National, Progressive, Green, United Future and Maori.

NZF , A ,NP, G, UF Maori

NZ Maori PUFF GANja

Mmmmmm? very Da Vinci Code, but maybe I am stretching my imagination an ounce.

Youth Parliament and ministries of this and that but not the other...

The Youth Parliament is held every year and supported by the Ministry of Youth Development (yet another ministry). Candidates are selected by MPs and these young people get the chance to learn how to behave badly at tax payers' expense in the Beehive in Wellington. There are 121 odd MPs and numerous ministries. This means each member of the Cabinet has more than one portfolio. The PM and Justice Minister each have five portfolios!

Local Elections

The local elections are every three years like the national ones and candidates are elected by a mixture of the first past the post system and single transferable votes. The last election (October 2007) was a postal vote and we had to vote for a mayor, local council members, regional council members, health board members and some other bureaucratic tier which I can't now remember.

I don't know what it is like in other parts of the country but local elections here are highly amusing. One of the local mayoral candidates wants CCTV everywhere, 11pm curfews on 14 year olds and to move the prostitutes off Manchester Street as they lower the tone of the place. My guess is she'd be a Daily Mail reader if she were British. My favourite candidate, and the one who may get my vote, is opposed to the $100 million new town hall that is being built and wants to erect a six foot high statue of Mickey Mouse to represent those who work in the building. Hang on a minute won't he be working in the building if he gets elected? This same guy wants to employ "a red tape, extravagant spending PC assassin in the form of a low income earner who has to budget him or herself from week to week just to make ends meet- not a rich person who can't decide between a bottle of Moet or Bollinger, and buys both". Hang on another minute hasn't he just been politically correct himself by suggesting the job could be done by either a man or a woman? And he sounds a bit rich to me as most normal people wouldn't be able to list more than one brand of classy aftershave let alone two.

Reading the candidates' spiel it was hard to know who to vote for as everyone was so sincere and had more integrity than you could shake the proverbial stick at. All wanted the same things. I wondered why the local government is the way it is with such crusaders out there capable of wrestling such a Leviathan to the ground for it to rise, having seen the error of its ways to lead us to the promised land. Yeah right. I remember British politics being the same.

More than one candidate appeared in more than one election, suggesting they wanted power in whatever form. You shouldn't knock democracy though as it throws up some complete nutters who help you realize that middle of the road is good. The independent standing for mayor under the "Economic Euthenics" banner has tried to make us aware of the "offensive tingle ray" that slow cooks, annoys and looks inside buildings. Coupled with the "disgraceful" use of "stinging cellphone-lasers" he adds "this should not be happening during the time of a Labour Government." Try living under the Tories then mate.

This same candidate appeared in the Health Board elections under the "Electronic Schizophrenia" ticket declaring there is "no such thing as schizophrenia. It is all done with microphones, and microwave surveillance and the use of a ray that can go through walls to sting and annoy victims." That tingle ray again, now I am starting to get worried. I may have to go and construct some sort of blocking device using egg boxes and a coat hanger.

I finally realised the man was completely cuckoo when he stated that "Thrush in men is another neglected issue under Labour". Just shows you, you can't trust Labour to do anything (tut, deep irritated sigh). He ends his election statement with "You should not have to work with men with thrush". I agree completely, but Christchurch please, please, please do not elect this man to any position in local government. I will be on the first plane back to England if he is allowed anywhere near power unless it is 230v and he is in six inches of salty water with bare feet.

No, my vote is going to Jimmy Chen, a man who has lived in this ward eleven years and who knocked on my front door canvassing for votes. He stood there with a huge smile, wearing an old anorak and fingerless gloves and wore a piece of cardboard around his neck hanging there on a bit of "manky" string. I half expected it to say "spare 20p for a cup of tea?" It read something like "vote Jimmy Chen", or words to that effect. He shook my hand enthusiastically and he invited my family and I "to vote for Jimmy Chen in local election". He spoke just like Jackie Chan and then he thrust a leaflet into my hand pointing out all the things he was involved in within the community. Then with another big smile and an infectious laugh he was off out the front gate thanking me very much, presumably for that 20p I gave him.

Do you want to know why I will probably vote for him? Because he was prepared to come around to my house and ask me for my vote. In all the elections I have voted in I have never been canvassed by any candidate who was prepared to do the footwork and show that they are one of the people. But especially to show that they would make a cardboard sign as crappily as I would and to actually invite me to vote for him. I will investigate what he stands for, but best of luck Jimmy Chen.

In Christchurch the Council is structured, electorally into eight community boards. The ward where we live, gets to elect five members directly. The council appoints two more. There are canvassing boards everywhere around the city mainly on road intersections attached to people's fences. Large grinning faces are everywhere many showing teeth needing a little dental work or displaying the age of the candidate.

It is all very confusing because they aren't party candidates along the national political party lines. They have names like 2021, Save Our Water and Independent Citizens. Jimmy is part of 2021.

All the parties want to run the council more efficiently, often without the need of an assassin or giant Mickey Mouse statue. They all want to cut rates so this is obviously a hot potato here as much as in Britain. No one has suggested a Poll Tax yet. Everyone claims to be experienced, positive, strong and committed. Some candidates appear very young looking (judging by their teeth) and one or two good looking ones have had their boards stolen from the fences by admiring fans, or perhaps the opposition?

Footnote: Jimmy Chen came 4th in our ward (or community board) with 6073 and as there were 5 places up for grabs he was duly elected to represent us. Well done and I look forward to your next Rush Hour film with Chris Rock.

Space For Your Research

~~NZF A N~~ P ~~G UF~~ M   NZ MAN GUFF...

NZF ~~A N~~ P G ~~UF~~ ~~M~~   MAN U ...

~~NZF A N P G UF~~ M   NZ GAFF PUN

Maybe I'll just leave this space for your research and go and "yvan eht nioj".

http://2008.electionresults.govt.nz/
     Interesting if you like that sort of thing.

www.elections.org.nz
     Interesting if you like that sort of thing.

New Zealand Councils

You may have guessed by now that New Zealand likes bureaucracy and where better to propagate this desirable state than with lots and lots of regional councils. There are 85 councils that run NZ at a local level. To be fair there is some very good information on their websites, but it can be a bit of a nanny state. Apparently it was far worse thirty or forty years ago.

Dog registration

There are about 600,000 dogs in New Zealand, some of whom may even be quite nice. All require licensing, registering and since 2006 microchipping. These are all mandatory and failure to do so risks a $300-$1000 fine. Successful registration allows your dog to wear a dog tag. You can tell the age of the dog by the number and colour of the tags hanging from their collars. Really old dogs hang their heads under the weight of all they have collected over the years.

Current tariffs for Christchurch City are as follows but expect to pay this wherever you live:

Dogs classified as dangerous	$120	pa
Un-neutered dogs	$85	pa
Spayed or neutered dogs	$75	pa
Working dogs	$25	pa

Higher tariffs exist if the fee is paid after the cut-off period for the year, to illustrate, if it were really needed, once again, the bureaucracy of the country.

Dangerous dogs include the usual suspects, Rottweillers, Dobermans, Staffies and so on. The banned breeds include American Pit Bull Terrier, Brazilian Fila, Japanese Tosa and Dogo Argentino. Leave these latter breeds in the amnesty bin at the airport.

In Christchurch, newly registered dog owners receive an information pack which includes ten leaflets on animal control including "dog attacks: reducing the risk of being bitten", "barking dogs", "keeping two or more dogs", "dogs on the beach", "barking dogs: legislation". Talk about nanny state. I don't think my pack was complete because I couldn't find a leaflet on

"Patting your dog" or the one titled "Dogs can't open tinned food by themselves".

One of our neighbours tried to get his big old dog through on the working class tariff and the council told him to get on his bike. He appealed on the grounds that he was reconditioning the beast in a manner analogous to Graham Henry the All Black coach reconditioning badly behaved rugby players, and he got the discount. Unbelievable, but it shows you that red tape can be defeated.

When our dog passed away we applied for a partial refund for the licence which arrived by cheque together with a card from the animal control section of the council "conveying their sympathy at the recent sad loss of your dog and friend Maddie". Overleaf was the poem called The Rainbow Bridge which melts the toughest of constitutions. As a family we were touched by this simple gesture and while you can mock bureaucracy all you like, and I do, the human touch can't be beaten.

Legislation and by laws don't stop at registration and management. Many beaches are dog free zones during daylight saving time or it's a $300 fine. To be fair the restriction is around beaches where people and children congregate. You can walk you dog on the beach but well away from the well marked restrictions. You are also expected to deal with your dog's do-dos. Kicking them into the gutter or under a car is not acceptable.

Space For Your Research

www.consumerbuild.org.nz/publish/tools/councilfinder.php
>How to find a council in order to apply for planning or building consent but useful to use just to find a council.

www.ccc.govt.nz/animals/DogRegistrationFees.pdf
>The tariff for owning a pooch in Christchurch.

www.dogsafety.govt.nz
>"All about safety with dogs" which includes helpful advice on not tormenting your dog with lighter fuel and fireworks.

178

Newspapers, Mobiles and the Internet.

There are several dailies but each city leads with its own publication and regional news with national news thrown in. Sundays gives the reading public a couple more titles and at least one titivating title full of t.t.t..topics to generate controversy. Many of the articles are borrowed or bought presumably from other papers and you will see articles that have come from The Observer, The Sunday Times and the Los Angeles Times to name a few. Therefore the standard of journalism is good.

The main newspapers you will hear mentioned all have websites you can reach by "Googling" their names :

> The New Zealand Herald
> Auckland Herald
> Waikato Times
> The Otago Times
> The Press
> Dominion Post Wellington
> The Sunday Star Times

Each city has its freebies too and Christchurch seems to have plenty of hand delivered free newspapers. I have counted at least four so there is no reason not to be changing the guinea pig's bedding now.

The local broadsheet for the city is called The Press, though you will hear it called The Priss. This costs $1.20 a day and sometimes will only have ten pages in it and I should imagine somewhat reminiscent of The Times newspaper of 1864, though without the adverts for erectile dysfunction. They justify the charge by adding in various supplements on certain days of the week. So you get motoring and property and jobs and world supplements to pad it out. The property section full of rentals comes out twice a week.

You can have it delivered and it arrives in a rolled up tube in cellophane, thrown onto your forecourt. Interestingly no-one seems to pinch the ones on open display. Once in a while the publishers will deliver a free copy to houses they know don't subscribe in an attempt to encourage you to sign up. Days when that happens are good days because you get something for nothing, like sunburn.

Mobile phones

The big players in telecommunications are Vodaphone and Telecom. Telecom users have 027 prefixes, "Vodafoners" use 021.

3 G coverage is limited to the cities and big towns but Vodafone has 97% of the country covered for mobile reception. Mind you we all know when you really need your phone it will be when you are in the 3% black spot. Word in the field is despite the coverage users struggle with the mobile phone system here at times. I have never had a problem. Maybe this is because I don't have a phone.

There are some good deals out there though. One launched by Vodafone in November 2007 offered texting or calling to any UK mobile or land line for one hour between December and March 24/7 for just $2. That sounds great if only I had friends or someone to stalk.

Apple weren't going to, but it has now launched its i-Phone in New Zealand and July 2008 saw Steve Jobs announce the rolling out of the second generation i-Phone in NZ amongst other places.

The Internet

There is pretty good broadband coverage in the big cities and obviously more service will come on line. The big player is Telecom and delivers the broadband service via DSL (Digital Subscriber Line or telephone lines to you and me). Telecom is in the process of unbundling its network and opening it up for competition. When Broadband hits the wop wops there is the suggestion it is going to be twice the subscription the cities pay. This is tough because much of rural New Zealand has had to put up with poor communications for decades, be it telephone or TV reception. One company is addressing this issue and offering high speed wireless internet.

Telecom in August 2007 suffered a lot of embarrassment when having moved their email facilities over to Yahoo, hundreds of businesses email systems failed. They apologized but it meant companies had to resort to snail mail. Morale and productivity also dropped as hundreds of employees were unable to circulate emails like "why not to get drunk with your friends" and " just how does Ronaldinho get such good looking girl friends" followed by pictures of his multimillion Euro home.

180

I have to keep reminding myself that this is a sparsely populated country yet they have invested in broadband technology. We never had broadband in England, just the whiney old 56K modem, but I am now a convert to the high speed connection and while most of our telephone bill each month is broadband charge, it has been worth it.

For the nerds reading this the average advertised speed is about 13.5Mbps though this can fall to 2.4Mbps according to those organizations who test this sort of thing (speedtest.net).

Computer sockets receive the RJ45 type plug in case you were wondering, which actually means nothing to most people with a life.

In our first year here I bought a desktop computer from Dell. This is a brand I trusted in the UK and have purchased before. I liked the shape of the tower, it was tall, oblong, silver black, and had USB ports at the front. There are other factors I built into my choice of PC but these were the main ones. As in the UK you buy online or via telephone. It is manufactured in Malaysia. With shipping it took more time than a UK order would have taken but I did a comparison between one ordered in the UK and the closest one ordered in NZ, and I found that you got more for your money if ordered from NZ even with the exchange rate making the dollar high against the pound.

I would advise that if you come with laptops or a home PC you invest in a little web camera and microphone. This is a great way to keep in touch with friends and relatives back at home. Your contacts obviously have to have a web cam their end and have downloaded Skype or Microsoft Messenger to link up with you in real time otherwise it is just emails or instant messaging. In many ways this sort of investment can help your family feel less isolated as they integrate into a new life here.

A web cam is well worth the cost because linking up is free, apart from the electricity to run the computer and the carbon emissions, but we are able to talk with grandparents each Sunday. Obviously I mean the children's grandparents because mine don't seem to want to or can't communicate with me from where they are. In their defense this may be due to a configuration conflict in the software so for this reason it is easier to stick to the Ouija board for talking to them.

A word of advice to end this section: don't try to listen to the FA Cup Final Live on the internet. I waited up until 2am for the 3pm kick off, two years running, soaking up the BBC build up to the game only to have the coverage pulled for contractual reasons just as the whistle blew for the start. For this reason only get Sky TV or support a NZ rugby team.

Space For Your Research

www.ihug.co.nz

Phone and internet service provider. Cashing in on Telecom's misfortunes.

www.kropla.com/city_no.htm#new_zealand

For NZ city and country dialing codes.

www.scorch.co.nz

For wireless internet their aim is to cover as much of the rural area as fast as possible so that rural businesses can benefit.

www.slingshot.co.nz

Broadband ISP.

www.telstraclear.co.nz

Broadband and mobile provider.

www.vodafone.co.nz

Broadband ISP and other nerdy things.

www.xtra.co.nz

Telecom ISP (broadband).

Post Offices (known here as Post Shops)

You can set up a PO Box number called a "Private Bag" here, which can be handy for correspondence until you get a permanent address.

Posting back to the UK isn't free, though I believe it should be as Britain is the mother country. They don't like staples used to seal the padded envelopes but if you have to use them they have to be covered in tape to prevent postal workers cutting their fingers. This seems a bit odd to me because I thought any postal service only ever kicked parcels around the depot with their feet.

Parcels sent abroad as you'd expect are expensive and you have to fill in a customs declaration for when they x-ray the parcel. Careful how you describe the contents, do not put "drugs" on the sticker unless you want an early morning wake up call and no front door to close afterwards. Things like perfume can't be sent from within NZ as they are considered dangerous. However you can receive perfume sent from overseas without problems. Go figure that one out.

I watched a man in the queue at the post shop sorting out his large box at the cashier's window. It was a box with two pillows in it. I thought that rather odd. Why would you send someone two pillows? I guess the post shop staff have seen everything. I thought about sending a box of New Zealand air back to England, but then something shiny caught my eye and I moved onto the next disjointed thought in my pitiful existence.

Typical charges for sending letters and parcels might be:

Parcel to England economy rate 280g (world zone D)	T shirt plus its wrapping	$9.90
Letter to England	114mmx225mm (A4 folded)	$2.00
Letter	locally within the city	50 cent

Anything bigger than 260mm x 385mm x 20mm and more than 1kg sent within NZ is considered a parcel. Now isn't that interesting?

Considering that it costs about 77 pence to send an A4 folded letter from England to NZ it is about the same price as to send it the other way, but wages are lower here so relatively speaking it is more expensive. I save postage costs on birthday mail by sending godchildren cash attached to a postcard.

The quickest a parcel or letter has arrived from the UK has been four days. Typically they take around a week to ten days both ways. Plan any dispatches in advance and use economy post which is obviously cheaper. Urgent stuff can be airmailed but this costs more and I'm not convinced it is that much faster. Domestic and international destined mail is covered for $250 compensation. Up to $1500 additional insurance can be purchased too.

Despite the best of planning expect to need a personal loan to fund the Christmas postage. Twelve presents, carefully chosen for their light nature and low density were sent economy but it cost $168 in postage alone. The cut off date for economy post to Europe is mid Movember when moustaches are at their itchiest. Post anything after that and you need a second mortgage if you want them to arrive before Christmas.

Don't put jewelry on the customs declaration as they will charge you an extra $10 for insurance and it will get pinched. Such items are best described as "costume jewelry". The ladies in the Post Shop will offer extra advice like this, are lovely to deal with and as I have hinted have seen everything.

One final piece of advice is when labelling parcels it is best to put the sender and receiver addresses on different sides. If like us you put your own address in the top left hand corner you run the risk of it coming right back to you, which it did. It seems the casual labour employed at certain times of year are often Asian; and in China and Korea their convention is to put the receiver's address in that corner.

New Zealand post boxes look like this one which is the one outside my house. They are waist height, presumably for use by people with disability. Unfortunately it benefits lazy people more as they don't even have to get out of their cars to post a letter. They just pull up on the kerb, flatten the plants growing there and wind down the electric window to post the letter.

Place your letter in here

Some humans are so lazy. I have often watched these people in disbelief from my bed at 2 or 3 o'clock in the afternoon.

When you move house you fill in a mail redirection form from the post shop and they will forward your mail from the old address to the new one for six months. They also supply you with new address postcards to send to utility companies and friends to inform them of your change of address. These use free mail and save you having to write letters to everybody.

Space For Your Research

www.nzpost.co.nz
New Zealand Post.

Nationalities that make up New Zealand

Apart from the native New Zealanders there are a large number of countries represented in the migrant population who have made New Zealand their home. Consequently the big cities offer cosmopolitan eating experiences similar to anything in Britain. I have the impression that migrants from the Commonwealth countries prefer other Commonwealth countries to re-settle in rather than the Mother Land. When you think about it why would you want to come to a country everyone is trying to leave and where you have no chance of buying a house.

Some of the national communities represented in NZ and Christchurch are listed below, most live up to their stereotypes:

South Africans	Always up for a game of touch and a scrap.
Zimbabewans	Those who were wise to, or could left.
Canadians	Quieter than Americans, but still a bit loud.
Cubans	There are 36 in NZ. Not all arrived on a lilo.
British	Enough said.
Irish	Always up for a drink and a scrap.
Dutch	Some from Holland, some from Dutch East Indies.
Korean	I hear some come just to get their kids educated??
Japanese	A noble race, plenty of their cars here.
Pacific Islanders	These are people from the Cook Islands etc.
Chinese	Some locals give the Chinese a lot of stick.
Singaporians	I don't know any Singaporians here.
Thais	There are some fantastic Thai restaurants.
Greeks	Love their football, love that they <u>were</u> Champions.
Russians	I have only met one, worried most are gangsters.
Somalians	Illustrates NZ has welcomed many refugees.
Germans	Love football, and a punch-up twice a century.
Swiss	Only met one, he was not in the least bit German.
North Americans	Louder and more assertive than Canadians.
Malaysians	I don't know any.
Italians	Love football, their mamas but not punch ups.
Sri Lankans	I don't know any here.
Dalamations	At least 65 more than there are Cubans.

Brazilians have recently filled the labour shortage in Queenstown because they operate a fast track working visa system in the town. I would imagine though given the winter they've just had down there these migrants must be regretting stripping all that body hair.

186

I have just read an article in the paper that states there are more than 160 ethnicities (speaking 104 different languages including Geordie) represented in Christchurch, so that list is not exhaustive by any means. Romanians, Spanish, Chileans, Slovakians, Egyptians, Babylonians, Hittites and Etruscans are but a few more to add to that list.

It may be worth noting that with so many different driving experiences and driving styles you have to expect that other road users in the cities may not have the same superb driving skills that British middle aged men might have. Referring you to the section on the driving licence you cannot assume that all road users know how to handle a car. This is especially true for the Hittites who have only ever been used to chariots before they came to NZ.

Quite clearly many of the migrants can't all speak English as a first or even second language yet New Zealand has not turned its back on them. You the reader have the advantage of speaking the national tongue, though whether you can get the Kiwi accent is something else and it can even seem to be a different language they are speaking to us sometimes. This works both ways and Kiwis can have just as much difficulty comprehending us with our clipped vowels and BBC accents.

Three classic examples of this are:

- A lovely Kiwi bloke came to England to work and rented a room off one of my cousins. He is and will forever be known as Mack, even though his name is Mark. It's just the way he said it. For weeks they thought he was called Mack, and it stuck.

- Our dog was called Maddie and when the locals asked what her name was they repeated it with Middie, Maggie, Mattie, even Molly and all possible combinations of the syllables except the right ones.

- I work with a super lady who, in conversation with me and a fellow pom, kept going on about needing to sell some shears even though we were talking about banks and financing. It was several minutes of confusion before we could put the word into context. She needed to sell her company shears on the stick market.

Only the other day, and bear in mind I have been here three years now, I was in the supermarket at the cash desk, and as my bag of frozen hash browns was swiped through, the cashier asked me about my frozen nipples. I said pardon but I swear she asked me about my frozen nipples again. People think you are stupid if you keep saying pardon so I just said "yes it is very cold outside". I had no idea what it was she said originally but she stopped talking to me after I gave my response and I watched in uncomfortable silence as my bags were packed. After I got home and put the shopping away I noticed there was a competition offer on the hash browns' packaging for netball ("nipball", "nipples", whatever).

That great Labour Party anthem "Things can only git bitter" just wouldn't work here without appearing prophetic. I also have real problems differentiating the two words "effective" and "infective" when spoken in Kiwi.

"That's a very effective handshake you have there."

"Oh...... OK I get some antibiotics for it then."

Kiwi English also has its own rules that seem to override the Queen's grammar. The one I keep noticing is the phrase "the couple was". This is the past singular first person. Now I would have thought the correct way to structure that triplet is "the couple were" as it, that is the couple, are more than one person, or plural and hence the need for the past plural of "be" ergo "were". As Manuel would say to Mr Fawlty, "I speak Inglish very well , I learn it from a booook". Well I must be tolerant as I suppose anyfings betta dan dat txt speek.

I wait nervously, for any English teachers reading, to correct my above comments and to also bring me up on all the split infinitives I have used throughout the book so far. To save you the research, all feedback is welcomed through nerdsinnewzealand@hotmail.com.

Space For Your Research

Language

I have put together some Kiwi-isms so that while the accent will play havoc with your ears at least you have a fighting chance with the common turns of phrase.

Bach or crib
A small weekend or holiday home. Often basic in their comfort the term "bach" stems from the type of place the early pioneering bachelors would inhabit.

Bashing
A serious physical assault, not as you would expect from the term, a slapstick inflatable hammer, but usually the fists or something harder.

Biff it
To throw something away, in a bin usually.

Bring a plate (or a glass)
Means come with some prepared food on a platter. It is also good manners to return a plate to its owner with something on it. Try last night's spag bol stains and see what happens.

Bro
Brother, sister, dude. You do not have to be Maori to use it but you look and sound cooler if you are.

Bucket of arse
A pleasant way of saying "what a load of old rubbish". Given that 50% of Kiwis are overweight or obese I think the order of the day is two buckets.

Budgie Smugglers
Speedos or swimming costume (male), also known as "man skins" or Togs.

Cab
This is a rather politically incorrect term for someone who is a bit thick. Cab is short for cabbage. Do not confuse it with Cab Sav, which is not an "idiot savant" but an abbreviation for a rather nice red wine.

Caucus
In politics over here, it describes the meeting of all the members of parliament for a particular party. Buns for the bun fighting are provided by the tax payer.

Chillie bin
Cool box usually on wheels and usually full of beer.

Chook
As in a live chicken not a plucked one in the supermarket.

Chips
Are potato crisps (not pickled onion Monster Munch though).

Chips
An example of a not very good homonym. These "chips" are chips as we understand them as in "Fush and Chups". Fat and greasy like Ron Jeremy.

Crook
This means you're ill, not a criminal, unless you are a convict with a cold then you would be a crook crook and if you worked in the prison kitchens you'd be a crook crook cook.

Domain
A piece of common ground, a reserve or park often in rural areas as opposed to cities but not necessarily so.

Flip Flop
This a u-turn in politics. Thatcher's speech wouldn't work here.
"You flip flop if you want to. The lady's not for flopping" doesn't have the same zip about it.

Glad wrap
Cling film. An essential component to the Grundy Run.

Hick
A resident of Hickville, a country bumpkin from the Wop wops.

Jandals
Flip flops but not the political kind. Essential summer and winter wardrobe. It originally stems from the Japanese Sandal, (obvious really).

190

Judder bar
Speed bump. These do not stop Hooners who love to accelerate once they are through them. Though at times I have seen their "exhaust" scrape the road and I whoop and jump with delight.

L & P
Lemon and Paeroa. A NZ soft drink marketed under the brilliant tagline "famous in New Zealand since ages ago"? Now owned by Coca Cola.

Lolly
Sweets. The more unnatural in colour and the more additives they contain the more they honour the name. Most lolly looks horrible and artificial but kids and dentists seem to love them.

Look
Look, this used to really get my goat, until I realised it is not meant in the "Look listen to me" sort of way, it is used as the start of a sentence like "Hey" would be.

Manchester
I believe this is what the Kiwis call bedding. I am not entirely sure. They mention Manchester a lot in adverts for pillow cases and duvet covers, so I am only putting two and two together.

Metal road
Is a local term for a gravel road.

Mufti
Can be mufti cops or mufti day at school or work. It means civilian clothes. Stems from Arabic society where legal advisors were civilians.

OE
The right of passage to adulthood, the "Overseas Expedition" that all young Kiwis seem to undertake. Many take years to return and why there is always a bloody Kiwi at the scene of every incident around the world.

Sausage Sizzle
Bar-b-que for fund raising or socializing purposes. Expect Sausages to be the only protein on offer.

Scarfies
University students (often referring to Otago University Dunedin).

Shifting
Moving house. Sometimes they take it literally and move the house on giant trailers to a new site. This doesn't work well with brick houses so is reserved for the older wooden villa types.

Station Wagon
Another Americanism. Something we would call an estate car.

Stoked
Happy, delighted or elated.

Stubbies
These are the tight, short shorts like footballers wore in the 1970's. Sadly they are favoured by middle-aged men who wear them tighter than they were ever designed to be worn. I have three pairs. All snug.

Sweet as
Cool, no worries.

The Ditch
The Tasman Sea separating NZ and Australia. Reflecting their understated humour it is 2000 km wide.

Tramping
Rambling, not in a nerdy, garrulous way but as in a walking way and often employing an overnight stay in the bush. Try "www.tramper.co.nz" if interested.

Twink
Tippex or correction fluid. A stupid name if you ask me but then I suppose Tippex is as well.

Unsealed
A road which is unmade and has no Tarmac finish. You can't usually take your hire car down these but everyone does.

Wee
A reminder of the Scottish influence. Used far more often than "little".

Westie
A West Aucklander. Brits would know them as Chavs.

Wop wops
Rural New Zealand.

Wine cask
Wine box or if you are English a whine box. I could not make the man in the liquor store understand me, he kept wanting to give me an empty cardboard box, but at least my nipples weren't involved. I bought a bottle of Scotch instead.

Maori Language

It is fair to say, like many Brits, I slaughter any foreign language given the chance to speak it. What hope then does spoken Maori have. Despite this I find Te Reo (the Maori language) very agreeable on the ear. Many more people are speaking it now than a few years ago, and a bit like Welsh it has been rescued and spoken with pride. The third week in July is Maori Language Week, which has been celebrated since 1975.

As the language is part of the culture and history of New Zealand lots of Maori words have slipped into common use or if not common use, will be heard a lot. The secret to pronouncing the words, I understand, is to break the syllables at the consonants.

Harakeke becomes Ha-ra-ke-ke

Maori words in common use

Historically Maori wasn't a written language so the words are Anglicized. There are only 15 letters in the "alphabet" and some sounds can't be defined. The closest pronunciation sound for "wh" is an "f". So wherever you see a "wh" together in a word it is a "fer" sound. When you come across "ng" it is a nasal sound like the syllable "ng" in good Kentish words like sing, ring, fing, bling etc. Some words have numerous meanings.

The table overleaf gives the most commonly heard Moari words I have encountered say when watching the news, reading the paper or pertaining to the Maori culture.

Aotearoa	"Land of the long white cloud" or New Zealand.
Haka	War dance or challenge. It's great to see large Australian rugby players gulp when watching this performed at the start of the game six feet from them. There are all sorts of Hakas.
Hangi	Underground earth oven used for cooking food, or possibly the first missionaries.
Kia Ora	Newscasters and presenters open with this greeting.
Mana	Reputation, charisma, kudos or street credibility in today's language. Also spiritual power.
Marae	Meeting house, the traditional wood carved buildings you see. You must remove your shoes to enter.
Matariki	Maori New Year and a group of stars whose appearance starts the New Year (NZ Winter time).
Moko	Tattoos on the face, they are highly symbolic and are a privilege to wear. Bit scary looking though.
Pa	Settlement or village, maybe fortified.
Pakeha	Kiwis of European descent originally, but now anyone not Maori.
Paua	Pronounced "power" they are the giant mollusc that is a delicacy in NZ and whose shell polishes up beautifully.
Poi	Little balls on strings like numb-chuckers but without the serious injury, used in traditional dance.
Pounamu	Greenstone or jade: sacred to the Maori.
Powhiri	Greeting ceremony. It is considered rude to clap (or laugh) during or after this ceremony.

Tane Mahuta	The world's largest Kauri tree and sacred. "www.kauricoast.co.nz"
Tangi	To cry or mourn, or the funeral. You will hear this term used on the news after Maori die.
Tapu	Sacred, forbidden or prohibited.
Waka	War canoe
Whanau	Family, tribe, close friends
Te reo	The Maori language.
Iwi	Tribe.
Wai	Water. Any word with wai in it is a good bet it has something to do with water.
Hongi	Nose rub greeting. Participants are sharing the breath of life.
Whakapapa	Greeting verse telling someone who you are and your ancestry. They sound really cool. Our daughter can do hers but our surname sticks out like a nose on a face when she says it. Though to be fair, as a family, we do have big noses.

The Whakapapa for our family goes as follows:

Ko tenei taku whakapapa	This is my whakapapa
Ko White Cliffs te Maunga	White Cliffs is the mountain
Ko Thames te Awa	Thames is the river
Ko wakarererangi te Waka	Plane (aeroplane) is the canoe
Ko Ngati Ingarangi	English is the tribe
Ko Nerd te ingoa whanua	Nerd is the family name
No Ingarangi ahua	I am from England
Ko Knobby taku ingoa	My name is Knobby
No reira	Therefore
Tena koutou, tena koutou, tena koutou katoa.	Greetings, greetings, greetings to you all.

In March 2008 a car rental company got into trouble by hijacking the language for an advert. In typical Kiwi fashion it ran "Rent a car from us for $25 and visit any whaka".

Maui (pronounced Mow-ee) and the legend of Ao-tea-roa

The legend behind the creation of New Zealand or Aotearoa in Maori is pretty cool. The South Island is the "waka" or canoe that a hero called Maui was sailing when he pulled up the giant fish which became the North Island. Stewart Island at the bottom of NZ is the anchor. The bit at the top of the South Island is all wibbly and wobbly and that is where the canoe got damaged by the fish. Christchurch is where the drink holder was. A truly amazing interpretation of the coastline when you think this was the 11th century and cartography was centuries away.

The story of Maui and his life is portrayed in a stage production which tours the country, called funnily enough, Maui. If ever you see it advertised

196

go watch it. It is brilliant. I don't do theatre or cinema because there is always someone who wants to eat, talk, text, fidget, kick my seat, or procreate during the performance and they are often in my own party. Anyway if you like great stage sets, wires, counterweights and booming voices Maui is great. I barely understood a word of it, so it is worth buying a programme. It was one of the best musicals I have seen. Sung in Maori I did catch the word Maui a couple of times in it and it knocked the fur off Cats.

The Treaty of Waitangi

You will hear this mentioned a lot. The Treaty of Waitangi was signed by the Maori chiefs and the British on the 6th of February 1840 at Waitangi in the North Island. It is an agreement between Maori and Britain (later the NZ government) to protect their way of life and recognizes them as the people of Aotearoa. Obviously it has developed over the years as times change and it now asserts the right of the government of NZ to make laws and run the country but allows Maori to organize themselves and have control over the land and resources they own. It also stresses that all New Zealanders are equal in the eyes of the law. It is not without its critics and there is an anti treaty movement that mobilises to demonstrate on Waitangi Day each year. Some Maori desire a separate state. There is also a Maori flag which gets flown on Waitangi Day which seems to upset the Prime Minister. I believe it is every citizen's duty to upset their prime minister, why should their job be easy?

The Maori Monarchy is a well respected part of New Zealand's culture. The Maori Queen Dame Te Atairangikaahu died in 2006 after 40 years on the throne. Her son, the now King, Tuheitia Paki has succeeded her as monarch. It is not necessarily a hereditary title, the chiefs of the tribes chose the person they feel will represent them best. An enlightened democratic approach I feel.

Maori are rightly proud of their heritage and traditions and they have some deep set beliefs which are important to them. I am a firm believer in respecting other people (apart from those I have already dissed) and as the saying goes when in Rome, so if you come to New Zealand and have the fortune to witness a Pouwhouri or blessing ceremony watch respectfully. Do not do as some have and laugh at the body movement and language of the performer, they may just pop you one with their club as one disrespectful tourist discovered. Smile, wiping and face all sprang to mind along with quite a lot of blood.

197

I was lent a book to read called "Our Country's Story a new illustrated history of New Zealand" by KC McDonald. Published in 1963 I think "new" is stretching it a bit but I warmed to the last line of the chapter on Maori and Pakeha.

"Meanwhile it is perhaps fair to say that there is no country in the world where two races of different colour live together with more goodwill towards each other."

Forty years on there is still widespread ignorance, a degree of apathy or even hostility to Maori from some European New Zealanders or Pakeha with respect to Maori culture, land claims and perceived preferential treatment.

Space For Your Research

www.nzhistory.net.nz/politics-and-government
The Treaty of Waitangi and lots of other New Zealand history.

Emergency services

Dial 111 to summon an emergency service, but don't do it more than once a day as they get a bit tetchy about it.

Use 111 when dialling from your mobile as well. Best not use text as it could be misunderstood. For instance "local lads trapped in old mine shaft please send Lassie as soon as possible" may translate as "Bois frm d hood shft d btch L8er" and may be misinterpreted by the operator.

Police

Policing in New Zealand is by, and with the consent of the people, so like most democracies. Old photographs of the police uniform looked very similar to the British bobby. Nowadays the uniform looks much like the Australian force's but without the side arm and perhaps some of their attitude. A sad reflection of the times has the beat bobby in the populated areas wearing body armour and carrying night sticks and tasers, which they aren't afraid of using.

In recent months the force has taken a nose dive in the public's eye with incidents of inappropriate use of mace spray, drink driving and several high profile court cases of historical rape allegations, involving on-duty police officers.

If it wasn't for the serious nature of the charges around it the following would have been quite funny. One senior officer issued a warning to his force threatening serious consequences to any officer caught using police equipment in a sexual manner. The mind boggles, just what can you do with a HO/RT1 road traffic reporting form and a pair of police issue socks?

My contact with the police here has been minimal, because I am a good boy, though I did get breathalysed in a police road block the first Christmas I was here. The nice police officer was very polite gave me some pens for my trouble and didn't mace, taser or violate me with any police equipment, but then women offer the gentle touch to policing.

The local force offer a series of "bluelight" events where they take young people from school to sporting events like rugby and basketball or all night discos run by the police. The kids get to ride in the police cars as the officers chaperone the youngsters to the events. At the disco they will do light shows with their torches and then it's home via the police car. It is all designed to improve relations with the community. In the Kiwi way it gets everyone on first name terms for when they have to nick them for something in a few years time.

There is a form of community policing here in the city where volunteers sit in marked cars in crime hotspots looking out for anything suspicious. Community Watch vehicles are quite distinctive because they have net curtains on the inside which twitch when anything suspicious happens outside. They are just there as the eyes of the community and radio in anyone wearing a loud shirt or sporting a mullet haircut.

There are Neighbourhood Watch schemes here and if you register you get a weekly update showing the crimes in your part of the city. But making friends with your neighbours is the best way. Gerry over the road is an excellent neighbour especially when it comes to crime prevention and property protection. He works from home and is the good egg that comes to explore a burglar alarm when it goes off. I first met him when mine went off in the evening. We'd not long moved in and didn't know the burglar alarm number to work the alarm and it was on our list of things to sort out. I was wrestling with a large fly that had been evading the rolled up newspaper I held, so reluctantly I resorted to a chemical spray. I caught up with the fly in the hall around the vicinity of the smoke detector which I now know to be connected directly to the alarm system. This is a good thing, if you know the alarm code to deactivate it when it goes off, which of course it did in response to the aerosol I had just sprayed into its workings.

The only solution I could think of was to go into the loft to open the control box and disconnect the power to the siren. Have you ever come across a square headed screw? Neither had I until then. The door to the control box was secured with two screws that needed a square headed screwdriver to fit them. I climbed down the loft ladder to mop the blood that was leaking from my ears and to get a screwdriver while being chastised by The Evey, who in such situations of my wrongdoing is about 3 decibels louder than the space shuttle taking off. More blood leaked from my ears. Acting under pressure the only thing I could think of was to cut the wire to the claxon. Do you think I could find a pair of scissors anywhere? I cut the wire (and myself) with a pair of baby nail clippers, that have been knocking around the kitchen drawer of everywhere we have ever lived since the children were babies.

200

There were eight wires that went to the siren which I mended the following day with a junction block I had, though I needed to buy a small screwdriver, some wire-strippers, wire cutters, insulating tape and a set of square headed screwdrivers. The Evey sat there shaking her head and muttered the standard response to such events "another costly mistake".

Anyway before I ended up on my favourite topic, me, this was about Gerry. He actually witnessed a burglary in action. A dodgy looking character came down his drive and was surprised to find someone in, let alone challenging him in a gruff "what do you want" tone of voice. The man gave a lame response asking if so and so lived here and Gerry said no they don't who's asking? This guy gives him a name and leaves with a flea in his ear. Gerry goes back to work and the character then goes next door and proceeds to burgle that property. Gerry is gobsmacked as we all would be but he phones the police while watching it unfold next door giving the Bill a description of the man, his car and number plate and as it happens his real name. Result.

Ambulance

There aren't any Ambulance Trusts here, but there is the good old St John's Ambulance though. While the cities are well represented rural areas can lose out a bit on the ambulance service.

I heard a story from an Emergency Department nurse working here that they don't get as many really serious car crash patients presenting to casualty in New Zealand. This is because they die at the scene. There are apparently only two trained paramedics outside of Auckland, though surely this will change in time? I can't independently verify this though I am aware that helicopter rescue teams have an advanced paramedic on board as part of the crew. However I do know that some rural areas of New Zealand are manned by single crew (driver only) ambulances.

The lesson is to drive carefully, especially in the rural areas. There is the rescue helicopter sponsored by the Lions and another by the bank, Westpac. Known as the Lion and Westpac helicopters respectively, they are very busy moving seriously ill or injured people around the country. This knowledge helps to focus the spirit of self reliance that exists here that I have mentioned before. The Westpac helicopter can airlift you off Mount Hutt and into Christchurch Hospital in 35 minutes. A journey that takes nearly two hours by road. As we live under the flight path I have wondered if they'd be prepared to do their bit for global warming and take one car off the road once in a while, preferably in the winter ski season and on a Sunday.

I have to confirm it but my understanding is there is a charge to call the ambulance out, something in the region of $50-$80. This can be claimed back when all the dust has settled and the paperwork and ACC sorted out, however it has the potential to leave a good Samaritan out of pocket. Most people have done some sort of first aid training. Almost the same rules apply here. Know your ABC: airway, breathing, circulation though I would add it should be ABC Mobile. Check the victim for a mobile phone and ring the ambulance on that.

Fire

New Zealand Fire Service has around 800 appliances, which doesn't sound a lot. It has 1700 professionals and backed up by 8000 volunteers who make up the part time crews. They seem to fight a lot of scrub fires and attend a lot of car crashes. On your travels you will see lots of road side boards indicating the fire risk for the area you are travelling through. In a dry summer, scrub fires can be devastating. Farmers needing to burn off land as part of land management have to have permits to light any fires but even they can find the fires burn out of control. Discarded bottles act like magnifying glasses and careless cigarettes and camp fires all add to the risk.

Quite amazingly 40% of their call outs can be false alarms, which I find staggering and more than a little alarming if you will excuse the pun. On examination most of these are due to faulty fire alarm systems. False alarms are charged at a $1000 a go plus GST which strikes me as a high price to pay to get close to a fireman. Buy the calendar as it works out cheaper.

Coastguard

Like our coastguard, this is a volunteer run service but they also have spotter planes. The North Island may have better coverage because the whole of the west coast in the South Island isn't covered. As the country is surrounded by sea, the ocean is in their blood and they love their fishing, many kiwis have boats.

We sat and watched a group of four young lads launch their tiny aluminium boat in crashing foam off Northland a few years back. It was about an hour from twilight, it was autumn, they were in t shirts and shorts and of course no life jackets. Oh to be young and foolhardy again. Whether they ever made it back to shore I never knew because it was getting near bedtime, I needed my Ovaltine and the six o'clock news was due to start.....in an hour.

Civil Defence

The Ministry of Civil Defence and Emergency Management helps prepare the country for the potential natural disasters that could befall it. These include:

Earthquake	A fault line runs through the entire country where two tectonic plates meet.
Tsunami	Following an earthquake most probably in Chile the next stop is the east coast of New Zealand. My mother in England phoned us one morning to tell us a Tsunami warning had been issued. The government here never issued one. Fortunately nothing happened, but people were a little upset (but stoic). In Christchurch there is an 80% risk of a two metre high tsunami reaching the coast in the next 100 years.
Volcanic eruptions	New Zealand has been formed from volcanic activity. The Banks Peninsula off Christchurch is a huge volcano that erupted for two million years. Fortunately extinct now as you could get a bit bored with such a long eruption. There is a great publication on "Living with Volcanoes" complete with the national contingency plan summarised as … Ruunnn.
Flooding	A risk in many places around New Zealand.
Twisters	Taranaki and New Plymouth were hit in 2007. It swept through a trailer park, and when interviewed for the telly, one very large Englishman said he was saved from injury only by his fridge falling on him (I believe he ate himself out to raise the alarm).

One thing I like about the style of government here is the large amount of websites and information to educate people. It illustrates my belief that Kiwis are a self reliant breed and the government probably likes to keep it that way. It's cheaper.

Schools including pre-schools practice regularly what to do for tsunamis and earthquakes. My teenage children react instinctively to three long notes on the recorder leaping up to rescue the class hamster and vacating the Wendy house in a calm and sensible manner.

Everyone is encouraged to put together a survival kit and have an emergency plan. Now that I have lived in New Zealand if I ever go back to the UK I will definitely put together a survival kit. The one I have here has never been used, thankfully, except to pinch the UHT milk out of it when we have run dry of proper milk. I am rightly proud of this kit. My family has mocked me for the cost of it and the space it takes up. I have thought of everything, though. There are thick polythene bags for putting daily body waste into and four sheets of triple ply loo roll per person per day.

The Evey and the small people have asked for Imodium tablets to be included because they refuse to do their constitution in a polythene bag no matter how thick it is and request a drug induced constipation for the duration of the emergency. I, for one, am happy to use this set up provided there is a good supply of magazines to read and some rope to support my squatting frame as I don't think my leg muscles are up to it.

Earthquake Commission

This is the governmental organization that provides insurance cover for all the potentially nasty natural disasters that could befall you here as listed above. Earthquake insurance cover is automatic when you take out a home insurance policy. I like the website because it has a page listing the last earthquake to hit New Zealand. At the time of writing the last one was south of Nelson at 5.58am two days ago and measured 4.0. The biggest earthquake, to hit NZ since the Europeans arrived in 1830, was in 1968 on the West Coast. It measured 7.1 on the Richter Scale. The Richter scale is logarithmic which means a 4.0 is ten times stronger than a 3.0. The 2004 Boxing Day Tsunami was a huge 9.3.

Justices of the Peace

Just a quick comment about JPs. They are not an emergency service I know but there is something comforting in the knowledge they are everywhere, living amongst us. You wouldn't know it unless you looked in the telephone book. There appears to be pages of them. This gives the impression that every street has one. Ordinary people need not worry they do no harm and will not spring into action unless the world is threatened and there are lots of citizens needing documents to validate. They are extremely helpful and carry out many civic duties free of charge. We have had many a document verified by our local JPs who have so much integrity they would accept nothing more than a slice of chocolate cake for their troubles.

Jury Service

You don't have to vote but it is illegal not to register on the electoral roll. Consequently you may be called for jury service. You don't have to be a Kiwi or have permanent residency. The Evey got called up for service within eighteen months of us being here.

Space For Your Research

www.justice.govt.nz
   For more information on how to buy a jury in NZ

www.nzcoastguard.org.nz
   The RNLI kiwi style.

http://eqiq.org.nz/iqhome.aspx

Everything about earthquakes in NZ. There is a really great
animated house in which you can create your own quake and see the
damage each magnitude causes. I liked the fruit rolling off the table
shortly before you get squidged by your furniture and your "family
treasures become shattered memories" a bit like your tibia, fibula
and pelvis. Are you still sure you want to come here? If you go to
Wellington go to Te Papa museum and try the shaking house display
they have in their earthquake section. Some extra advice: don't wear
roller skates in an earthquake as you'll likely do yourself a mischief.

www.geonet.org.nz

Up to the minute information on where the latest earthquake was.

www.civildefence.govt.nz

"Don't panic Mr Mainwaring".

www.getthru.govt.nz/

A good site with lists of things you will need or what to think about
if a disaster strikes. Accessed from anywhere in the world the lists
may be useful to Brits following the dreadful Summer of 2007.

Insurance in New Zealand

www.ami.co.nz

AMI (Assured Mutual Insurance) an 81 year old New Zealand
owned company.

www.state.co.nz

STATE a 100 year old company but now owned by the Australians.

www.aa.co.nz

The AA wins as it is *104* years old and started life as the Auckland
Automobile Association.

206

Cuisine in New Zealand

When you talk to the natives you realize that it wasn't that long ago they existed on "meat and two veg" and they had nothing to do with this fancy foreign food. In the last ten years or so with its place in the world tourism economy and its immigration policies, New Zealand has embraced world cuisine.

If you go to the main centres of population you will be spoilt for choice and whatever takes your fancy is available, though I doubt you will get ortolan, on any menu here (even in "French" Akaroa). The Kiwi's national dish is still "fush and chups": at least that's what it sounds like. Eggs Benedict appears on a lot of breakfast menus and I have sampled this all over NZ and it has always been very good.

On the tourist routes there are some excellent cafes, restaurants and hotels delivering high quality food. I have had some really lovely meals here and I struggle to think of a poor meal I've consumed. There is even a small vegetarian Chinese restaurant and take away within 1 km of where we live that is exceptional.

I left a town in the southeast of England with a very good Indian restaurant and as human nature is the way it is you compare every curry you have with the gold standard of your favourite takeaway. However one of Christchurch's Indians comes pretty close.

You have to keep reminding yourself this is a country with a population of just over four million as they seem to deliver high standards on many fronts, in a typically unpretentious Kiwi sort of way. You can dine pretentiously if you want but in my limited experience here those restaurants don't ever seem to be full. This may be because only tourists and the elite can afford it but I suspect it is more that the average Kiwi feels at home in a place where he or she can dress casually and eat in a laid back fashion, but not in the laid back Roman way as that path always leads to indigestion.

I remind you again that New Zealanders are a resourceful, self reliant breed and to feel at home here you have to possess a bit of that yourself. I will say however that too many of their recipes have desiccated coconut in them. That stringy, distinct flavour and texture reminds me of school dinner desserts and ruins anything it has been added to.

I have embraced some of this self reliance and have started making bread. I really like the workout you get from kneading the dough as it tightens all those torso and arm muscles while removing old paint, car grease and the ancient grime from under your fingernails. If anyone asks I say it is coconut bread. Incidentally on the subject of bread, folic acid will be added to all bread except unleavened and organic within the next two years. So if you object to this you will have to make your own anyway.

New Zealand has in one way gone to the other extreme with the hugely popular annual Wildfoods Festival in Hokitika held in March. Bushtucker delights such as Mountain Oysters and Huhu grubs are just some of the dishes on the menu. Like me the first time you hear the term you could be forgiven for your initial flash of understanding. Yes there are sea level fossils on Everest so why not oysters in the mountains? The Homer Simpson reaction "d'oh" quickly follows when the penny drops and you realize the morsel is a euphemism for the reproductive organs of the male goat. This lends itself quite literally to the meat and two veg food analogy. One dish to side step if you ask me. Give me a plain old sausage and two boiled potatoes arranged in a creative way on a plate any day.

A note if you are eating out. Kiwi service-staff do not expect a tip. It is very welcomed if you do but it is not mandatory. This was a very hard habit to get out of when we arrived because we have always tipped. I offer stock market tips and The Evey offers handy advice on how to remove stains. This reminds me of Tommy Cooper who, at the end of any cab ride would pop a tea bag in the top pocket of the cabby's shirt and say "Have a drink on me".

There are essentially two sorts of eateries in New Zealand. Restaurants where you book a table, wait to be seated and there is a full "waitering" service. The less formal, café style eating or bar food establishments, run on you ordering your meal at the till and a order number on a stick changes hands and you sit at the nearest spare table. It doesn't have to be the nearest, you can sit by the door if you want or anywhere really. Sometimes it can be a little difficult to work out which system the place runs on. I always let The Evey go in first then she can make a fool of herself at the till while I fiddle with my wristwatch or do important work on my shoelaces at the door.

Both the small people that share my house are vegetarian and when we first came here on our reconnaissance in 2003 it was very hard to find vegetarian food. In the four and a half years since then, things have got better, both in the supermarket choices and when eating out. From a

208

vegetarian point of view, New Zealanders are definitely realizing that cows are for leather sofas and sheep are for wool. Vegetarian protein is now here with tofu, soya and legumes appearing in supermarkets.

If you are vegetarian some establishments and brands assume you will eat fish and chicken is apparently not a proper meat (not nearly red enough). One of my daughters went on a field trip and was given chicken because she was vegetarian. As we are all aware chickens are for eggs and for sacrificing to the gods of the Pacific Ocean and not for eating.

Supermarkets offering cheese made with vegetarian rennet (if that isn't another oxymoron) include Woolworth's, Countdown and Fresh Choice. Look for cheeses in the "Signature" range. In 2008 we noticed the brand "Mainland" producing a veggie cheese too.

Space For Your Research

www.hokitika.com/wildfoods/
    Despite this Hokitika is a nice place and worth a visit. I know people who go each year to the festival and think it is great and by all accounts the atmosphere is, with bands and alcohol and the motels are all booked up early on.

www.wildfoods.co.nz
    Bushtucker and a bucket to throw up in.

Arts and Farts

The World of Wearable (WoW) Arts museum in Nelson and WoW Showcase Wellington are great events and venues. They demonstrate Kiwi ingenuity and resourcefulness turning anything and everything into fashion. My favourite outfit was the traditional Japanese kimono made of wrinkly tin closely followed by the ballerina costume made out of recycled ballet shoes.

NZ fashion week

Grab a ticket and you may be lucky enough to bump into Stacey's mum, Rachel Hunter. (Now there's a situation when four arms would be useful).

Music

Apart from generating its own legends like Crowded House, the Mint Chicks and Head Like A Hole, New Zealand embraces other peoples' legends too. Everyone got really excited when Justin Timberlake toured in November 2007. I for one did not.

For young adults there are world tours that stop off at New Zealand, usually at the end of the world tour and usually for the artists to buy a bit of the South Island for investment and tax purposes. Groups that have toured recently include:

U2, Rod Stewart, Linkin Park, Gwen Stefani, Pink and the Red Hot Chillis. In 2008 Ozzy Osbourne, Kiss and Westlife appeared in New Zealand, though the latter were without their charismatic main man Robbie Williams. (Yes I know).

Some great names, I will concede, so much so that at times I regret never have been able to play the air guitar, although I think I mentioned I can play the air piano when I'm nervous.

Mostly these acts go to Auckland and Wellington where they can sell out and do several shows. Some do come to Christchurch like Muse and Snow Patrol.

Radio stations organize the "Big Day Out" in summer. Basically a one day festival. Top names in the country and some from Britain attend. Chavs like Kate Nash and Lily Allen have played here.

For really old people there are The Stones, and I mean The Rolling Stones not gall stones, who have toured on several occasions and are always well received unlike the latter. Lionel Ritchie has ventured to the South Island but without Nicole, his drummer preferring to use his own drumsticks, and recently (Mar 2008) Tom Jones swayed his hips to a delighted older audience before wrestling his way through corsets. It is not clear whether these were his or theirs.

For the very old crusty cultured types there is Englebert Humperdink who toured in 2006 and I believe he was very good for a German who has been dead for 86 years. Bon Jovi visited Christchurch in early 2008 and looked younger than ever. I don't know how he does it?

Placido Domingo is a patron of Christchurch based Southern Opera, although this may be to secure him some South Island real estate like Shania Twain who is most people's landlord in the South Island.

Christchurch has hosted its 31st International Film Festival, with many a popular French or German title securing the crowds with promises of nudity only to disappoint with the subtitles obscuring the best bits. This city also hosts the World Buskers' Festival each year. Unusual acts from all over the world eke out a living on the popular tourist streets in late January. Expect to get pulled from the crowd with this sort of thing.

Space For Your Research

www.booksellers.co.nz/mba_main.htm
  Find out more about their version of the Booker prize.

www.worldofwearableart.com
  The International Arts Festival Wellington and Nelson.

www.worldbuskersfestival.com
  The World Buskers' Festival held over ten days. Performers come
  from all over the planet to do odd things. Some of which are funny.

Chapter 13

New Zealand Shopping

New Zealanders have embraced EFTPOS big time. They use this system twice as much as any other country and in over half of all transactions. For this reason it is becoming increasing more difficult to find dropped change on the ground. It also takes a bit of getting use to using a card to pay for small things like a newspaper or a pack of chewing gum. Each card transaction costs the card holder so you do need to be careful.

There have been occasions where the system goes down and you can imagine the chaos with so many transactions going through. The run up to Christmas 2005 saw the system collapse several times as it struggled to keep up with the cash registers. Most people made do with an orange, a shiny penny and some Brazil nuts. It was a stoic Christmas that year.

"Do not forget your PIN number" is always sound advice but your UK PIN number may not work if you are using a credit card here. We found that in *some* shops the UK PIN will work but mostly it is safer to ask to sign the transaction receipt if you use an active UK card here.

People are employed at supermarkets to put your shopping into carrier bags. It's like having a servant for a few minutes. However I have real problems with what to do with fidgety hands as I would normally be filling the bags. Instead you stand around looking uncomfortable and wanting to help. I could never have a man servant. I would be wanting to help him iron my shirts. Funny though in twenty four years I have never wanted to help The Evey iron my shirts.

When making the big purchases it is always worth asking if they are able to do a deal on the purchase. There is scope to knock a bit off the total price particularly if you play one store against the other or have a big shopping list. We achieved some good discount on three beds we bought and then the bed linen was thrown in for free. We have found you can't haggle over grocery shopping.

Rounding Up and rounding down

In late 2006 or was it early 2007 the five cent coin was removed from circulation, following the one and two cent coins years earlier. Prices in shops, or indeed services bought, and the effect of adding GST (Kiwi VAT) means that bills and price tags are still labelled in these denominations. So you may get something priced $3.97 or a bill for $79.01.

The lowest coin is a 10c so if an item is priced for $3.97 they will charge you $4. Generally they will use the Swedish rounding method so the price is rounded up if it is 5-9 cents and rounded down if it is 1-4 cents. New Zealand must be one of the few places in the world where you pay more "for cash".

What I have said here applies to cash sales. If you are paying with credit or debit cards you should be paying the list price and there should be no rounding. Sometimes this does not happen and this contravenes the Fair Trading Act. Always check your receipt at the till and complain very loudly in your best English accent. Whine if you can because that always helps. If they don't address your complaint there and then you can return the goods there and then and make the poor Saturday girl blush as much as you can. You WILL get results because no shop is going to lose the sale for 5 cents. If they don't honour the mistake you can take your complaint to the Commerce Commission.

Below is a list of stores and their UK equivalent and their sometimes bizarre catch phrases. Many chain stores here are Australian so may be familiar to anyone who has visited Australia before.

Animates
Animates for all your animal mates. A pet care chain if you hadn't caught on. "For the love of pets" but when spoken "For the love of Pits"?
www.animates.com

Bond and Bond
Electrical. Bond and Bond, (looks like a palindrome but not quite). "You want it, we've got it, let's talk". Will you take less for cash? Doubt it? They started in Auckland in 1875 selling Play Stations which took a while to catch on, but now have 30 stores nationwide.
www.bondandbond.co.nz

Bunnings

A huge DIY chainsaw sorry chain store. They advertise under the slogan "Lowest prices are just the beginning". I thought "death is just the beginning"? (© The Mummy). You can lose yourself in here for days and I mean days. Go in for just 3 washers and come out with a light for under the stairs, a pouch to put nails in, three litres of boiled linseed oil and a set of garden furniture for midgets.

www.bunnings.co.nz

Countdown

Like Tesco (food hall part of Tesco). The parent company holds 45% of the grocery market and also owns Foodtown and Woolworths.

www.progressive.co.nz

Briscoes

Briscoes "You'll never buy better" These people have a permanent sale on judging by the adverts. Unbelievable and more than a little irritating. Mind you I've had some good bargains from here.

www.briscoes.co.nz

Dick Smith Electronics

Tandy meets Curry's and I hope they will be very happy together. Dick Smith Electronics is a nerd's paradise, even Dick Smith looks nerdy, check out the site and see what I mean.

www.dse.co.nz

Farmers

Very much like Marks and Spencer's or top quality BHS

www.farmers.co.nz

Flight Centre

Like an NZ Thomas Cook. Many branches have a life sized fibre glass "Airline Captain" outside the shops. Catch it out of the corner of your eye and it scares the bejesus out of you. I thought I was about to be mugged on more than one occasion.

www.flightcentre.co.nz

Fresh Choice

Sainsbury's. Also owned by the Progressive Group of companies.

www.progressive.co.nz

214

Harvey Norman

A bit like Courts plus electrical and computers. "NZ home of furniture". (Electrical and computing *and* bedding, an odd combination?)

www.harveynorman.co.nz

Just Jeans

Very like River Island and Top Shop. The trade descriptions people may be interested to know they don't just sell jeans which is confusing for people like me who take everything too literally.

www.justjeans.co.nz

K-Mart

A bit like ASDA but without the food "where good times start". OK, I'm not sure about their logo but there are bargains to be had here by the bucket load so someone is going out of business somewhere, or being exploited.

www.kmart.co.nz

Michael Hill

A jewelry store with more than a passing resemblance to Ratner's. Sorry about that Mr Hill but I wouldn't put just any jewelry through my navel and I already have a number of green stains from my 2 carat "gold" sovereign rings.

www.michaelhill.co.nz

New World

Resembles Sainsbury's supermarket. Very good one, but a bit pricey by NZ standards. Proudly 100% NZ owned and operated. Hooray.

www.newworld.co.nz

Noel Leeming

Electrical store. "The Real Deal" as opposed to a raw deal I suppose? The Noel Leeming group owns Bond and Bond too.

www.noelleeming.co.nz

Pack N Save

Very like Lidl. Piled high branded goods but pack your own bags no slaves here. **However you must get your carrier bags on the way into the store.** In the rougher areas it is known as Pack N Run. This supermarket gets a huge advert on recycling day because everyone, rich and poor alike, show they like a bargain by putting their old newspapers out in the yellow Pak 'n Save bags for collection.

www.paknsave.co.nz

Powerstore

Another electrical store. I can't say much more about them except we get our vacuum cleaner bags from here.

www.powerstore.co.nz

Repco

Like Halfords. The staff are very helpful. Their tag line is "Cars are our life too". Oh please.... Every nerd knows electronics and computing are our life. Cars are for getting from A to B and that's all.

www.repco.co.nz

Smith City

Everything except food. No relation to Dick Smith though? Smith City "Has it all" and it does very nearly.

www.smithscity.co.nz

The Warehouse

Posher than Matalan or Ma'aland as we say in Kent but run on the same lines. Seems to have a little of everything. Some of it even tasteful. Mostly of it very cheap. This is bargain city but not quality central. "The Warehouse, The Warehouse where everyone gets a bargain". I guarantee you this dreadful ditty will become an earworm and bounce around your grey matter forever.

www.thewarehouse.co.nz

Warehouse Stationery

Ryman's or Staples. For pens, paper, furry gonk pencil cases and those funny little fruit people with arms that sit on top of an HB.

www.warehousestationery.co.nz

Westfield

An Australian company and the world's biggest retailer. Soon to be in Britain, if they aren't already, they specialize in shopping malls. I guess when you've seen one shopping centre you've seen them mall. The experience is rather like Lakeside, Bluewater or Manchester's Arndale Centre but maybe on a smaller scale.

www.westfield.com

216

Whitcoulls

Like W H Smith. In fact they seem to sell some of W H Smith lines that may not have sold as well in Britain. They own Borders, another book shop big in Australasia.

www.whitcoulls.co.nz

Woolworths

A food supermarket and not at all like the shoplifters' heaven we were used to in the UK Woolworths (RIP). This company allows you to order on line and have it delivered. One of the few who do.

www.woolworths.co.nz

Sale of Alcohol

You can't buy what I call proper booze from a supermarket. The supermarkets carry wine and beer, but if you want anything above 14% alcohol you have to go to a liquor store. Another American influence I think. These places sell alcohol in all its forms. As I have mentioned before you can buy alcohol at 18 years of age but if you look under 25 they will ask you for identification. It is a real hassle to get them to look at my ID. I have it ready and wave it at them but they say "it's OK grandad we believe you."

As I keep reiterating most kids who are under 18 and who want to drink have fake ID anyway so the law only has so much power to deter.

You may come across "laybys" and "rainchecks" where you can set aside stuff in a shop paying a bit here and there each week and take possession on full payment. I like to take advantage of this with Burger King and KFC meals. You will find sale stock will stipulate on the adverts on TV and in papers that the sale does not entertain laybys or rainchecks in which case you will have to buy it outright or shoplift it.

The top end of the market is well covered with Italian fashion, furniture, bathrooms and so on but with a big tariff attached. There is a Louis Vuitton shop in Christchurch. I have never seen anyone in it and nothing has a price on it. Despite this the children were wanting a dog carrying bag like Paris Hilton, but then she doesn't have to lug a 22 kg border collie around.

Being a bloke I don't do much shopping. Like many of my breed the deed is executed in typical SAS fashion. Knowing exactly what you want you

217

nip in under the cover of a diversion, pay for it and then out before anyone knew you were even there. You take up less than two frames on the security camera. There is none of this female method of shopping where you cover three or four kilometres and have only been to two shops. Anyway, to date there hasn't been anything I haven't found available in Christchurch. Sometimes there is a poor selection and the quality isn't good but every conceivable shop and service seems to exist here. There are also high end services such as laser eye correction surgery and plastic surgery often with lots of competition in the marketplace. I find it hard to believe all these shops and services are supported by a base population of only 420,000 people plus the occasional visitor. Pretty impressive as you forget sometimes you are in a lowly populated country antipode to Britain with all its retail outlets, opportunities and bargains.

While there is a big move to buy Kiwi made items, New Zealand still imports a lot of manufactured goods, some of these are made in China and there have been problems with the occasional product. Now I know this isn't like the Chinese to cut corners so that we western consumers get a bargain, but it has upset a few people who for some reason don't like their children playing with toys dipped in lead.

Refunds and customer service

In the first three weeks here and while setting up home, nothing we bought seemed to work. The iron and the fridge never worked from the start, the toaster broke, the fan heater worked for a day and the table and chairs never arrived when promised. I could go on with other things. Oh all right then, the phone kept deprogramming itself, we waited in for the sofa to arrive and it never did and the outside furniture was stuck in Auckland.

Footnote: Everything comes from Auckland. Don't expect the stores outside Auckland to stock big stuff. Expect to wait while it comes from Auckland which is the centre of the New Zealand universe.

Anyway, on with the story. The ATM took our card AND kept the $600 we were trying to withdraw. The previous tenant kept opening our post box to retrieve her mail as she hadn't told anyone she had changed addresses and we had to padlock the post box shut and lie in wait with baseball bats to dissuade her. Our next door neighbour was an abusive alcoholic who kept wanting money, so we had to lie in wait with baseball bats. (To this day he believes he fell down the stairs in his bungalow). Then our baseball bats
218

broke because they were not up to the job. The oven only fired on three rings and The Evey destroyed the rubber thermal backing on the curtains in our rental flat by putting them on a hot wash. And all this happened in the first three weeks of being in New Zealand. We couldn't wait for week four.

The point I am making before I got carried away was that customer service can be a little below what we would expect in the UK. To be fair when the fridge packed up the store lent us a replacement fridge until a new one could be sent from Auckland. Their policy was a customer could not be without a fridge as it is considered a health risk as beer should never be drunk warm.

Most shops won't offer a refund unless the product is faulty, then you can have your money back. If you decide you don't want something and provided you haven't used it and it is still brand new, you won't get a refund but you can bring it back and exchange it for something else.

Expensive to buy in New Zealand

Books
Both paperbacks and hardbacks are expensive as they are often imports from UK and US publishers. Expect to pay $25-30 for a paperback unless it is a classic by Austen or Hardy and then you pay about $15, but who wants to read those?

Mobile telephone upkeep
It is worth researching the best plan for you and your mobile as talking on such devices can be expensive due to the lack of competition. Many just use the text facility which may explain why car drivers appear to be texting so much.

Paint
You buy the base paint and pay for it to be tinted. It costs $2.50 to $5 for the colour to be added. I advise investing in the best paint you can afford. Cheaper ones will be offered to you because Kiwis love a bargain but with many things it is a false economy when you need to apply 5 coats to stop the darker colour showing through as I had to when I painted the kitchen.

Certain foods

Usually these are the imported brands like Marmite, Bouillon powder and anything Italian. I also think pork can be expensive to buy. Please don't be disgruntled about it. It is because the pigs get sun burnt in the NZ climate. They need more husbandry input, factor 30+ rubbed in the places they can't reach, shades and keeping out of the sun between 10 am and 2 pm, that sort of thing. Butter went up 25% overnight in line with a surge in world demand for dairy and food stuffs. Indeed all dairy produce has gone up hugely in price over recent months. A local newspaper recently reported an increase in old people being caught shoplifting cheese which is both funny and sad at the same time which ever whey you look at it.

Clothes

Ladies' clothes for petite people can be tricky to source as are trousers for short or tall men. I am six foot three and a half. The length of the trousers seems only to increase with waist size so you may have to buy bigger and have them altered. The Evey is only three feet tall so consequently has to have her clothing changed. This makes certain clothes expensive to buy and the circus that employs us does not pay well. Girlie fashion can take a few months to appear out here because the seasons are out of sync.

Petrol

Petrol is now too expensive for anyone to buy. The latest Tui beer poster states:

Oil companies are hurting too.   Yeah Right

Cheap to buy in New Zealand

There isn't much that is cheap if you aren't a tourist on a good exchange rate for your currency. However I bought a bucket last week for 75c (about 25 pence). It was yellow and the handle broke on day two when it was full of dirty water. I suppose it could have been worse, it could have been a red bucket. I did also buy the Kevin Costner DVD "Waterworld" for $5 which is quite a good price for a frisbie. A quick word on plastic and UV light. If you buy anything made of plastic that will be left outside check that it is UV stabilised or of good quality. Anything else is a false economy as the strong sun makes everything made of cheap plastic very brittle. We seem to get through lots of pegs here as they snap when you are hanging the washing out.

220

Shopping loyalty cards

Like the Brits the Kiwis love a bargain and shops love selling New Zealanders bargains and securing their return with loyalty cards. The Evey has a purse bulging with them. She is great at utilizing them efficiently, employing compounding techniques to stretch that dollar.

I cite the day she went to Animates to get the dog a bag of food. These normally cost $38 each but over the months she had used her Animates' loyalty card to accrue a free bag which she cashed in. So that's two bags for $38, result. But wait she also had a coupon from the vets to save $ 7 and at the check out there was a $10 special offer for next time. I say a full house beats the casino. A saving of $45 and the dog was fed for nearly two months. Now if that had been me, I may have been able to make the cumulative savings at a stretch but the dog would have got run over within a day and I would be eating Eukanuba Adult Senior at breakfast for the next eight weeks.

Fly buys

Many shops and services offer fly buys. These are loyalty points that you can save up for prizes. Essentially digital Green Shield Stamps. A large number of stores offer these as rewards and even real estate agents will offer you Fly Buys to secure your business either as a landlord or as a vendor. When I first heard a check out operator ask me if I had Fly Buys I hadn't a clue what she was talking about. I thought she may have mistaken me for Tom Cruise in Top Gun?

For Your Research

www.flybuys.co.nz
>Fly buys, fly boys, whatever.

www.smilecity.co.nz
>On line shopping with reward points for using the sites and answering surveys etc.

www.vouchermate.co.nz
>Free discount vouchers on all sorts of things.

Brands but not as we know them?

Heinz brands and especially baked beans appear here in all but name. The corporate image is that of Heinz, labels, colours and so on, the taste however is not. Marketed under the name Watties, a New Zealand company established in 1934, they are now owned by H J Heinz and the range is distinctly Kiwi in taste. Kiwis love everything in the Watties range. Watties baked beans and Heinz baked beans are not the same so do not be fooled into buying them. They appear to use chilli as a flavour. "English recipe" Heinz baked beans are now available in the bigger supermarkets but at a premium. Try $2.37 or 91 pence for a standard tin they are almost as expensive as printer ink. Read the label carefully to make sure you pick up the right one or watch and follow the English families in the supermarket to lead you to them.

Marmite exists but also not as we know it. An Australian version pretends to be the real thing but it is quite disgusting. "My mate Marmite" proper is now available but Linda McCartney sausages however are not; even from specialist English shops.

An extra note on these English specialist shops. As mentioned earlier they can supply lots of English staple foods and culinary delights like Quality Street, proper Cadbury chocolate and Pickled Onion Monster Munch and on the whole they are very good but watch out for two things. I reiterate that the prices are considerably marked up and the shelf life is often short. This is hardly surprising because they travel by container ship to NZ. We were talking to the owner of one of the shops and her container with all her Christmas stock was being held by the ministry in Auckland and they were having problems with the customs paperwork to clear some of the products. For instance they needed to know which part of a horse, horseradish came from. Given some of the chinese medicinal ingredients that ends up in the country I would consider a horse's radish the least thing to worry about.

Space For Your Research

www.sanitarium.co.nz
    A big food manufacturer here, making the Kiwi version of Weetabix
    and Marmite (bears no resemblance, let alone taste, to UK Marmite).

Chapter 14

The section with no name

This is a small part of the book which lumps together all those useful things that don't really fit in the other sections, or more likely the information I forgot to put in the earlier pages. I don't want to upset the formatting as the "tabs" and "justifications" are complete nightmares to get right as I am sure you know. Getting the page numbers and index to work properly was as painful as knowing Manchester united have won the Premiership *again* so I hope you will forgive the poor flow of the book at this point. Normal service will resume as soon as page 230.

Planning your migration to New Zealand

The following list may prove a helpful starting point for a checklist you can personalize.

Birth certificates	For every member of the family.
Certificates for qualifications you own.	
Children's schooling reports, history and letters of support from head teachers	May help support a school application especially if living "out of zone".
Curriculum vitae.	Bring a hard copy and one saved to a storage media. I have all our documents scanned onto computer and backed up onto a portable hard drive.
Copy of itinerary of anything shipped out here along with serial numbers and model types.	Allows you to describe and then claim for any breakages or missing items and allows you to check off what you sent against what finally arrives.
Credit card protection insurance.	If you intend to keep a UK credit card here.
Fuses	Sounds odd but if you have a piece of electrical equipment you bring out and need to leave the UK plug on it, it will be a job to get fuses. NZ plugs don't have fuses in them, they are wired straight to the prongs that go in the wall socket. Fuse protection happens at the fuse box under the stairs.
Letter of good standing from your professional body if relevant.	Letters of bad standing are best left at home.

Letters of good standing or references from your last employer or bank manager or past (paid) bills from utilities etc	A formal letter from someone in authority eg bank manager, credit facility or previous landlord which you can use to help with a non-existent credit history you will have here or to rent a property. I guess the modern equivalent of a letter of introduction. Best not use your mum to write it as they can be a bit biased, unless your mum is the Queen.
List of personal belongings and receipts for big items like cameras.	Allows you to describe and claim for the item in the event of theft or damage.
Marriage certificates.	Adoption papers etc included if relevant.
No claims bonus certificate from your UK car insurer.	Allows you to support a no claims application when applying for NZ car insurance.
Passports.	You must have valid visas. Make sure you have a decent length of expiry on your passport if you intend to keep a UK one. It is expensive and quite fiddly to renew your passport out here.
Professional Registration or Trade Qualifications	You must bring that fake PhD you bought from the University of Springfield USA. Save the planet a bit and don't bring the frame like I did. They have frames in NZ. I wish I'd known that.
Summary of medical history and vaccinations etc	Ask your doctor's receptionist for a print out. They are happy to do this for you because it gives them a chance to nose your medical notes. Particularly useful for children's vaccination history because NZ immunization programme is different to the UK's.

Sun cream	UV light is 40% stronger here than in northern Europe. Invest in good sunglasses too and your retinas will thank you.
Toothbrush	I jest, NZ does have toothbrushes (and sun cream).
Travel plug	One is enough probably. It will save you having to cut off the UK plug and rewiring a NZ one. Note you will need power socket adaptors for UK phone chargers as their transformers are usually built into the plug.
Medicines (regular or unusual ones)	Bring empty boxes or packets rather than names as they can be mispelt ! Or get your local pharmacy to print out your medicine history. They like to nose as well.
UK driver's licence	Must be kept on you whenever you drive here.
Cash or a solvent bank account	There will be a lot of incidentals in the first few weeks. Unless you have a fully furnished rental accommodation in mind you will need lots of things: like something to sleep on.

Don't forget when boarding a plane you can only have 100 ml or less of liquid, gels and aerosol per passenger and they must be carried in re-sealable 1 litre transparent bags if you wish to have them as hand luggage. So better add some re-sealable transparent bags to the list.

New Zealand is DVD region 4. You can bring out you DVDs we did. If you have a region free DVD it should be OK. Our DVDs from the UK work here on a NZ DVD player. Watch it if you are playing them on a laptop some media software only lets you play them a number of times before it locks the driver down.

Space For Your Research

www.flysmart.govt.nz
> For the most up to date information on liquids, gels, duty free etc.

www.immigration.govt.nz
> The government's immigration site (again).

www.immigrationlaw-nz.com
> Immigration consultancy service.

www.migrationbureau.com
> An immigration consulting group. Everyone looks happy on this site and so they should they are in NZ.

www.malcolmpacific.com
> A big player in the migration industry.

www.nzami.org.nz
> Professional association for migration advisors. Use search facility to find an advisor.

Rentals and Car Hire

Car rentals

www.hertz.co.nz

www.avis.co.nz

www.autorentals.co.nz

www.rentadent.co.nz

www.thrifty.co.nz

Some Motorvan rentals

www.nzkiwicampers.co.nz

www.spaceships.tv

www.keacampers.com

www.wickedcampers.com

Motorcycles

www.motorbiketours.co.nz

www.mongrelmob.co.nz

Space For Your Research

Check out soccer's superheroes from the past like Dutch striker Hertz van Hire.

Typical of Kiwi humour.

Great looking vans with unique graffiti. Definitely for fun loving types.

Please recognize my humour when you see it.

Planning visits within New Zealand or days out when you are here

Use these ideas and links to plan NZ based holidays, day trips and what to do when visitors you don't really want invite themselves out to stay with you. A great little website for last minute deals is wotif. If you are looking for accommodation and planning your trips just a few days in advance, then try this site. We've had some great overnight stays in motels and hotels with some good discounts.

When in New Zealand please give some thought to travelling outside the country. We decided to go to the Cook Islands in late 2006 and it was a great holiday. If you do go to the Cooks then also consider a day trip to Aitutaki, an island 45 minutes plane journey from the main group. It has to be one of the best days of my life, a truly beautiful place with some of the best sunburn I have ever experienced.

Space For Your Research

www.aatravel.co.nz/101-must-dos-for-kiwis/index.php
    Voted for by kiwis, so if they don't know their own country what
    hope is there.

www.destination-nz.com
    Some travel ideas for NZ.

www.i-site.org
    New Zealand's official visitor information network. These centres
    are excellent sources of info and advice in 86 locations nationwide.

www.itag.co.nz
    Publishers of "Local Know & Go". A useful guide to the regions
    and facts like the where the police station and supermarkets are.

www.marlboroughsounds.com
    For a range of things to do in the beautiful Marlborough Sounds.

Chapter 15

Christchurch, things to do, people to see

As you probably already know Christchurch is known as The Garden City. This is because it has last year's "must have" Christmas present discarded in one corner, a hole dug by the dog in another and like most gardens the last person to mow the lawn didn't empty the grass collector and it's all gone slimy and smelly. When you overlook these, it is truly a lovely city with lots to do.

www.artsfestival.co.nz

> Christchurch Arts Festival.

www.artinagarden.co.nz

> Visit a garden with some art in it.

www.bankspeninsula.info

> French fest in Akaroa, an annual event in September or October for garlicky types. Plus things to do in Little River, Lyttleton and Christchurch city.

www.bethere.co.nz

> Check out the latest events and those scheduled for the future in Christchurch.

www.dosomething.co.nz

> "Never be bored again". A slightly ambitious tagline but a useful site for things to do all over New Zealand. Together with the associated blog it offers ideas of activities to do with children (other than lock them in the coal bunker with snakes).

www.ellerslieflowershow.co.nz

> Ellerslie International Flower Show will be moving to Christchurch from Auckland in 2008. This is the NZ equivalent of Chelsea or Malvern.

www.kidsfest.co.nz

Help make the school holidays the best ever for your kids which does not involve burning the school down.

www.nzcupandshow.co.nz

Fillies and fashion and the regions Agricultural and Pastoral Show (A&P) all in November. Well worth a look. Lots of other things happen in this week, for instance New Zealand cup and a rodeo to name two 'horsey' themed activities.

www.tranzscenic.co.nz

The Tranz Alpine is a four hour trip on one of the world's greatest train journeys. Unlike Von Ryan's Express the ending is happy.

Things to do on sunny days

Cycle hire and trip around city.
Botanic gardens.
Punt ride down the Avon or hire a canoe.
Gondola ride (cable car) into the hills.
Mona Vale garden walk and meal in their restaurant.

Things to do on rainy days

Why not go shopping in one of the city's many malls. Quite what you'd do for the remaining twenty three and a half hours is really up to you but you could try:

Canterbury Museum

Anyone not a nerd can skip this bit, but if you want to know how the Nor'wester that blows across the Canterbury Plains makes people go a little loopy or gives them migraines then you will be happy here for a few hours. It also has a huge globe that rotates above you and you can see just how far from Blighty you really are and just how huge the Pacific Ocean and Australia are. Oh yes and it has an Egyptian display too. A couple of Mummies, cats I think, but nothing Brendon Fraser's sawn-off couldn't deal with.

Art Gallery with meal in their restaurant

We recently saw the exhibition of the photographer Cecil Beaton on the last leg of its world tour before returning home. It was very popular with the locals but there were far too many pictures of the Queen Mother for my liking. I am not and have never been a fan of the Queen Mother. I do however believe Her Majesty is worth the two pints of milk it cost me to fund her each year but I am not keen on the rest. Maybe we could just keep her and become a Republic. Anyway the meal in the restaurant was very nice though, so I didn't let the Queen Mother spoil my day too much.

Art centre shopping and history tour

The old university was going to be demolished but thankfully is now home to artisans like silversmiths and weavers. This venue is great for watching how bone is modeled into Maori artifacts, or to see how a piece of swamp Kauri or Mountain beech is turned into a pot for the storing of your belly button banana bars. There are numerous crafty shops, galleries, a ghost tour, a theatre and a shop to buy merino wool nipple warmers (and very warm they are too).

Tram ride

About 45 minutes long for the whole circuit with great commentary by the driver. A good way to see the city centre, but don't go all wistful and let your imagination run riot as my kids did when we first came here. They thought they would be taking the tram to school and be living in a riverside penthouse condominium. Border collies and penthouse condos don't really go together. The journey to school would have been awfully long as the tram goes in a continuous loop and does not pass anywhere near their school. The tram is due to complete its one hundred thousandth circuit any day soon. Amazing.

QE II pool complex

This is a great venue especially for kids and the kids in all of us. There are water-slides, a wave machine and a powerful "lazy river" that you can use to workout the abs and upper body. Within the river is a real life whirlpool, just like in the Tarzan movies of old, and very difficult to get out of once in it, guaranteed to reintroduce you to your breakfast. After such a great work out you can enjoy fish and chips, pizza and chips or lasagne and chips in the on-site café. September 2007 saw the opening of the world's first indoor waterslide with inbuilt visual, sound and sensory experience. Not a bit like being reborn, unless you were delivered at a Motorhead concert.

Antarctic centre

A ride on a hagglund snow vehicle, cute little blue penguins and real ice, snow and synthetic Antarctic blasts all add to the atmosphere of this attraction right by ......the airport. New Zealand is a big player in Antartica and with many ships bound for the Ice Continent they use NZ as a base to stock up on cup-a-soup, marshmallows and hot water bottles. It is also the very last place where you can buy Pickled Onion Monster Munch.

In your first winter here you will probably notice everyone hibernating and you may not even see your neighbours for weeks at a time. Activities are going on in an underground sort of way. There are plenty of night classes here from learning Maori to Silversmithing, wine tasting and understanding coffee. The local papers carry details.

Some other indoor activities in Christchurch for rainy days are listed below. Children are not necessarily needed as an excuse to do these, though a degree of nerdism is.

Archery	Aimtru	www.aimtru.com
Go karting	Action Karts	www.actionkarts.co.nz
Science Alive	NZ's Science Centre	www.sciencealive.co.nz
Rock Wall	The Roxx	www.theroxx.co.nz
Laser Tag	Laser Strike	www.laserstrike.co.nz
Christchurch Libraries	Dotted around the city	www.ccc.govt.nz
		Very well resourced with magazines, music, audiobooks, **internet access**, DVDs as well as that ancient medium most know as books.

Some other things to do and see in Christchurch can be found at the following websites. I am amazed at how much there is to participate in and how some of these businesses survive within the smallish population of Canterbury when you take into account certain overheads. Whether it be high insurance premiums for ballooning or the finite amount of skin available to tattoo. I guess the tourist industry contributes a lot of bodies to such activities. We wait and see how the global credit crunch affects tourist numbers to New Zealand and if these companies are still here in three years time when the Rugby World Cup sails into town.

Space For Your Research

www.brownbear.co.nz

    A website offering restaurant information, shopping places, things to explore that sort of thing.

www.summertimes.co.nz

    What's going on in Christchurch (but only in summertime).

www.sinzexpo.co.nz

    Get a tattoo. Why not? It seemed like a good idea at the time.

www.ballooning.co.nz

    Get in a balloon a see the great plains of Canterbury. A must for agoraphobics and acrophobics alike.

www.airforcemuseum.co.nz

    Air Force Museum. This is a great day out.

www.iceberg.co.nz

    International Antarctic Centre.

Somewhere to stay

"Everybody needs a bosom for a pillow"... because hire cars are one of the most uncomfortable places to sleep. There is no shortage of places to rest your head in the cities, but small townships or settlements need booking in advance. I recall that Haast on the west coast has only one place to stay and you are a long way from anywhere else if you turn up unexpected.

Like the three S's the five P's (prior preparation prevents poor performance) rely on not leaving everything to the last minute. It is worth noting that it is considered good manners to phone ahead to your booked motel if you are running late and will not be able to check in before 8 pm. After 9 pm some motels in the cities will light their NO VACANCY signs to discourage the world's oldest profession and their punters from booking rooms. Plus the owner operators like to give themselves some uninterrupted evening. If push comes to shove you may be able to knock up a "motelier" if the sign is lit and still get a room. Grizzly, tired children help your cause. A string of NO VACANCY lights where every motel seems full, may be due to a Super 14 match happening in town. Fridays and Saturdays are usually rugby nights.

On the whole we have found motels and hotels to be of a good standard in New Zealand and we are pretty discerning. If there isn't a decent range of soaps, shampoos, conditioners and sewing sets to thieve we don't use that sleepover again. Motel group loyalty cards operate and you can earn a room for free if you stay with just one chain in your travels around the country.

Qualmark

Operators displaying the Qualmark logo and stars are quality assured motels, hotels, complexes and even tourist activities who are awarded "quality" on a star basis. One star meets minimum requirements, so is clean and comfortable. Four stars indicates an excellent rating with high quality and a wide range of facilities and services. A five star grade is "exceptional" and probably means black satin sheets, mirrors on the ceiling and a waterbed with leopard print pillows.

Do watch out for self rated systems. We have been caught out with places outside of the Qualmark system giving themselves stars. One place we stayed was a three star backpackers. We did not know it was a backpackers until we got there. Yes it was good for a backpackers but I have

235

snobbish reasons in avoiding back packer hostels. Loud talking, snow boarding, action man alpha males for one.

For Your Research

www.backpack.co.nz
>Backpacker hostels in NZ.

www.bookabach.co.nz
>Allows you to lease direct from the owners and stay in some very nice rental property in some beautiful areas. Care: some owners show their best as "vacant" but on enquiry they aren't. They only have the crappy ones left. The old wheel them in scam (allegedly).

www.greenwoodguides.com
>B&B stays in NZ for the discerning traveller.

www.wotif.com
>Last minute hotel and motel rooms that need to be sold. Watch that you are not booking in the school holidays as the rates go up.

www.livingspace.net
>Short and long term accommodation in stylish surroundings for people who like being around other people.

www.nzmotels.co.nz
>The Motel Association of NZ.

www.qualmark.co.nz
>New Zealand tourism's official mark of quality.

www.scenic-circle.co.nz
>A New Zealand owned and operated hotel chain.

www.unitedtravel.co.nz
>Holiday deals on line.

www.yha.co.nz
>The Youth Hostel Association of NZ.

Good places to eat in Christchurch

At great expense to my heart, waistline and life expectancy I have forced myself to eat out as much as possible. I am very discerning, though not in a pretentious food critic sort of way. I like well presented food in nice surroundings and reasonably priced. Consequently the following eateries in Christchurch are my recommendations.

A note to potential migrants: it may be more cost effective in the long run to buy crockery so once in a while you can eat at home.

Café Roma
In a building with lots of character and cosy fires.
www.caffe-roma.co.nz

The Boatshed
On the Avon River and very atmospheric.
www.boatsheds.co.nz

Brigitte's
In Merivale the posh part of town.

Dux de Lux
Very atmospheric. Order your food at the till. They brew their own beers. I recommend Ginger Tom, an alcoholic ginger beer that the famous five would kill for. They are also in Queenstown.
www.thedux.co.nz

The Bard on Avon
An English pub, decent bar meals too.
www.bardonavon.co.nz

Drexel's
American diner, opens early but shuts at 2 pm.
www.dineout.co.nz

Raspberry Cafe
Outside the city in Tai Tapu, very popular so you must book. Worth a visit for brunch or lunch. Rhodes Road Tai Tapu Tel: 3296979
www.dineout.co.nz

Strawberry Fare
> Desserts to die for. They quote "Desserts is stressed backwards" My blonde daughter told her English friends that "Desserts is chocolate spelled backwards". She later retracted this statement.
> 114 Peterborough St Tel: 3654897
> www.dineout.co.nz

Speight's Alehouse
> Bit like a Beefeater. Provides lots of food in a portion. Good beer.
> www.speights.co.nz

Thai Samura
> Restaurants all over the South Island and reasonably priced and excellent.
> www.thaifood.co.nz

Tutto Bene
> Popular Italian restaurant in Merivale run by proper Italians or at least with very good accents. 192 Papanui Road Tel:3554744

Café Valentino
> Buzzy at night, good food. Nice prawns.
> www.cafevalentino.co.nz

Viaduct
> One of a very nice row of eateries in this part of town.
> www.viaduct-bar.co.nz

The Loaded Hog
> Not a Pickled Onion Monster Munch in sight. Good bar food and breakfast in the red light district.
> www.theloadedhogchristchurch.co.nz

Lyttleton Fisheries Chip Shop (Lyttleton)
> NZ's favourite dish is not curry but Fish and Chips.In Nov 2007 this chippie was voted NZ best Chip shop and very good it is too.

There are numerous other places to eat out, covering all budgets. Check out other dining venues for yourself at www.dineout.co.nz

238

The Entertainment book

This publication is a discount voucher book supporting numerous charities in New Zealand. It is a restaurant and activity guide providing up to 50% off meals, 2 for 1 discounts, 15% off the final bill, that sort of thing.

Services and experiences it covers includes:

Garden Services
Pilates Classes
Golfing
More restaurants than you can imagine (except the one you are in)
Holidays
Apartments and Motels
Skiing
Sightseeing tours and so on......

It costs $60 a year to buy but it is well worth it and you are helping charities too. They are hard to come by and sell out quickly, so you need to ask a local where you get them. We got our one through the school and they are available from around March time. There are editions for Auckland, Wellington and Christchurch and Australian regions.

Space For Your Research

www.entertainmentbook.co.nz

The Entertainment Book on line. I can vouch that the reasonably small outlay of $60 is more than covered by the savings that can be made, if only in Burger King tokens. I know how to treat The Evey to a slap up meal with fries.

Skiing in New Zealand and Canterbury

Now it's always nice to test out the healthcare system of any new country. Most of us do this on holiday when we contract the local gastric viruses, but sometimes it's nice to test out the orthopedic services available as well and what better way to do this than to ski. This section is really for people who fancy to learn rather those who can, so forgive my patronizing tone later on when I give tips on slope safety.

The Evey and I hadn't skied since we went on the school ski trip to Italy in 1982. That was the year when everybody in Britain was introduced to the Falkland Islands. We heard it on the Italian news and everyone wanted to know where they were. My friend Douglas thought they were off Scotland and we didn't have laptops and WiFi and the internet in those days to check it so we all believed him. We asked the teachers that accompanied us but they didn't know either, not even the geography teacher but he could draw us a diagram of land use and soil erosion in Patagonia. There was a niggle of doubt because we did wonder why the Argentinians had come such a long way to invade a group of Scottish Islands and wouldn't it stretch their supply lines a bit?

Well twenty four years later and we found we could still ski, though I could still only turn to the right. It was a bit tricky finding a ski field long enough to only do right turns on.

We have skied two ski fields so far, both pretty good I think. I have tasted the snow on two of the fields in the South Island, Mount Hutt and Porter Heights and very pure it is too. I like the way snow always finds its way into your underpants when you kiss the mountain at speed.

Approach roads to the mountains are scary especially with locals overtaking you to get to the slopes quicker. It is wise to get there early as lessons are popular and parking at these fields can be tight. You also don't want to be doing three point turns on the mountain, I can tell you, as safety barriers on the access roads haven't been invented yet.

On the second visit to Porter Heights I was introduced to the mountain parrot called a Kea. Cheeky little fellows they are. Unlike the Norwegian blue this breed seems to like rubber and I have heard stories of them stripping the rubber seals off windscreens which I can believe having seen one steal a Wellington boot from a child not 3 feet from it. It wouldn't surprise me if they can do wedgies as well which is why I believe your ski pants are designed to come half way up your back to stop this happening.

Most of the ski fields are in the South Island though there are some in the north notably Mount Ruapehu with three separate fields on this active volcano. There was a small eruption here in August 2007 and a climber lost part of his leg. Within 24 hours of the eruption the skiers were back on the mountain. He took a little longer to return there.

If you are an experienced skier I am afraid I couldn't tell you if the NZ fields are truly top quality. You would have to use your contacts or the book mentioned below in the references to make that judgement.

I will say as a reasonably competent beginner that the learner slope at Mount Hutt is very gentle but with nothing intermediate to move onto except the mountain itself. This was pretty scary when you've only been on skies for three hours in the last 25 years or in the case of my children for only three hours, ever. Porter Heights had a better learner slope and so it appears, does Round Hill near Tekapo. It is also wise to buy lessons as the learner pass gets you to the front of the ski lift which makes you feel a bit like royalty as jealous crowds look on from the slow moving queue.

Gentleman be aware that some of the ski lifts in the smaller fields are essentially knots on a piece of rope so always wear a thick pair of underpants to avoid empathizing with James Bond in that scene from Casino Royale.

Safety first

If you are new to skiing or haven't skied for a long while then the following is useful to know or to be reminded of again.

- Prepare yourself before you finally go skiing. Walk up stairs to build stamina and strength. Running everywhere would be better, but will make you look odd.

- Don't wear jeans on the slopes. They get wet and you get cold. Wear thin layers that can be put on or taken off as needed as it can be hot when the sun's out and cold in the shadows.

- Most heat is lost from the head so leave it at home. If you have to use a head wear a hat. Make sure it is stylish and matches as you don't want to look unfashionable on the slopes as most people go skiing to be seen and very few people can ski. It is all a myth. We all look the part but no-one can actually do it.

- Goggles or shades preserve your retinas for the drive home and are a must. Google goggles to find good goggle suppliers.

- Sun screen is essential unless you are Scottish or English, in which case make sure you have the biggest goggles or glasses so that your facial sun burn has something equally big to contrast against.

- Don't forget to eat and drink on the slopes. You burn lots of energy and the air is very drying and you sweat like a p.i.g so you risk dehydration. Mount Hutt does a very good lasagne and chips. I like this dish after I have been measured for my skis, then again when I find some poles and then again before I start.

- Look both ways when starting off or crossing trails so you don't get hit by a bus.

- Skiers and boarders below or ahead of you have right of way.

- When stopping (intentionally as opposed to falling over) stop on the sides of the run so you won't be in the way.

242

- Wrist injuries are very common in snow boarders so if you like going down the mountain on a tea tray remember to fall onto knees or forearms because your wrists are very important, especially if you are male and a student.

A serious word of warning. You may well be leaving base camp early, possibly driving a distance or in the low light of a winter's morning. You will also be tired at the end of the day. This is Alpine and High Country, black ice is a big problem on shaded bends and the rush to be first on the slopes is tempting, after all the lasagne is very good. There have been several deaths and serious injury recently where cars have come off the road on black ice or gone down the mountain. Be safe: fly in by helicopter but if you don't have access to one take the bends slowly.

Space For Your Research

The Snow Guide to New Zealand Published by Penguin Books
> Covers 26 resorts with detailed maps of the ski fields and rating system described as a must have travel guide if skiing in New Zealand.

www.tourism.net.nz/ski-fields-new-zealand.html
> New Zealand ski fields with information on skiing and boarding.

www.nzski.com
> Allows you to buy two day lift passes, not today but in advance.

www.skidealsnz.com/new-zealand/webcams-christchurch
> Check out the web cams on the various mountains and more deals.

www.roundhill.co.nz
> 3 hours from Christchurch and safe gentle slopes for beginners.

www.mtruapehu.com
> The website for Mount Ruapehu.

Some final thoughts

I hope you have found this publication useful and you have been able to dissect the facts from the flippancy, I have tried to keep them obvious. There are some subtle jokes and some spelling mistakes throughout. These were intentional… (yeah right).

The facts are correct to the best of my research. The subjective stuff is just that, our subjective experiences that have helped form our time here. You will have a different set of problems and possibly not the ones we fell into, in which case the book has succeeded. Good luck solving the problems you end up with instead. If you survive them and you feel others need to know, drop me a line. If there is ever another book I will include them.

There are an infinite number of things that can go wrong in life and reading the future would be a handy skill to have. Back in England I liked to examine the entrails of a freshly slaughtered sheep before embarking on any life changing decision. It's more difficult to do this in New Zealand as I have found sheep are hard to come by.

While no animal was harmed in the production of this book unless you buy the goat skin edition, I feel *I* may have suffered a little in writing this tome. Both psychologically, as well as physically (I experienced a thrombosed haemorrhoid from prolonged sitting, but I don't suppose you wanted to know that). I have spent many a long hour tapping away at the keyboard over the last eighteen months and still do not fully appreciate the destructive nature of tabs, tables and margins.

I will eventually get to the message I want to convey to you I promise. The world is a smaller place in the 21st century and people are far more mobile than ever before. If you ignore the environmental issues of flying, the world is within your reach and New Zealand is accessible within 36 hours of Britain, though you may need a 75c bucket from The Warehouse, if you try to do it within 24 hours. Of course New Zealand has its faults, especially that big one which runs down the backbone of the country, but I feel privileged to have lived here.

We only have so many days on this planet, so if you have a dream to live in New Zealand, just do it. You can make it happen. The inertia not to do it is you. It is hard work. It will be expensive. It took us lots of planning, but you stand every chance of enjoying the experience and you will be richer and wiser and quite possibly happier for it. I know I am. I think The Evey is too?

244

We would both like to one day find a piece of land in New Zealand and grow long, grey, bushy beards together. Though I may need some hormonal help in the latter of these two desires.

I believe that happiness above all else is the state of mind we humans seek. If you have found the book useful but not funny, or likewise short on facts but quite amusing I am very pleased. If you found it both useful <u>and</u> funny you will have made me really happy and I thank you from that state of mind I now inhabit, with its white rabbit skin bean bags and huge canvasses of modern art. Thank you.

I started the book with a quote and I think it completes the cycle to end the book with a quote.

"If you think you can do something or if you think you can't, either way you are right."

Henry Ford
Industrialist and innovator
(1863-1947)

Once again your guess is as good as mine as to what it means, but a **"Henry"** is the slang for an eighth of Cannabis (Henry VIII) which as a plant grows very well in New Zealand.

Appendix I

Facts and figures about New Zealand

Population

In 1952 the population milestone of two million was reached. It is now 4,180,554 but check the population clock at Statistics New Zealand as humans enjoy increasing their numbers and seem to be good at this so the figure is sure to be out of date from the moment I put the full stop on the sentence (so I won't put one)

Life Expectancy

Female 81.7 years.
Male   77.5 years.

Sadly it is up to 8 years less for Maori, and not a good indictment on society.

The National Anthem

New Zealand has two national anthems: God Defend New Zealand and God Save the Queen. When the Head of state is not present they are allowed to sing the first. God Defend New Zealand was declared as the second national anthem by the Queen in 1977, before that it was the national hymn. I have to say that it brings a lump to my throat when I hear it and I'm not a Kiwi. Actually it is far nicer than ours and sounds beautiful sung in Maori, The first verse is sung in Maori and then again in English. I feel like John Redwood attempting to sing the Welsh National Anthem in Welsh when the NZ anthem comes up.

Daylight Saving

In April 2007 a three week extension to the period of daylight saving was made. Daylight saving now runs from the last Sunday in September until the first Sunday in April. I helped do that. I was one of just 42,000 who signed a petition and the government changed the legislation. No petition I have ever signed has ever changed anything. I love New Zealand democracy. I feel so empowered we can do anything now even free Nelson Mandela.

As a general rule we are 12 hours ahead of UK time. This can, for a few weeks be 11 or even 13 hours depending on the time of year and whether the clocks have gone back or forward. (UK clocks go forward on the 25th March).

Please, if you see my brother-in-law can you remind him to text us at anytime that's *not* afternoon in England. Also my mate Mark settled down with a nice cup of tea and a biscuit one rainy Saturday afternoon in England and thought it would be good to have a catch up chat with us over the phone. We thought someone had died.

Father's Day and Mother's Day

Father's Day is the first Sunday in September and I'll have an Xbox 360 and some games please. Mother's day is some time in the first half of the year, early to mid May I think, and we can let The Evey off dish duty for the day and instead put them on the floor for the dog to clean.

You can use this disparity as an excuse for not buying the parents a gift back home. When your mother phones up to ask if there was anything on its way in the post, you just say it isn't Mother's Day here. You can then ignore the Kiwi Mother's Day because it isn't the UK one and your mother probably doesn't know when it is in NZ. Result.

Space For Your Research

www.stats.govt.nz
    There's that link again. Use it to check the NZ population clock.

www.mch.govt.nz/anthem/index.html
    Hear the National Anthem or Hymn and reflect how much nicer it
    is than ours.

www.rasnz.org.nz
    The Royal Astronomy Society of NZ. A really nerdy site for
    checking when the sun sets but also to keep an eye on when that
    meteor will hit Earth ending all the angst to do with the credit
    crunch.

Appendix Ia

Some Canterbury and Christchurch facts and figures

- Canterbury is the largest region in New Zealand with 400,000 square km, and is the third largest urbanised area in NZ. Guess the others?

- Christchurch has 2.5 million visitors annually with 12% of its workforce employed in tourism. Tourism is one of NZ's strongest industries contributing $17.5 billion a year to the economy second only to exporting New Zealanders to the rest of the world.

- From 2001 to 2006 some 25,870 new jobs have been created in Christchurch and one of the highest growth rates in the country.

- The population of greater Christchurch in 2006 was 414,000. Greater Christchurch includes all the little townships around the city like Rangiora, Kaipoi, Lincoln, Rolleston, Lyttleton, Woodend, Prebbleton and Templeton. The population is expected to rise to 501,000 by 2026.

- 8,000 people migrate to Christchurch each year (through internal and external migration). Excluding NZ European and Maori the top seven ethnic groups in Christchurch (2006) were:

Chinese	12,477
British/ Irish	8,427
Samoan	6,102
Other European	5,574
Korean	4,566
Indian	3,057
Dutch	2,835

- Street furniture like benches only last between 5 and 10 years. Amazing.

Appendix II

The Super 14 Rugby Teams and where they come from.

Team	Country	Region	Includes
Blues	New Zealand	Auckland & Northland	
Brumbies	Australia	Australian Capital Territory.	
Bulls	South Africa	Pretoria	
Cheetahs	South Africa	Bloemfontein	
Chiefs	New Zealand	Central & Eastern North Island	Waikato, Bay of Plenty, S Auckland.
Crusaders	New Zealand	Canterbury & Tasman	
Force	Australia	Western Australia	
Highlanders	New Zealand	Otago and Southland	
Hurricanes	New Zealand	South / SW region of North Island	Wellington & Taranaki.
Lions	South Africa	Johannesburg	
Reds	Australia	Queensland	
Sharks	South Africa	Durban	
Stormers	South Africa	Cape Town	
Waratahs	Australia	New South Wales	

Appendix IIa

Regions of New Zealand

I include this because Kiwis often refer to the regions especially in relation to rugby teams and it takes a while to place them. Here are some of the regions that they seem to use and some of the main settlements that they include. You could use the list to place a regional council or heaven forbid; a rugby team. The regions seem to be loosely defined depending on what they are referring to, (wine, rugby, telephone numbers and weather forecasts). A map might be handy?

	Region	Includes places like:
North Island	Northland	The tip of the North Island: Bay of Islands, Doubtless Bay, Kaitaia, Whangarei
	Auckland	As in the metropolitan district of the city.
	Waikato	The region below Auckland to the west: Cambridge, Hamilton.
	Coromandel	The peninsula level with and right of Auckland.
	Taranaki	West Coast at the bottom. New Plymouth.
	Bay of Plenty	The big bay below Coromandel in the East Whakatane, Rotoroa.
	Waiarapa	To the right of Wellington: Masterton.
	Hawkes Bay	Napier, Hastings and Havelock North.
	Eastland or East Cape	The sticky out bit that will cop any tsunamis: Gisborne.
	Manawatu Wanganui	Region above Wellington: Palmerston North, Levin.
	Wellington	As in the metropolitan district of the city.
South Island	Tasman	Richmond.
	Nelson	Nelson which often includes Richmond.
	Marlborough	Blenheim.
	West Coast	The wet side of the Alps: Westport and Greymouth.
	Canterbury	The plains to the sea: Christchurch.
	Otago	Below Canterbury: Dunedin and Queenstown.
	Southland	Bottom tip of the South Island: Invercargill.

Appendix IIb

Would you look at that…a map! More professional maps can be found at 'www.terralink.co.nz' and 'www.wises.co.nz'. While the website "www.nztourmaps.com" has a large number of touring maps and route planners.

Appendix III

Cost of living

Rough guide prices from 2005-7 and using the exchange rate from these dates which averaged about 35 p to the dollar.

4 people (excluding mortgage payments or rent).

	Per month	Approximate UK equiv
School sundries	$ 50	£ 18
Broadband (10Mb)	$ 60	£ 21
Telephone	$ 50	£ 18
Electricity	$ 200	£ 70
Food	$ 1300	£ 460
Rates	$ 190	£ 67
Diesel heating fuel	$ 160	£ 56
Water is included in the council rates		
Bank charges	$ 10	£ 3.5
Total	**$ 2020**	**£ 710**
Miscellaneous costs		
Burglar alarm call out fee	$ 85	£ 32
Drs/Dentist consultation	$ 90	£ 32
Vet consultation	$ 44	£ 16
X-ray (dog)	$90-$200	£ 30-£70
Car tax	$ 16	£ 6
Petrol (tank full)	$ 100	£ 40
Insurance (house, 2 cars)	$ 125	£ 44
Typical car service	$ 120	£ 42
Warrant of Fitness	$ 5	£ 2
Car HP payment	$ 580	£ 205

www.sorted.org.nz	Try these sites for information on budgeting tips
www.familybudget.org.nz	

Appendix VI

British	Kiwi equivalents	Further Information
Armistice Day	ANZAC Day	Held on different days though.
Bank Base Rate	Official Cash Rate	Set by the Reserve Bank.
Bookmakers	TAB bar www.tab.co.nz	Pronounced "Tee Ay Bee". A betting agency accessible on line or in some pubs.
British Legion	RSA www.rsa.org.nz	The Returned Services Association.
Corner Shop	Dairy	Convenience stores with overpriced milk.
Council Housing	State Housing	As in the UK you can easily spot this housing.
Desert Island Discs	8 Months to Mars	www.radionz.co.nz
Ebay	Trade Me	www.trademe.co.nz
Electrolux	Fisher & Paykel	www.fisherpaykel.co.nz
Estate agent	Real Estate agent	As opposed to a make believe estate agent.

Fruit machines	Pokies	Gambling is a bit of a problem in NZ.
Highway Code	Road Code	The Road Code is like The Da Vinci Code only better written.
Jehovah Witnesses	Jehovah Witnesses	You can't escape them anywhere in the world so don't try.
Non uniform day (at school or work)	Mufti day	Usually costs you a gold coin ($1).
Plain Clothes Cop	Mufti Cop	Would Regan and Carter be cool as 'Mufti Cops'?
Premium Bonds	Bonus Bonds	www.bonusbonds.co.nz
Teletext	Teletext	Available on Channels 1,2 and 3.
VAT	GST (Goods & Services Tax) levied at 12.5% and on everything including food, clothes and books etc.	Taxes and death, the only certainties as they say. www.ird.govt.nz/gst/
Which?	Consumers' Institute	www.consumer.org.nz

Appendix V

Other websites not mentioned earlier but useful maybe?

www.accommodationz.co.nz
> Find a motel or somewhere to stay for the night that isn't the hire car in a lay-by.

www.areyouok.org.nz
> A campaign website to help in preventing family violence. You can easily knock any government (bad use of words there-sorry) but the NZ Government does try in its way to help people.

www.yellowpages.co.nz
> Let your fingers do the walking (in work time). Good for locating places on street maps.

www.cityofdunedin.com or www.dunedinnz.com
> Some websites for the "Edinburgh of the southern hemisphere". In a similar vein 'www.christchurchnz.com' and, I'm sure you get the format now, 'www.wellingtonnz.com' are useful starting points for researching these cities.

www.commtrust.org.nz
> The Canterbury Community Trust. Worth a look for all the work it does.

www.dia.govt.nz
> The Department of Internal Affairs. Do they mean swingers? No! It is passports, registers and civil union type stuff.

www.donatenz.com
> Someone, somewhere is in need of that collection of Spanish dancing dolls you have, if only to be smashed with a hammer by an anger management charity.

www.ferrit.co.nz
> On line retail. "Ferrit. Find it. Buy it" Break it. Biff it.

www.google.co.nz
> Get a New Zealand slant on things with this Google domain.

www.jasons.com
> Travel information with thousands of listings in NZ and Australia and the Pacific.

www.localeye.info
> Information of all sorts but especially useful for locating post shops, bus routes, maps and mobile phone coverage.

www.newzealand.com
> Official tourism New Zealand site.

www.nzct.org.nz
> New Zealand Community Trust doing nice things for the community (this time of a sporting nature).

www.nzis.co.nz
> New Zealand Institute for Sport. A tertiary education centre for people who know how to catch and throw and jump and… (boring)

www.nzlotteries.co.nz
> Lotto and Big Wednesday where you can win a lot of NZ dollars. Divide by 3 to get the equivalent in Sterling. The top prize is about £7 a week or threepence halfpenny old money.

www.nzs.com
> Web directory and search engine for NZ websites.

www.nzsoccer.com
> Wellington Phoenix FC is the country's soccer team to support even when the oval ball is being rested.

www.ticketek.co.nz
> NZ equivalent of "ticketmaster.co.uk" Great place to get those Lionel Richie or Lions tickets.

Appendix VI

Dictionary of pretentious words used (as promised)

Antipode — Diametrically opposite to something. Hayley v Lemmy.

Crapulent — Sick from excessive drinking (or eating).

Didactic — Instruct in a moral or lecturing sort of way. "You will come to New Zealand and you will like it."

Discombobulating — Confusing, but too long a word for Scrabble.

Expostulation — Reason earnestly to dissuade or correct. "Honestly you don't need to give me a dictionary at the back of the book." I am proud of you for looking it up.

Garrulous — Excessively talkative and rambling.

Homonym — A word that sounds the same as another but has a different meaning, as opposed to a homonym like Quentin. Windy and windy would be examples.

Ortolan — That little French delicacy of eating tiny whole songbirds, which are netted, force fed, drowned in Argmagnac, roasted to perfection and consumed, bones and all, from under a napkin. Comes with chips.

Patronizing — What this "in-book" dictionary idea is.

Phenotype — The outward expression of our genes. What a person looks like, big nose, lanky, hairy ears: Hey that's me?

Postprandial — After you've eaten. Postprandial hyperglycaemia was invented for afternoon siestas.

Sesquipedalian — Someone who uses long words. Lengthy, that's a long word.

Tautology — What's the matter with you can't you use a dictionary?

Appendix VII

Some places we have stayed and highly recommend

Being a Virgo and anal I have very high standards so I would not recommend a place to stay unless I would be prepared to go back there again or enjoyed a place a lot while I was there. Below are some places we have stayed where I would be comfortable recommending to total strangers. Well, I think by the time you have got to appendix VII we are more than just strangers now. I feel I know you and maybe even like you, provided you haven't bent those pages back or broken the spine of the book.

Awaroa
> Awaroa Lodge, Abel Tasman National Park.
> Crystal clear water and very nice rooms and food.
> > www.awaroalodge.co.nz

Hamner Springs
> Alpine Villa.
> Expensive but you get your own hot tub in the top priced room.
> > www.albergo.co.nz

Hokitika (West Coast)
> Bella Vista motel chain.
> Modern, well equipped, clean and all their motels nationwide are exactly the same so you know what you are getting.
> > www.west-coast.co.nz
> > www.bellavistamotels.co.nz

Kaikoura
> Kaikoura Gateway Motor Lodge.
> Very smart and clean but with the smallest swimming pool I have ever seen.
> > www.kaikouragateway.co.nz

Nelson
> Te Puna Wai Bed & Breakfast.
> A beautiful house, warm welcoming hosts. Dog friendly.
> > www.tepunawai.co.nz

Queen Charlotte Sound

Bay of Many Coves Resort.

Well worth pinching the soap from this great place. Has a good hot tub and fantastic scenery, access is by water taxi from Picton.

www.bayofmanycovesresort.co.nz

Queenstown

Spinnaker Bay Apartments.

Nice rooms, décor a bit dated, though my parents loved it. Great indoor swimming pool we had to ourselves.

www.spinnakerbay.co.nz

Queenstown

Onsen Hot Pools

Private hot tubs. Bath in pure alpine water overlooking the Shotover River. Fantastic views in all weathers. Don't park on the helicopter pad or keep playing with the retractable roof like I did.

www.onsen.co.nz

Rotorua

Novotel Hotel

International chain, basic but perfectly adequate. Superb breakfast.

www.novotelrotorua.co.nz

The Cook Islands

Lagoon Lodges Rarotonga

Basic but pleasant enough. Within metres of the beach.

www.islandhoppervacations.com

www.cook-islands.com

The Cook Islands

Aitutaki Day trip

Expensive at $400 each but that's what you work for. Truly magical day. Organised through Air Rarotonga at the air port.

www.airraro.com

<u>The Cook Islands</u>

    Pa's Island walk day trip Rarotonga.

    Strenuous in places but a great day out. He is a real character and does the trip barefoot. Check out the leaflets in your hotel room for his telephone number as he doesn't have a website.

<u>Wanaka</u>

    Oakridge Resort Grand Mecure

    Bit of a pretentious name but very nice.

       www.oakridge.co.nz

Space For Your Research

Appendix VIII

Really Nerdy Stuff

New Zealand Plugs

For those of you who don't do electrical stuff, I agree, the plug sockets do look kind of sad. I also challenge anyone to successfully insert a NZ plug into one of these sockets in the pitch dark. Almost impossible.

Note the plugs are smaller than UK ones. This is because they do not contain a fuse. They are moulded in two types those with three prongs (on earthed appliances) and those with two prongs that are not earthed. Please also note that the earth terminal is inverted compared to the UK power outlet. If you have to cut a UK plug off and wire a NZ one, "wireable" plugs can be bought. Get all electrical work checked by a registered electrician to avoid me being sued.

For your information only, New Zealand wiring follows this convention:

Red = LIVE

Black = Neutral

Green & Yellow = Earth or ground

Space For Your Design of an Electronic Circuit

Appendix IX

Property evaluation for buying or renting

Property aspect

Is it sunny? Take a compass. Remember North facing is good.
Consider how much sun will it get in winter when the sun is low, are there trees, is it dark?
Is it windy? (if on hill or exposed coast etc).
Consider a visit at a different time of the day, and in different weather.
Does it have a view (if so of what).
Is access difficult? (eg convenience when you move in).
Is it on public sewerage or a septic tank?
Is there a garage or off-road parking? Does there seem to be good drainage?

Amenities

How close is the nearest school?
What type of school is it? (co-ed or not)
How far are the nearest shops and are they a broad selection?
Nearest dairy? (corner shop)
How far is the hospital, doctors or dental surgery?
Public transport close by?

Neighbours & neighbourhood

How private is it?
What do the neighbours seem like?
Are their houses well-kept?
Check with neighbours if TV reception or mobile phone reception is good?
Are there overhanging trees that could cause a nuisance?
Could there be a noise problem from the neighbours or their pets?
Drive around the neighbourhood (different times of the day, and weekend)
Is there traffic noise, sports field noise, hooners. Is there a basketball hoop on the garage next door?
(bounce, bounce, bounce at 7 am and 11pm after the pubs shut).
Is there any empty land nearby? Check with council regarding any plans.
If rural or semi-rural are there smells, noise from farms or livestock etc?

Appendix X

Buying a house at auction

This is pretty alien to the British as we like to get a bargain and offer low to meet half way with the vendor. Many agents sell the majority of listed properties on their books at auction so it can limit your choice if you are like me and a bit scared of bidding. Below is some advice specifically for buying a house by auction.

- View the property and have a LIM report and survey conducted. (A LIM is a Land Information Memorandum, basically a land search). Some vendors supply a LIM report. This is not a guarantee or warranty though.

- Register your interest at the open home with the agent. Ask the agent for the guide price. Some sales never go to auction if a decent offer is made and there isn't enough interest.

- You need all you finances in place by auction day and have 10% of the price in "cash" for the deposit.

- Your bid is TOTALLY UNCONDITIONAL. When that hammer falls you have to buy it. Eeeeeeeek!

- Secure a legal advisor who can help with anything unfamiliar.

- Attend some auctions of houses you aren't interested in to see the process in action.

- Bid confidently. Be aware that by the very nature of auctions you will be bidding with someone who also wants the place. Have an absolute top price you will pay in your head and don't go over it.

- Don't touch your nose, scratch your head or point at interesting things in the room.

- Some sales can be completed after the auction if the reserve price isn't met for instance.

<u>There should be further information available at the auction house so don't be afraid to ask for it.</u>

Please note I have never bought a house at auction so the information above is just my basic research on the subject. I have never been wrong before but twice in my life I have been mistaken.

Appendix XI

New Zealand Films

New Zealand has been the backdrop or subject matter of many films. I can't leave you without some suggestions for films to rent out to get a feel for New Zealand, its culture, scenery, people, humour and way of life.

Feel good films

Whale Rider (nice)
Secondhand wedding (chick flick)
Sione's Wedding (not a chick flick but not a bloke flick either)

Depresssinngggggg

In My Father's Den (deep and disturbing)
Once Were Warriors (violent: eggs will never seem the same again)
Heavenly Creatures (murder)
Out of the Blue (mass murder)
An Angel at My Table (powerful and humbling)

Cartoons or humour

Footrot Flats (cartoon series)
Bro Town (self deprecating cartoon series)
Eagle vs Shark (wacky)

Scenery films

Black Sheep (comic horror)
The Piano (starring naughty Harvey Keitel)
LOTR trilogy (Rugged scenery and rugged Orlando, Yeah Right)
River Queen (Watch with a good sound system to hear dialogue)
Narnia films (Plain stupid, animals that talk? What would Buzz say?)

Index

267